Project Manager Street Smarts

Project Manager Street Smarts

A Real World Guide to PMP® Skills

Linda Kretz Zaval, PMP

Terri A. Wagner, MA, PMP

WILEY

Wiley Publishing, Inc.

Acquisitions Editor: Jeff Kellum
Development Editor: Toni Zuccarini Ackley
Technical Editor: Brett Feddersen
Production Editor: Liz Britten
Copy Editor: Sharon Wilkey
Editorial Manager: Pete Gaughan
Production Manager: Tim Tate
Vice President and Executive Group Publisher: Richard Swadley
Vice President and Publisher: Neil Edde
Book Designer: Judy Fung and Bill Gibson
Compositor: Jeffrey Lytle, Happenstance Type-O-Rama
Proofreader: Jen Larsen, Word One
Indexer: Ted Laux
Project Coordinator, Cover: Lynsey Stanford
Cover Designer: Ryan Sneed

Library of Congress Cataloging-in-Publication Data

Zaval, Linda Kretz, 1948-

   Project manager street smarts : a real world guide to PMP skills / Linda Kretz Zaval, Terri Wagner. -- 1st ed.

      p. cm.

   ISBN-13: 978-0-470-47959-9 (pbk.)

   ISBN-10: 0-470-47959-0 (pbk.)

   1. Project management. I. Wagner, Terri, 1959- II. Title.

   HD69.P75.Z38 2009

   658.4'04--dc22

2009019175

10 9 8 7 6 5 4 3 2 1

Dear Reader,

Thank you for choosing *Project Manager Street Smarts: A Real World Guide to PMP®
Skills*. This book is part of a family of premium-quality Sybex books, all of which are
written by outstanding authors who combine practical experience with a gift for teaching.

Sybex was founded in 1976. More than 30 years later, we're still committed to producing
consistently exceptional books. With each of our titles, we're working hard to set a new
standard for the industry. From the paper we print on, to the authors we work with, our
goal is to bring you the best books available.

I hope you see all that reflected in these pages. I'd be very interested to hear your comments and get your feedback on how we're doing. Feel free to let me know what you think
about this or any other Sybex book by sending me an email at `nedde@wiley.com`. If you
think you've found a technical error in this book, please visit `http://sybex.custhelp.com`.
Customer feedback is critical to our efforts at Sybex.

Best regards,

Neil Edde
Vice President and Publisher
Sybex, an Imprint of Wiley

Acknowledgments

It takes a village…to write a book. Thank you to the tireless team of folks supporting this effort. First to Neil Edde for his suggestion we venture down this path. Next, thanks go out to acquisitions editor Jeff Kellum for grabbing his book-publishing compass and mapping the course. Another shout out to editorial manager Pete Gaughan for gathering an awesome team. A special thank you also to Kim Heldman for walking the path before us, setting the example, and inspiring this work; we love you Kim. Liz Britten, our production editor, did a wonderful job. Thanks also to Sharon Wilkey, the copy editor, for grammatical help and suggestions. Hats off to development editor Toni Zuccarini Ackley for keeping the project on track and offering helpful recommendations along the way. Another thank you to Brett Feddersen, our technical editor, for reviewing every word and every exercise for clarity, usefulness, and accuracy. And finally, a very special thank you to the community of project managers who have taught us throughout our careers by words and by action, and who continue to lend wisdom to the profession.

About the Authors

Linda Kretz Zaval (PMP) has successfully managed several multi-million-dollar projects within the telecommunications, cable, and IT industries. Her most recent assignments have included training for many government agencies including the Department of Defense, the Department of Energy, the National Park Service, and the National Security Agency.

During her 40-year working career, Zaval held a variety of positions at US WEST, including Director of Project Management. She was a member of the core team that developed the Center for Program Management at the University of Denver. She has also served as Vice President of Training and Product Development for the International Institute for Learning in New York City and managed a global team of project managers for IBM.

Zaval is the owner/managing member of 20/20 Solutions, LLC, an Idaho-based project management consulting and training company.

She is also an active member of the Project Management Institute (PMI) and is the author of *The Project Manager's Toolkit*. She has taught several university-level seminars as well as public and custom programs in project management, finance, and systems development. She is an internationally sought after public speaker and consultant known for her ability to establish real world methodologies for implementing project management in a corporate environment.

Terri Wagner (PMP) has managed multi-million-dollar project management office portfolios for international consulting clients. Wagner also has led teams of project managers, business analysts, process specialists, operational groups, and trainers in the planning, design, development, and deployment of system and operational enhancements, as well as client-based initiatives. She has been awarded honors for being a creative thinker with the ability to successfully apply technology for the advancement of internal and external operational efficiencies and quality. She has taught project management, portfolio management, program management, business leadership, quality management, and other topics to state agencies, governmental entities, corporate clients, and at the graduate level in the university system. Wagner has delivered training, consulting, and project management in the United States, Canada, the Caribbean, and Europe while continuing to both run projects and consult with organizations on project management methodologies and strategies.

Wagner is owner/managing member of Mentor Source, Inc., a Colorado-based project management consulting and training company. She is an active member of Project Management Institute (PMI) and technical editor for several textbooks on the topic of project management.

Contents at a Glance

Contents

Introduction

The project management discipline is swiftly becoming the catalyst of choice for change in modern business models. The added value project management provides to the bottom line is now considered a corporate lifesaver, not a corporate cost center. Even though the discipline does not usually generate revenue (except in projectized organizations) it enables profit generation by maintaining tight controls on expenditures with a proactive view of project events.

Project managers today are provided the power and authority to establish, maintain, and forecast project results. It is a proactive instead of reactive process. Project managers today participate with finance and marketing analysts in the financial justification of projects. Their contribution to the corporate bottom line makes the discipline of project management a twenty-first century core business process.

If used correctly, the process of project management can impact revenue-to-expense ratios in a positive way. It can curtail expenses and assist senior management in choosing one project over another by providing a realistic and defendable cost structure designed to increase competitive advantage and maximize shareholder wealth. In other words, project management is a cost saver rather than a cost center.

So just how does a project fit within an organization's goals and strategies? How can a project manager get others excited about the project? Complex projects challenge the capabilities of contemporary organizations, requiring new structures, sophisticated management skills, and new roles and relationships. This book addresses these challenges. Novice project managers will be able to follow a project from beginning to end. Seasoned project practitioners will be able to see how real world project management and the Project Management Body of Knowledge® are aligned. While learning project processes and the activities associated with, them the reader will be able to:

- Describe how project management principles and techniques apply to the real word challenges of project management

- Understand how to define project scope and explain the steps needed for successful project plan execution

- Develop competency in creating a work breakdown structure (WBS)

- Contrast the accountabilities of functional managers with those of project managers

- Develop schedule logic

- Develop competency in evaluating schedule performance

- Understand how to determine corrective action when plans go awry

- Utilize human resources effectively

- Understand appropriate communications with project stakeholders

- Get a glimpse of project portfolio management and how it relates to project selection

- Understand the characteristics of high performance teams and their challenges

- Understand motivation techniques through constructive counsel
- Understand how to communicate more effectively in conflict situations
- Understand and demonstrate listening, persuasion, and delegation techniques
- Describe risk management components and concepts
- Understand uncertainty and its role in decision making

Project Success Factors

Before we begin, let's take a look at the factors that can make or break projects. As you move forward, keep these factors in mind so that your project will start out on a positive note. If these success factors do not exist in your organization, perhaps more up front work will be needed before you begin your project management journey.

Project Success Factor 1

In order for project management to be successful within an organization, it must have top down, *senior-level or executive support*. The project owner must support the benefits of the project, accept responsibility for funding and budget status, concur with project and charter requirements, sign off on risk plans, and be knowledgeable of the status of both planned and actual results.

Project Success Factor 2

Clients and users must have ownership of the project. This is demonstrated by providing resources, being involved in the project initiative, signing off on requirements once the plan is completed, signing off on the schedule, participating in the risk management processes, and concurring with scope changes.

Project Success Factor 3

Business processes must be fully known. The project manager and the team must demonstrate knowledge of business processes. Many projects are generated due to a business problem, and the team must understand that problem and define how the project solution will change business processes. When there are changes, the impacts should be documented and fully understood by the client. Process improvement metrics must also be identified so that it can be determined whether the project has met its intended purpose relative to the business problem.

Project Success Factor 4

Projects should be chosen based on a sound business plan that is completed for a particular stage or effort. The infrastructure and business solution units must be identified and synched with the corporate plan and economically validated.

Project Success Factor 5

The project scope should be clearly defined and identified in the project charter. Impact analysis relative to budget and schedule must be performed when scope changes occur, and the focus of the team must be limited to approved changes only. Owners must step up to the risks and benefits for all scope changes.

Project Success Factor 6

An effective change control process must exist that is followed by all stakeholders. The project manager must regularly review all changes and their impacts with the owner, who must approve change requests and associated funding.

Project Success Factor 7

The *business drivers must be fully identified* and agreed upon by the owner and user community. In other words, the project must *add value* to the business. The solution elements of the project should be traced back to business drivers, with success criteria defined at the onset and benchmarked at each phase. A means to collect data should be established so that the metrics can be demonstrated.

Project Success Factor 8

There should be *limited experimentation with new technology*. Previous use must be demonstrated prior to commitment for mission-critical projects. Previous industry application must be demonstrated before application for customer-affecting projects. The appropriate technology group must agree to support the technology in a deployed state.

What Is PMP Certification?

The Project Management Institute (PMI) was founded in 1969 with the goal of developing standards for project management practices across industries and across the globe. It has outlined processes and techniques in its own publication, *A Guide to the Project Management Body of Knowledge (PMBOK® Guide)*, which has also been approved as the American National Standard by ANSI, the American National Standards Institute. PMI also administers a certification process granting several different credentials depending on experience, education, and specialties such as risk, scheduling, program management, and project management. The Project Management Professional (PMP) is their most recognized credential, as of this printing.

According to its web site at www.pmi.org, "The PMP® credential recognizes demonstrated knowledge and skill in leading and directing project teams and in delivering project results within the constraints of schedule, budget and resources." To sit for the PMP exam, you must demonstrate experience by filling out their application and capturing hours leading project tasks during the last 8 years of your career. At the time of publication of this book, PMI required that professionals holding a bachelor's degree document a minimum of 4,500 hours of experience covering at least 36 unique months during the past eight years while those with a high school diploma need to demonstrate 7,500 hours of experience covering at least 60 unique months during the past 8 years. Along with that experience, applicants must also show that they have accumulated at least 35 contact hours of project management education prior to submitting the application to sit for the professional exam. Once the application is accepted, and the applicant agrees to abide by the organization's Code of Ethics, the applicant must then take and pass the proctored exam, consisting of 200 multiple choice questions, within a 4-hour period of time. The tests are offered by a third-party professional test facility with locations around the globe. For more details on the professional exam, go to www.pmi.org.

Is This Book for You?

Project Manager Street Smarts is designed to give a project manager all of the tools and techniques to be successful. Whether you are a Project Management Professional (PMP), aspiring to become one, or are a novice project practitioner, this book will guide you from the beginning of a project to the end.

One case study is used throughout the book to bring reality to the challenges and successes a project manager faces. The book contains more than 65 exercises to challenge your knowledge of project management principals as they relate to real world situations. We've also provided dozens of templates that you can use if you do not have access to them in your own work environment.

This is not a PMP Study Guide, although *Project Management Street Smarts* does align with the *Project Management Body of Knowledge,* 4th ed. *(PMBOK® Guide)*. It is a companion book to Kim Heldman's *PMP® Project Management Professional Study Guide*

How This Book Is Organized

This book is organized into five phases, which represent the five main process groups of project management according to the *PMBOK® Guide*. Each phase is separated into individual tasks. The tasks within each phase lead you step-by-step toward completion of that phase.

Phase 1: Initiating Process This process includes financial information needed for a project, creating the charter, and defining the scope of the project.

Phase 2: Planning Process This process guides you through all of the project management plans needed for the master project management plan.

Phase 3: Executing Process This process brings you to the implementation of all plans as well as management of team personnel.

Phase 4: Monitoring and Controlling Process This process provides real-world situations to keep the project on track as well as how to manage performance issues related to cost, schedule, scope, quality, risk, communications, procurement, and so forth.

Phase 5: Closing Process This process walks you through all of the steps to close out a contract as well as the project.

Each task in this book is organized into sections aimed at giving you what you need when you need it. The first section introduces you to the task. Descriptions of the remaining sections follow.

Scenario This section places you in the shoes of the project manager, describing a situation in which you will likely find yourself.

Scope of Task This section is all about preparing for the task. It gives you an idea of how much time is required to complete the task, what setup procedure is needed before beginning, and any concerns or issues to look out for.

Procedure This section is an outline of what will be learned in the task.

Details This is where the learning takes place. This section informs you how to complete the individual items included in the task.

Project Management Tasks

The tasks included in *Project Management Street Smarts* include:

Phase 1:

- Understanding finance principals
- Conducting project selection methods
- Establishing a progressive business case with built-in feasibility analysis
- Conducting a stakeholder analysis
- Creating a scope statement
- Developing the charter
- Documenting high level risks, assumptions, and constraints

Phase 2:

- Identifying team members
- Defining roles and responsibilities in this phase
- Creating a project organization structure
- Developing a communications plan
- Creating the work breakdown structure (WBS)
- Creating subsidiary plans
- Determining project risks
- Creating the master project management plan
- Obtaining plan approval
- Developing a change management plan

Phase 3:
- Directing and managing project execution
- Acquiring team
- Developing team
- Managing team
- Performing quality assurance
- Executing the communication plan
- Managing stakeholder expectations
- Conducting procurements

Phase 4:
- Monitoring and controlling work
- Managing risks
- Administering procurements

Phase 5:
- Formalizing customer acceptance
- Performing personnel performance reviews
- Obtaining contract closure
- Understanding lessons learned
- Creating and distributing final reports

How to Contact the Publisher

Sybex welcomes feedback on all of its titles. Visit the Sybex website at www.sybex.com for book updates and additional certification information. You'll also find forms you can use to submit comments or suggestions regarding this or any other Sybex title.

How to Contact the Authors

Linda Kretz Zaval and Terri A. Wagner welcome your questions and comments. You can reach them by email at zaval@wildblue.net and Terri@mentor-source.com.

Phase

1

Initiating Process

Workers may think that projects are launched on nothing more than a grab out of thin air. Some feel that "sweetheart deals" are made before the project is cost justified. Others use sophisticated feasibility analysis as well as business cases to determine whether a project should be launched.

Regardless of how your project is approved, at some point, trusted and experienced project managers may have to challenge the rationale of senior managers before placing the project into the portfolio or moving on to the next phase. Let's face it: these senior managers don't always have all of the information that we project managers may have. We do this based on data and facts. Emotions have no place here.

For example, some project managers working on internal projects (for example, capital improvement projects) are advised not to be concerned with the cost; "just do whatever it takes to get the job done" seems to be the order from the sponsor and senior management. We as project managers are stewards of company funds. We can help launch projects that will not only provide benefit to the company, but also be cost-effective. But first we have to start at the beginning. This phase explores several ways you as the project manager can make a difference as projects are initiated:

- Understand finance principles
- Conduct project selection methods
- Establish a progressive business case with built-in feasibility analysis
- Conduct a stakeholder analysis
- Create a scope statement
- Develop the charter
- Document high-level risks, assumptions, and constraints

Task 1.1: Understanding Finance Principles

Project managers play a pivotal role in the economic engineering of projects and participate in feasibility studies as well as economic justification of projects, so we must have a broad understanding of the concepts of how money is used. In no way is this information intended to be all-inclusive—people earn degrees to master this topic.

Scenario

Cimarron Industries is a multimillion dollar corporation that had very humble beginnings. It is now in the Fortune 500 ranks and owns 200 stores as well as a centralized textile mill that produces fabrics.

The company was started to produce a series of children's books that were being written by the company founder and current CEO, Olivia Ross. The books were a total success, and the revenues from the books provided seed money to open a line of children's clothing stores patterned after the principal characters in the books.

The lines of clothing for each character were originally designed and created by Ms. Ross and were consigned to a children's boutique of a large clothing chain. They sold out immediately. Later, the apparel stores were also wildly successful. Marketing continues to focus on the superior quality of the clothing at discount store prices.

Based on that success, Ms. Ross would now like to open a line of women's clothing stores called Apples and Pears. Ms. Ross believes that the store would provide what women everywhere are looking for, that is, chic clothing tailored to body types. Those women with expanded waistlines would be "apples" and those with large derrières and legs would be "pears." The target audience would be middle-age to senior women, but Apples and Pears (A&P) would also have a line for younger women with less-than-perfect shapes. It will not focus on plus sizes, just body types in all sizes.

Ms. Ross does not consider herself business savvy. Her degree is in textiles and merchandising, so she counts on Skylar Reese, MBA, chief financial officer (CFO), to guide her business and financial decisions. During the discussions between Ms. Reese and Ms. Ross, Ms. Reese reminded Ms. Ross that several other projects are under consideration. One of these is the remodel of the five top-producing stores. Another is the upgrade of equipment at the textile mill.

Ms. Reese believes that to start another project now would tighten their cash flow, but has suggested that a market analysis and economic study of the proposal be conducted and the decision made after that. Ms. Ross agrees.

Scope of Task

Duration

This task should take several days, if not weeks, depending on the size of the project and your level of involvement in project selection methods.

Setup

For this task you need an understanding, if not a working knowledge, of key financial principles. The project manager collects data pertinent to the project, and a financial person crunches the numbers. You have to know what the crunched numbers mean and be able to use them to help create your project plan.

Caveat

During project selection, the project manager usually partners with a financial person to the extent needed to clarify the project to senior management.

Procedure

In this task you will learn how businesses and organizations use money and understand its relevance in project management. We will review the following:

- Time value of money
- Capital budgeting concepts
- Cash flow concepts
- Future value of money
- Present value of money

Details

It has been our experience that even though complete finance concepts are not generally taught in a project management class, business leaders expect project managers to be able to discuss issues relevant to finance. You may not be involved in the actual selection of projects, but given a basic knowledge of project selection methods and the way your project was chosen, you will be able to provide logical answers to problems along the way. Our intention is to provide simple finance concepts relevant to the project manager's role in the money game.

Time Value of Money

One of the basic concepts of business economics and managerial decision making is that the value of an amount of money is a function of the time of receipt or disbursement of cash. A dollar received today is more valuable than a dollar to be received at some future period of time. The only requirement for this concept to be valid is that there exists a positive rate of interest wherever you invest your funds. We will further explore this concept by showing you how to find the present value of a future amount and the future equivalent of a present amount. Time value of money is the heart of capital budgeting.

Capital Budgeting Concepts

Capital budgeting is used for investment decision making. Some decision-making criteria include the following:

- Maximize shareholder wealth
- Consider all cash flows
- Discount cash flows at the cost of capital
- Attempt to place an economic value on the strategic implications of new projects and include them in the economic analysis

- Quantify the strategic benefits of new projects in nonfinancial terms (for example, quality improvement, reduced lead time, and so forth)

  Capital budgeting's purpose is to

- Generate and gather investment ideas

- Estimate/forecast investment costs and benefits

- Analyze/evaluate the costs and benefits of each alternative

- Select among the alternatives and implement the investment chosen

- Evaluate the implemented investment

Cash Flow Concepts

Because investment decision making requires knowledge of cash flows, let's take a brief look at a simple cash flow illustration (see Table 1.1). A company spends $100,000 on a concept study and uses the following facts to determine cash flow:

Equipment $2,400 (year 0)

Depreciation $450, $360, $270, $180, $90

Training costs $816 (year 0)

Incremental sales $7,500 with a 10% increase over six years

Incremental operating expenses $6,500 with a 6% increase over five years

TABLE 1.1   Sample Cash Flow

	Year 0	Year 1	Year 2	Year 3	Year 4	Year 5
Equipment	$–2,400.00					
Depreciation		–$450.00	–$360.00	–$270.00	$–180.00	–$90.00
Training Costs	–$816.00					
Incremental Sales		$7,500.00	$8,250.00	$9,075.00	$9,982.50	$10,980.75
Operating Expenses		–$6,500.00	–$6,890.00	–$7,303.40	–$7,741.60	–$8,206.10
Earnings before Interest and Taxes—Total Expenses (EBIT)		$550.00	$1,000.00	$1,501.60	$2,060.90	$2,684.65
Taxes = 40%		–$220.00	–$400.00	–$600.64	–$824.36	–$1,073.86
Cash Flow	–$3,216.00	$330.00	$600.00	$900.96	$1,236.54	$1,610.79

Notice that in year 0, there are only expenses. The following years show depreciation as a negative number, which is subtracted from the incremental revenue as well as the operating expenses to come up with the EBIT figures. Taxes are then subtracted to find the cash flow. Most cash flows are more complicated and include adding back the depreciation to receive a net cash flow.

Present Value

Most large companies today use some form of discounted cash flow (DCF) techniques in investment decision making (capital budgeting). To perform a DCF analysis, we must find the present value of future sums of money. If you are entitled to receive $200 at the end of two years, you might consider receiving a lesser amount today (say, $188.68), provided that you could invest it over the next two years and earn enough to receive the $200.

The formula for present value is $PV = FV/(1 + i)^n$, where $(1 + i)^n$ is the present value of a dollar to be received at the end of period n when the time value of money is i. The term $/(1 + i)^n$ is called the *present value factor* or *discount factor*.

These discount factors determine potential growth. Present value is equal to the future value times the discount factor. These factors can be computed in three ways: via tables, hand calculators, or computer programs. Tables are the easiest. Table 1.2 is an example of discount factors.

TABLE 1.2 Discount Factors

n/r	1%	2%	3%	4%	5%	6%	7%
1	0.9901	0.9804	0.9709	0.9615	0.9524	0.9434	0.9346
2	0.9803	0.9612	0.9426	0.9246	0.9070	0.8900	0.8734
3	0.9706	0.8423	0.9151	0.8890	0.8638	0.8396	0.8163
4	0.9610	0.9238	0.8885	0.8548	0.8227	0.7921	0.7639
5	0.9515	0.9057	0.8626	0.8219	0.7835	0.7473	0.7130
6	0.9420	0.8880	0.8375	0.7903	0.7462	0.7050	0.6663
7	0.9327	0.8706	0.8131	0.7599	0.7107	0.6651	0.6227
8	0.9235	0.8535	0.7894	0.7307	0.6768	0.6274	0.5820
9	0.9143	0.8363	0.7664	0.7026	0.6448	0.5919	0.5439
10	0.9053	0.8303	0.7441	0.6756	0.6139	0.5584	0.5083

TABLE 1.2   *Discount Factors (continued)*

8%	9%	10%	11%	12%	13%	14%	15%
0.9259	0.9174	0.9091	0.9009	0.8929	0.8850	0.8772	0.8696
0.8573	0.8417	0.8264	0.8116	0.7972	0.7831	0.7695	0.7561
0.7938	0.7722	0.7513	0.7312	0.7118	0.6931	0.6750	0.6575
0.7350	0.7084	0.6830	0.6587	0.6355	0.6133	0.5921	0.5718
0.6806	0.6499	0.6209	0.5935	0.5674	0.5428	0.5194	0.4972
0.6302	0.5963	0.5645	0.5346	0.5066	0.4803	0.4556	0.4323
0.5835	0.5470	0.5132	0.4817	0.4523	0.4251	0.3996	0.3759
0.5403	0.5019	0.4665	0.4339	0.4039	0.3762	0.3506	0.3269
0.5002	0.4604	0.4241	0.3909	0.3606	0.3329	0.3075	0.2472
0.4632	0.4224	0.3855	0.3522	0.3220	0.2946	0.2697	0.2472

What is the present value of $1 to be received three time periods from now if the time value of money is 0.10 per period?

In Table 1.2 at the intersection of 10% and 3 time periods, the value equals 0.7513. Therefore, if you invest $0.7513 to earn 10% per year, after three years you will have $1.

What is the present value of $100 to be received three time periods from now if the time value of money is 0.10 per period? Because $(1 + 0.1)^3 = 0.7513$ (according to the discount table in Table 1.2), you can see in Table 1.3 that the present value of $100 is $75.13 at time 1, $82.64 at time 2, and finally $100 at time 3.

TABLE 1.3   Present Value Example

Time Period	Investment at Beginning of Period	Interest	Investment at End of Period
1	$75.13	7.513	$82.64
2	$82.64	8.264	$90.91
3	$90.91	9.091	$100.00

With discount factors, we can compute the present value of any single cash flow. But in most applications we need to be able to calculate the present value of any sequence of cash flows.

Present Value Addition Rule

The *present value addition rule* states that the value of any set of cash flows is the sum of the present value of each of the cash flows in the set. For example, using Table 1.2, what is the present value of two cash flows, $100 to be received at the end of one period from now and $200 to be received two periods from now, if the time value of money is 0.10? Table 1.4 shows an example of how to compute this.

TABLE 1.4   Present Value Addition Rule

Period	Cash Flow	Discount Factor	Present Value
1	$100.00	0.9091	$90.91
			$165.28
2	$200.00	0.8264	$256.19
		Present value using 0.10 =	

By using the formula for the present value of a future cash flow and the present value addition rule, you can calculate the present value of any possible cash flow.

Future Value

Assume that you have $1 now and can invest it to earn i interest. After one period, you will have $1 plus the interest earned on the $1. Let FV be the future value and i be the annual interest.

Repeating the process, at time 2 you will have

$$FV = (1 + i) + (1 + i)$$

or to be precise,

$$FV = PV(1 + i)^2.$$

If $i = 0.1$ and $n = 2$, we have

$$FV = PV (1 + i)^2 = (1 + 0.1)^2 = \$1.21.$$

If, instead of starting with $1, we start with a present value, PV, of $50, the value at time 2 is

$$FV = PV (1 + i)^n = \$50 (1.0 + 0.1)^2 = \$60.50.$$

At 10% interest, $50.00 grows to $55.00 at time 1. The $55.00 (still at 10% interest) grows to $60.50 at time 2. This equation is the standard compound interest formula for the future value of a present sum. The term $(1 + i)^n$ is called the *accumulation factor*. It shows how to calculate future values of a present sum: the dollar amount you will have in n periods (which could be months, quarters, years, and so on) in the future if a present sum of PV dollars is compounded for n periods at an interest rate of i per period. Instead of computing future values, business decisions are frequently made based on present values.

Hands-on 1.1: Testing Your Knowledge of Finance Principles

Make the calculations necessary to show which of the following statements are true and which are false if the interest rate is 5% per year. Remember that *n* is an accumulation factor and not a multiplier.

1. $98.00 now is equivalent to $105.60 one year from now. (True or false?)

2. $200.00 one year past is equivalent to $205.00 now. (True or false?)

3. $3,000.00 now is equivalent to $3,150.00 one year from now. (True or false?)

4. $3,000.00 now is equivalent to $2,887.14 one year ago. (True or false?)

5. Interest accumulated in one year on an investment of $2,000.00 is $100.00. (True or false?)

Task 1.2: Understanding Project Selection Methods

Internal projects are selected in a variety of ways. Most come from internal customers wanting to change the way they operate, the systems they use, their location, and so on.

Project selection methods help decision makers choose projects based on some criteria. There are several types of project selection methods. In this task we will show you economic models using net present value and internal rate of return as well as benefit measurement methods that compare projects based on prearranged criteria. We will also look at a weighted scoring model.

Scenario

You have been assigned as the project manager of the Apples and Pears project and are to assist Ms. Reese any way you can. Ms. Reese has chosen you because your previous position was that of a business analyst. You have been a successful project manager for five years now, and know your way around the company and most of its processes.

You gathered data about cash flows, and considered operating expenses and earnings before interest, taxes, depreciation, and amortization (EBITDA) as well as the availability of personnel to work on the project, the training needed, strategic fit, competitive advantage, and a high-level comparative analysis. You have taken a recent class on capital budgeting and are anxious to try out what you have learned. It all looks promising, but the answer is in the money.

Scope of Task

Duration

This task may take hours or days, depending on the complexity of the project and your involvement in financial decision making.

Setup

Now that you have an understanding, if not a working knowledge, of key financial principles, you are ready to make some financial calculations.

Caveat

None.

Procedure

In this task you will learn different approaches to determine whether projects should be approved or denied. We will discuss the following:

- Net present value
- Internal rate of return
- Benefit measurement methods
- Economic methods such as net present value (NPV) and internal rate of return (IRR)
- Benefit measurement methods such as comparative approaches and scoring models

Details

Sometimes it is difficult to choose one project over another. You may have a variety of project selection methods, but one of them should at least include an objective economic model such as NPV or IRR. You want to be able to defend your logic with facts and figures as well as your own subjective thoughts and ideas.

Economic Model: Net Present Value

NPV is the current market value of a cash flow amount at time n if the discount factor Dn is based on a discount rate r that is the market price for the use of one dollar. It is an application of the present value concept, in which the values are summed over time. NPV is also known as the market value for the stream of cash.

If the NPV is greater than 0, the investment is always considered acceptable. With zero taxes, the NPV of an investment may be described as the maximum amount a firm could pay for the opportunity of making the investment without being financially worse off.

The NPV of the investment is the sum of the present values of the cash flow minus the initial investment. NPV is determined by following these steps:

1. Choose an appropriate rate of discount.
2. Compute the present value of the cash proceeds expected from the investment.

3. Compute the present values of the cash outlays required by the investment.

4. Sum the present values of the proceeds minus the present values of the outlays.

Following along in Table 1.5, assume that an investment costs $10,000,000 and returns $12,100,000 a year later. If the rate of discount is 10%, a company could make a maximum immediate outlay of $11,000,110 in the expectation of receiving $12,100,000 a year later. If it can receive the $12,100,000 with an actual outlay of only $10,000,000, the NPV of the investment will be $1,000,110. In other words, the $1,000,110 represents the difference between the present value of the proceeds, $11,000,110, and the actual outlay of $10,000,000. The value in period 0 is negative because that is our original investment.

TABLE 1.5   Net Present Value Example

Period	Cash Flow	Present Value Factor	Present Value
0	−$10,000,000	1.000	−$10,000,000
			$11,000,110
1	$12,100,000	0.9091	$1,000,110
		NPV =	

NPV is widely used and accepted by most organizations. It is simple to calculate and easy to understand. Additionally, NPV in this example is positive, indicating that the investment is acceptable. NPV has the following advantages:

NPV is valid. It directly measures the present market value of one or more cash flows considered separately or in combination.

NPV is effective. As a decision variable, NPV provides all the usefulness of any other variable and also provides additional strengths.

NPV is reliable. If the rules for calculating NPV are followed, any analyst will produce the same result for a given stream of cash flows and a discount rate based on the market cost of money.

NPV is flexible. After the NPV has been calculated for a portion of any project, it can be used without recalculation to include that portion in any other investment.

In several examples we have shown the use of NPV at either time 0 or time 1. If we start with time 0, that is the *beginning* of the time period. If we use time 1, we are saying that the investment has been working for a period of time (for example, the *end* of the first year).

It is also important to note that if you start with time 0, you stay with time 0 to calculate NPV. If you start with time 1, you stay with time 1 to calculate NPV.

Now that you know the steps needed to calculate NPV, let's try it.

Hands-on 1.2: Testing Your Knowledge of NPV

1. Assume that there is an investment to pursue. The initial investment is $12,337 (year 0). Because this amount is the initial investment, it appears as a negative number. The cash flow at the end of the first year (period 1) is $10,000. The cash flow at the end of the second year is $5,000. Using Table 1.6, compute the NPV of this investment by using 10% as the discount rate.

TABLE 1.6   Determine NPV Problem 1

Period	Cash Flow	Present Value Factor	Present Value
		NPV =	

2. The remodel project initial investment is $5 million, and the cost of money is 9%. Cash flow for year 1 is $1 million, for years 2–3 is $900,000, and for years 4–6 is $750,000. Using Table 1.7, determine the present values for each year of the remodel project.

TABLE 1.7   PV for Remodel Project

Period	Cash Flow	Present Value Factor	Present Value
		NPV =	

3. What is the NPV for the remodel project?

4. The Apples and Pears project initial investment is $7,000,000, and the cost of money is 9%. Assume cash flow for year 1 is $3,000,000, for years 2–3 is $2,000,000, and for years 4–6 is $1,500,000. Using Table 1.8, determine the present values for each year of the Apples and Pears project.

TABLE 1.8   PV for Apples and Pears Project

Period	Cash Flow	Present Value Factor	Present Value
		NPV =	

5. What is the NPV of the Apples and Pears project?

6. If the investment for the Apples and Pears project increased to $8,750,000, how would that change the NPV?

7. Which project should be pursued?

8. What other project selection methods could you pursue?

Economic Model: Internal Rate of Return (IRR)

The internal rate of return (IRR) is the value of r that makes the NPV = 0. The IRR is, therefore, a summary measure of an investment (not just of the cash flows) that is useful only when comparing that investment with another identical investment. For example, comparing two capital improvement projects is considered acceptable when using IRR. Comparing a construction project and an IT project is not.

Using IRR can create serious challenges for those who manage capital budgets. When managers decide to finance only the projects with the highest IRR, they may be making a decision that is not as favorable as they think. For example, when all elements of the cash flow stream are known, the IRR provides some information about a particular stream of cash. Each financial investment in Table 1.9 has an IRR of 10%.

TABLE 1.9   Internal Rate of Return Example

Time Period	0	1	2
A	−$100	$0	$110
B	−$100	$10	$110
C	−$100	$110.	$110

- In scenario A $100 is invested at 10% for two years before there is a return on the investment of $100.

- In scenario B $100 is invested at 10% for two years also, but the interest payment is made at the end of year 1 and principal is returned at the end of year 2 along with an interest payment for the last year.

- In scenario C principal *and* interest are paid at the end of year 1. The principal ($100) is then invested for the second year at the same rate (10%).

These examples have quite different scenarios, but all have the same IRR. Be careful when using IRR.

Although it is quite possible that each of the alternatives A, B, and C would be viewed as the same by one or more investors, it is also possible to alter the differences of the scale so the IRR would be the same for financial investment opportunities that would otherwise appear very different—say, when compared with one another using NPV.

Benefit Measurement Method: Comparative Approach

There are several comparative approaches you can use to select one project over another. Table 1.10 illustrates one of them. There are three steps:

1. Criteria are determined. (These are typically preassigned.)

2. Each criterion is compared.

3. The decision is weighed.

TABLE 1.10   Comparative Approach

Criteria	Project 1	Project 2
1. Project maps to business vision, mission, goals, and corporate strategy.	Yes No	Yes No
2. Project delivers sufficient value to the business.	Yes No	Yes No
3. Project impacts or relates to a project or application within other business units.	Yes No	Yes No

TABLE 1.10 Comparative Approach *(continued)*

Criteria	Project 1	Project 2
4. Alternative analysis done.	Yes No	Yes No
5. Project follows company standards.	Yes No	Yes No
6. Team members have appropriate skill set and are available.	Yes No	Yes No
7. Other projects similar to this project address similar requirements.	Yes No	Yes No
8. Would any existing projects have to be discontinued when this project is completed?	Yes No	Yes No

It is important to remember that most projects also use an economic model before a decision is made or include an economic model as one of the criteria.

Benefit Measurement Methods: Weighted Scoring Models

The same comparison can be used but with a weight associated with each question. Each weight should be described to avoid confusion (for example, 5 = Mission critical, 4 = Very important, 3 = Important, 2 = Nice to have, 1 = Not important). In this case the scale is 1–5, with 5 being the highest. Other scoring models may have a different range. There are three steps for this process:

1. Assign a weight to each criterion.
2. Rate each criterion.
3. Multiply the weight by the rating to get the score.

Table 1.11 shows an example of weighted scoring.

TABLE 1.11 Weighted Scoring

Criteria	Project 1			Project 2		
	Weight	Rate	Score	Weight	Rate	Score
1. Project maps to business vision, mission, goals, and corporate strategy.	5	5	25	5	3	15
2. Project delivers sufficient value to the business.	5	4	20	5	5	25
3. Project impacts or relates to a project or application within other business units.	4	4	16	4	4	16

TABLE 1.11   Weighted Scoring *(continued)*

Criteria	Project 1			Project 2		
	Weight	Rate	Score	Weight	Rate	Score
4. Alternative analysis done.	4	3	12	4	2	8
5. Project follows company standards.	4	3	12	4	4	16
6. Team members have appropriate skill set and are available.	3	3	9	3	3	9
7. Other projects relate that address similar requirements.	4	2	8	4	3	12
8. Would any existing projects have to be discontinued when this project is completed?	3	2	6	3	1	3
		Total	108		Total	104

Weighted scoring models are simple and provide consistency in their approach. For small projects (and your company would have to decide what is considered *small*), weighted scoring models may be enough. But most companies use an economic model as well.

There could be challenges with scoring models. Projects may be ranked and scored subjectively (without data and facts) instead of objectively. There may be inconsistencies in the selection committee based on politics, a personal agenda, and so on. Senior management may override the decision. If these challenges do exist, consider revamping the criteria so that all are in agreement.

Hands-on 1.3: Testing Your Knowledge of Benefit Measurement Methods—Scoring Models

Answer the following questions:

1. For each criterion found in Table 1.11, what information could you provide that would justify the rating and score?

2. Select five additional criteria. Weight and rank them. Determine the score. How could this impact the result in question 1?

3. What are the advantages of scoring models?

4. Is a comparative approach enough? Why or why not?

5. What problems could you have with this approach?

Task 1.3: Using Business Cases with Built-in Feasibility Analysis

Now that you have a good grasp of business finance, you are ready to look at a business case and its value to project management. Business cases are only as good as the people who prepare them and their knowledge of corporate finance and project management. A progressive business case has built-in feasibility analysis and provides a *score* at the completion of each phase. A minimum score is needed in order to move to the next phase. Each phase has its own *scorecard* that measures progress by the use of a minimum score. The scorecards for three activities are as follows:

- Project selection scorecard
- Project charter sign-off scorecard
- Project planning scorecard

Scenario

Although Ms. Reese is 99% sure that Ms. Ross would approve the project, based on what is known to date, Ms. Reese wants to take a closer look at the real world implications to their business. You have apprised Ms. Reese that there are operational issues, revenue tests, and other elements besides financials that could impact the bottom line. Ms Reese has discussed your suggestion with James Stevens, a member of the finance committee they both attend, and he agrees that a progressive business case should be used. He believes that it would bring reality to their assumptions and solidify support from those who may oppose the project.

Scope of Task

Duration

This task should take several days, if not weeks, depending on the size of the project and your level of involvement in project selection.

Setup

For this task you need a basic understanding of how business operates. With that, you can easily assist in the preparation of a business case. Again you will work with other managers—all of whom will own a piece of the pie.

Caveat

The project manager is typically given the operations criteria of the business case segment, called *probability of success* and *milestones*, because that is where project managers typically have expertise.

Procedure

In this task you will learn the elements of a progressive business case and see how they are iteratively refined. You will look at the five segments of a business case and compare their iterative scorecards. Those five segments are:

- Program assessment
- Financials
- Internal issues
- Alternatives and recommendations
- Milestones

Details

The difference between a business case and other project selection methods is that a business case affords a higher level of confidence to decision makers, because it takes a holistic view of the company. The business case is completed through the planning phase, thus before major expenditures occur. Additionally, the business case can be followed through the end of the project and beyond. For instance, if the business goal of the project were to increase revenues, it may take another year or more to see whether revenues have increased.

A minimum score is assigned to each of the criteria within a segment of the business case. If the total minimum score is not achieved, the project cannot proceed to the next activity.

The minimum values have been preassigned to each criteria. A project selection committee usually decides the minimum score for each scorecard. In the real world, this business case is repeated for the project charter sign-off and planning activities. Each progressive phase increases the minimum score that enables a decision maker to decide whether the project should continue.

For example, if the minimum score through project charter sign-off does not meet the minimum score for both activities (selection and charter), the project cannot advance to planning. Rather than show the table in its entirety for charter and planning, we include only summary minimums. Table 1.12 is an example of a minimum scorecard for the project selection activities.

TABLE 1.12   Project Selection Scorecard

1. PROGRAM ASSESSMENT				
A.	MARKET ANALYSIS			SCORE
	Customer-Initiated Request or Customer Expectation	Minimum Score	0	
	0	No request		
	5	Informal request		
	10	Formal request/expectation		
	Meets Customer Need	Minimum Score	5	
	0	No needs identified		
	5	Perceived fit with need(s)		
	10	Known fit with need(s)		
	Market Window	Minimum Score	4	
	0	Can't meet—delivery time exceeds customer requirements		
	5	Perceived ability to meet customer requirements		
	10	Known ability to meet customer requirements		
	Willingness to Pay	Minimum Score	5	
	0	Known unwillingness		
	5	Perceived willingness		
	10	Known willingness at proposed price		
	Market Potential	Minimum Score	3	
	0	No potential		
	3	Perceived potential		
	5	Some customers want		
	10	Most customers want		
	Forecast	Minimum Score	3	
	0	No forecast		
	5	Draft forecast		
	10	Firm forecast from customers with commitments from account teams and customers		
B.	STRATEGIC FIT			SCORE
	Product Alignment with Strategy	Minimum Score	3	
	0	No fit with any business unit strategy		
	5	Fits with half of business unit's strategies		
	10	Fits with all of business unit's strategies		
C.	COMPETITIVE ADVANTAGE			SCORE
	Creates Competitive Advantage	Minimum Score	0	
	0	No advantage		
	5	Perceived advantage or meets competition		
	10	Clear advantage		
D.	PROBABILITY OF SUCCESS			SCORE
	Availability of Technology	Minimum Score	5	
	0	No advantage		
	5	Perceived advantage or meets competition		
	10	Clear advantage		
	Ordering	Minimum Score	3	
	0	Means not available		
	5	Perceived feasibility		
	10	Known feasibility—mechanized systems ready when needed		

TABLE 1.12   Project Selection Scorecard *(continued)*

	Billing		Minimum Score	3	
	0	Means not available			
	5	Perceived feasibility			
	10	Known feasibility—mechanized systems ready when needed			
	Fraud Control		Minimum Score	3	
	0	No advantage			
	5	Perceived advantage or meets competition			
	10	Clear advantage			
	Maintenance		Minimum Score	3	
	0	Means not available			
	5	Perceived feasibility			
	10	Known feasibility—available when needed			
	Installation/Deployment		Minimum Score	3	
	0	Means not available			
	5	Perceived feasibility			
	10	Known feasibility—available when needed			
	Systems Synergy		Minimum Score	3	
	0	All new systems needed			
	5	Major modifications needed			
	10	Minimal modifications needed			
	Risk Versus Benefits		Minimum Score	3	
	0	Risks outweigh benefits			
	5	Risks and benefits are equal			
	10	Benefits outweigh risks			
		PROGRAM ASSESSMENT MINIMUM SCORE			49
		PROGRAM ASSESSMENT ACTUAL SCORE			
		DIFFERENCE			
2.	**FINANCIALS**				
A.	**Quality of Financial Analysis**		Minimum Score	3	**SCORE**
	0	Not done			
	1	Rough estimate of revenue, expense, capital or price, and estimated incremental investment (per unit basis)			
	3	Estimated demand, revenue, expense, capital in business case format (income statement, etc.)			
	5	Preliminary financial analysis including sensitivity analysis of variables, functional units involved in estimating costs where appropriate			
	7	Financial analysis including best/worst case scenarios, sensitivity analysis, and functional units involved in estimating costs where appropriate			
	10	Financial analysis including Monte Carlo risk analysis, best/worse case scenarios, sensitivity analysis, and service units involved in estimating costs where appropriate			
B.	**Financial Desirability of Program**		Minimum Score	1	**SCORE**
	0	Not done			
	1	Project/Program is expected to break even within 5 years			
	3	Project/Program has a positive NPV within the study life and has a discounted break even of 5 years or less			
	5	Project has significant gross margin/EBITDA opportunity and impact			

TABLE 1.12   Project Selection Scorecard *(continued)*

	7	Project/Program meets 3 of the 4 following criteria:
		  1. A modified profitability index of 2.0 or greater
		  2. A program rate of return 10% above the cost of capital
		  3. A discounted break even of 5 years or less
		  4. Shareholder value greater than $5M			

	10	Project/Program has:
		  1. A modified profitability index of 3.0 or greater
		  2. A program rate of return 15% above the cost of capital
		  3. A discounted break even of 3 years or less
		  4. Shareholder value greater than $10M			

		FINANCIALS MINIMUM SCORE		4	
		FINANCIALS ACTUAL SCORE			
		DIFFERENCE			
3.	**INTERNAL ISSUES**				
A.	**Effects of Preliminary Disclosure**	Minimum Score	3	**SCORE**	
	0	Effects of disclosure either have not been considered, or considered to be generally negative			
	1	Net impacts of full disclosure to competitors considered to be generally neutral			
	3	Net impacts of full disclosure to competitors considered to be generally positive			
B.	**Contract Development**	Minimum Score	2	**SCORE**	
	0	Not done			
	3	Outline completed			
	3	Draft completed, issues resolvable			
	10	Contract completed			
C.	**NET REVENUE TEST INPUTS/ANALYSIS**				
	Impact on Cross Elastic (CE) and Complimentary Services	Minimum Score	5	**SCORE**	
	0	Not done or negative net impact			
	3	Neutral net impact			
	3	Positive net impact			
	Demand Analysis for New Services, Cross Elastic, and Complimentary Services	Minimum Score	5	**SCORE**	
	0	Not done			
	5	Preliminary analysis completed, somewhat rough but much research either completed or in process			
	10	Analysis well developed and documented			
	Net Revenue Test Demand Relationships Analysis	Minimum Score	5	**SCORE**	
	0	Not done or negative net impact			
	5	Neutral net impact			
	10	Positive net impact			
	Legal	Minimum Score	4	**SCORE**	
	0	Violates rules/law			
	3	Issues identified			
	4	Legal department contacted			
	5	Perceived ability to resolve issues			
	10	Does not violate rules/laws			

TABLE 1.12 Project Selection Scorecard *(continued)*

		INTERNAL ISSUES MINIMUM SCORE			24
		INTERNAL ISSUES ACTUAL SCORE			
		DIFFERENCE			
4.	**ALTERNATIVES AND RECOMMENDATIONS**				
A.	**Pricing Plan (first year)**		Minimum Score	3	**SCORE**
	0	Not done			
	5	Rough draft			
	10	Completed			
		ALTERNATIVES AND RECOMMENDATIONS MINIMUM SCORE			3
		ALTERNATIVES AND RECOMMENDATIONS ACTUAL SCORE			
		DIFFERENCE			
4.	**MILESTONES**				
A.	**A. First Year Milestones by Quarter (including tracking mechanisms and contingencies)**		Minimum Score	0	**SCORE**
	0	Not done			
	5	Rough draft			
	10	Completed			
		MILESTONES MINIMUM SCORE			0
		MILESTONES ACTUAL SCORE			
		DIFFERENCE			

Now that you have reviewed the business case, take a look at the summaries for the project selection scorecard as well as the summaries for charter sign-off and planning (see Table 1.13). Notice how the scores progressively increase.

Hands-on 1.4: Testing Your Knowledge of Business Cases

Using your common sense and experience, please answer the following questions:

1. Who should prepare the business case? Why?

2. What do you think are the advantages of a project manager participating in the business case process?

3. Are there disadvantages? Why or why not?

4. Is a business case enough? Why or why not?

TABLE 1.13   Summary Scorecards for Project Selection, Charter Sign-off, and Planning

Summary Project Selection			
	Minimum Score	Actual Score	Difference
PROGRAM ASSESSMENT	49		
FINANCIALS	4		
INTERNAL ISSUES	24		
ALTERNATIVES AND RECOMMENDATIONS	4		
MILESTONES	0		
*TOTALS	81		

Summary Project Charter Sign-off			
	Minimum Score	Actual Score	Difference
PROGRAM ASSESSMENT	76		
FINANCIALS	8		
INTERNAL ISSUES	33		
ALTERNATIVES AND RECOMMENDATIONS	10		
MILESTONES	5		
*TOTALS	132		

Summary Project Planning			
	Minimum Score	Actual Score	Difference
PROGRAM ASSESSMENT	117		
FINANCIALS	12		
INTERNAL ISSUES	43		
ALTERNATIVES AND RECOMMENDATIONS	19		
MILESTONES	9		
*TOTALS	200		

Now that you have an overview on finance, how projects are selected, and how business cases evolve, you are ready to move forward! You now have the ability to map your project activities to the corporate issues that matter the most—money. Remember, at the top of the food chain, it's always about money. You can now plan your project brilliantly, present your project brilliantly, and defend your project brilliantly: with data and facts relative to money!

Task 1.4: Identifying Stakeholders— Who Are They?

Stakeholders are people. First and foremost, they are human beings. These folks can be an individual, a group, a community, or the like, but whatever we call them, they have an interest in your project. They may support your project with enthusiasm or they may have serious concerns about your project.

Some people may have serious concerns but have no power to change anything in the project. Others may be highly supportive but have no rank. And the opposite is also true: Some high-ranking corporate individuals may be the champions for your project or the harbingers of doom because they do not support the project at all.

In all cases it is important to listen to all of the stakeholders in your project. You may learn something you didn't understand or know. In this task you will discover who your stakeholders are, and their roles and responsibilities in a project.

Scenario

Ms. Reese, with help from her project manager from Cimarron Industries, has determined that the Apples and Pears project is a favorable project to pursue. It was determined that this project will generate more revenue in the short term than upgrades to the textile mill or a remodel of existing children's stores.

Creating clothing stores is the company's bread and butter. Ms. Ross believes they should use the same approach they used 20 years ago when the original children's stores were launched. Ms. Reese wants to bring in additional internal people who may have a better understanding of the more current way this type of project is handled. Ms. Ross thinks this is a waste of time but reluctantly agrees.

Ms. Reese also reminds Ms. Ross that if all goes well during this initiation phase, the planning work can be started in December and the project could be complete by the start of the next holiday season. Ms. Ross thinks that would be splendid but realizes those dates are not cast in stone until thorough planning has occurred.

Scope of Task

Duration

This task may take a few hours or several days, depending on the scope of the project and the availability of stakeholders.

Setup

None.

Caveat

For this task, you must be able to converse with senior management or others at their level.

Procedure

In this task we will

- Identify types of projects.
- Identify and analyze project stakeholders.
- Explore the roles and responsibilities of the project sponsor and project manager.
- Take a look at the management and leadership skills needed in a project manager.

Details

People are the most important resource on a project! Individuals are complex, and the project manager spends a great deal of time with them. We provide and receive information, overcome emotional hurdles, and provide and receive performance information in all manner of communications. First and foremost we must know and understand who these people are and their roles in the project. The stakeholders will come from different backgrounds, depending on the types of projects you're working on. Let's take a look at the types of projects you may manage someday.

Types of Projects

Different project types will dictate the appropriate stakeholders who will participate in the project. Most project managers do not have experience in all types of projects, and although it is helpful to have technical skills, the right project manager can manage many types of projects. Several types of projects seem to be common to most businesses and organizations from time to time, although this list is not all-inclusive:

Research and development projects are often likened to programs because they typically have an element of ongoing activity and exist as long as they are funded and achieve the desired result.

Strategic projects include reorganizations, mergers, acquisitions, reengineering, or enterprise-wide initiatives such as process improvement or quality efforts.

Information technology projects include new development, rapid application development, small and large maintenance, LAN/WAN creation, application acquisition, and the like.

Engineering and construction projects create buildings, bridges, and roads, among other things.

Capital improvement projects exist to upgrade internal or external infrastructures (roads, bridges, and the like) or equipment.

Product development projects create new products and services for internal or external use based on market demand and technology advances, and often involve manufacturing efforts.

Legal mandates or requirements can include, for example, a manufacturing facility that must comply with mandatory Environmental Protection Agency (EPA) emissions standards or a legal mandate that safety equipment be updated, perhaps based on a negligence lawsuit.

External customer requests are projects generated by customers that are not internal to your organization.

This list does not represent all types of projects—there are many more.

What Is a Stakeholder?

A stakeholder is anyone who will be impacted by or has an interest in the project. Who are these interested and involved people? The following is a list of some of the stakeholders on a project.

- Clients
- Sponsor
- Project manager
- Champion
- Performers
- Users
- Line managers
- Vendors
- Steering committee
- Support and operational staff
- Quality control staff
- Quality assurance staff

Some of the most important members of the project team are the project sponsor, project manager, and project team leaders. You need to understand their roles and responsibilities so there is no role confusion. We also will take a brief look at the leadership and management skills of a project manager.

ROLES OF THE PROJECT SPONSOR

The project sponsor plays a key role and has a defined set of responsibilities within a project:

- Participates in sales efforts and contract negotiations
- Establishes and maintains top-level client relationships
- Assists the project manager in launching the project
- Participates in the project steering committee, governance board, or oversight committee to assist in setting project priorities
- Interprets company policies if necessary
- Cuts through the red tape when that is required
- Optimizes corporate objectives

The sponsor should be in constant communication with the project manager. The project manager must keep the sponsor informed of project activities. The sponsor should never find out from someone else something they should have found out from the project manager.

ROLES OF THE PROJECT MANAGER: MANAGEMENT

Most people can be taught the tools of the trade, but a project manager must possess good management skills able to support the following disciplines:

- Financial management and accounting
- Purchasing and procurement
- Contracts and commercial law
- Manufacturing and distribution
- Logistics and supply chain
- Strategic planning, tactical planning, and operational planning
- Organizational structures, organizational behavior, personnel administration, compensation, benefits, and career paths
- Information technology

Additionally, project managers must have some technical skills, including the following:

- Able to manage the technology even if not skilled in the technology
- Can communicate with technical personnel
- Has a holistic perspective
- Can facilitate trade-offs
- Integrates technical, business, and human objectives
- Understands engineering tools and support methods
- Able to perform appropriate budgeting and estimating techniques
- Can plan and organize multifunctional teams
- Understands functional policies and operating procedures

So what else is a manager looking for when they hire a project manager? Not everyone is cut out to do this work. Do you fit the bill?

- You have to have a very thick skin.
- You need to be a technical generalist (not a specialist).
- You need to be able to live without structure and rules.
- Conversely, you also need to be able to live with structure and rules.
- You can accept the fact that you will (on occasion) have high-maintenance team members.
- You will manage conflict on a daily basis.
- You will have to decide whether an issue equates to the milk being left out or missing a job interview.

- You will deal with all ranks in the hierarchy but will have no significant rank.

- You must be willing to take the heat without it breaking your heart.

- You will smile when you see the client shaking hands with the president of your company on the company newsletter.

- You will be an honorable mention in the last paragraph of the company newsletter.

- Expect to be on the 6 o'clock news if things go wrong.

- You are in a place of notoriety and visibility (for good or ill).

- You will have a great sense of humor!

And remember, this is just a job—don't forget work/life balance.

Now that you know what the project manager's management roles are, let's take a look at the leadership roles of a project manager.

ROLES OF THE PROJECT MANAGER: LEADERSHIP

The project manager position is not for everyone. There is a discrete difference between management and leadership. The first woman general of the U.S. Army, Brigadier General Anna Mae Hays, Chief of the Army Nurse Corp, coined the phase, "You lead people. You manage time and things." Both are necessary, but in the project management role, quintessential leadership is the more important role.

Most project managers probably didn't tell their parents as they were growing up that they wanted to be a project manager. We landed that role in a variety of ways. You may have been asked if you wanted a "job enrichment opportunity." Of course you said yes, but in reality you knew nothing about managing projects. Thankfully, your boss saw good managerial and leadership skills in you and over time you became successful as a project manager.

Others were chosen to be a project manager because of their superior technical skills. This may sometimes be a hindrance to the project, however, as project managers focus their expertise in the technical field. It is difficult to remove your technical hat and become a generalist instead of a specialist. It takes a lot of trust that someone can do your technical job as well as you did.

Some project managers actually went to school and studied the topic, so they were prepared to be a project manager from the onset. Are you ready to take on the project management *leadership* role?

Hands-on 1.5: Testing Your Knowledge of Leadership Analysis

Table 1.14 represents key project management leadership skills. For each item, circle the number that represents your brutally honest answer. Your analysis is found in the Phase 1 Solutions section.

TABLE 1.14   Leadership Analysis

Little	Some		A Great Deal		SKILL
1	2	3	4	5	1. Ability to understand and work with group dynamics
1	2	3	4	5	2. Ability to differentiate between important and unimportant issues
1	2	3	4	5	3. Ability to know when to compromise
1	2	3	4	5	4. Possess both a flexible personality and a strong determination to succeed
1	2	3	4	5	5. Ability to state case well when needed
1	2	3	4	5	6. Ability to be assertive
1	2	3	4	5	7. Want to see things through
1	2	3	4	5	8. Ability to be persuasive and not be put off by potential confrontations or arguments
1	2	3	4	5	9. Feel comfortable with self-direction and do not become frustrated with unclear delegation of authority and/or from superiors
1	2	3	4	5	10. Ability to make fast, on-the-job decisions
1	2	3	4	5	11. Exhibit mature judgment
1	2	3	4	5	12. Ability to control costs
1	2	3	4	5	13. Ability to establish ties, and monitor and evaluate project accountability among team members
1	2	3	4	5	14. Ability to understand major technical issues
1	2	3	4	5	15. Ability to provide feedback for productive and creative efforts
1	2	3	4	5	16. Ability to communicate upward with clients and higher management and downward with key technical managers and professionals
1	2	3	4	5	17. Ability to take strong leadership in the beginning and willingness to delegate responsibility and authority to others as the project progresses
1	2	3	4	5	18. Ability to listen, probe, and objectively evaluate information
1	2	3	4	5	19. Ability to play unfamiliar roles as a manager
1	2	3	4	5	20. Politically astute
1	2	3	4	5	21. Ability to develop effective work relationships with peers and with individuals of different ranks
1	2	3	4	5	22. Willingness to participate in problem identification, problem solving, and decision making
1	2	3	4	5	23. Willingness to use, when needed, a trial and error approach rather than a sophisticated management approach
1	2	3	4	5	24. Well skilled in negotiating processes
1	2	3	4	5	25. Ability to be a political diplomat

ROLE OF THE PROJECT TEAM LEADER

Project managers usually work within the construct of a matrix organizational structure. Functional managers, line managers, or team leaders play a vital role in the success of projects. Their role, in addition to being accountable for their operational objectives, is to support the project manager. Here are some make or break roles that a project manager expects from team leaders:

- Demonstrates potential for innovative and creative behavior
- Supportive of project goals and objectives
- Flexible when changes are necessary
- Meets commitments for completion of deliverables
- Deals with conflicts within own area of authority
- Results oriented
- Maintains high morale
- Communicates clearly and concisely

Responsibility Assignment Matrix

Project managers have many things to be responsible for on a project, but what about the members of the team? The responsibility assignment matrix (RAM) is a simple tool to see at a glance who is responsible for what. Table 1.15 shows a RAM that represents a two-dimensional relationship between personnel on the project and their level of involvement in the project. They can be noted as responsible, accountable, provide support, must be consulted, or need to provide information (RASCI).

TABLE 1.15   Responsibility Assignment Matrix

Responsible	This person is usually a line manager responsible for individuals performing the work.
Accountable	An accountable party is a person or group who is liable for the outcome and having the authority to approve or reject deliverables based on acceptance criteria. This person is usually the owner of the project.
Support	A support person is usually the person performing the work. This may be an internal support person or an external vendor.
Contributor	This person is a contributor or a consultant who provides input to the project. These folks contribute expertise on an as-needed basis.
Information	This person is one who is informed of project information. This is usually the sponsor and members of the project team. Senior managers may wish to be informed if the project is highly visible.

Projects and the tasks within them are often complex. People want to know where they fit in the scheme of things. There are many models for identifying the roles of individuals in a project. A popular model is the RASCI model shown in Table 1.15 and described in Table 1.16.

TABLE 1.16 RASCI Model

Tasks	Project Manager	PMO	Team Members	Line Managers	Dept Manager	Sponsor	Senior Management

R	Responsible
A	Accountable
S	Support
C	Contributor
I	Information

Step 1 List the tasks.

Step 2 Use the letters of RASCI for each task as it corresponds to the title of the person listed above.

Step 3 Make sure there is only one accountable individual.

The RASCI model is simple. It can be made more complex by adding task numbers and any number of additional personnel titles. The RAM is a good executive overview tool enabling senior management to see at a glance what is being done by whom.

Now that you know who these people are, you should identify key stakeholders other than the sponsor, project manager, and team leaders. You need to do this because key stakeholders can influence a project in a positive or negative way. For example, a key stakeholder is concerned about exceeding the budget. In fact, that key stakeholder may be able to cancel your project if she does not feel that the project is staying on track and within the budget.

If you know this information, you can provide the key stakeholders with a level of confidence that the project is within the budget by giving them project cash flow data, earned value information, and so forth. So how do you determine these things? By conducting a stakeholder analysis.

Task 1.5: Conducting a Stakeholder Analysis

The stakeholders on your project can make or break the project. The project manager defines stakeholder assets or detriments and as a result will discover who supports your project and who does not.

You need to know who you can go to for help and support; but you especially want to know who may sabotage your project or cause you to "lose traction" as you move forward. People with high rank and high support should be leveraged fully. The project manager should create a response strategy that satisfies those with high power and no support.

Everyone has something of value to bring to the project, some more than others. Acknowledging contributions and feedback of stakeholders will go a long way toward project success. To accomplish this, you conduct a stakeholder analysis.

Scenario

Ms. Reese has prepared a list of potential stakeholders and provided them to the project manager.

- Megan Holly is a marketing manager who participated in the original market study. She has a sales background and is already planning her marketing strategy.

- James Stevens is on the finance committee with Ms. Reese. He believes that even though the initial numbers looked positive, it is risky to assume that the current economy will support the increasing revenue projections for the project.

- Jacob Patrick is the manager of engineering and construction. He believes that the cost of materials is decreasing because of the slowdown in new home sales and that the project could provide many jobs during its implementation.

- Jordyn Kelly is the human resources vice president who is all for the project because it will create new jobs in many new cities.

- Skylar Janes is the advertising manager for Cimarron Industries and is eager to pursue the brand project this will create.

- Carolyn Lee is the union representative for the manufacturing facility. She represents those who will ultimately design and manufacture the clothing.

- Madison Adams is the webmaster of Cimarron's web pages. She wants to know whether Apples and Pears customers will order clothing through the Internet and if so, will adequate funding be provided for additional servers and the like.

- Allison Jones is the IT manager and is concerned that traffic may double without adequate support systems being provided.

- Darcy Moore is the operations director for the West Coast children's stores.
- Louise Rose is the operations director for the East Coast children's stores.
- Todd Franks is a site superintendent for new stores.
- Harry Edwards is the procurement director for Cimarron.

Scope of Task

Duration

This task could take several hours to several days, depending on the complexity of the project.

Setup

The project manager should obtain a private place for interviews and a public space conducive to a free flow of information.

Caveat

None.

Procedure

As mentioned earlier, we conduct a stakeholder analysis to identify those who may have a positive or negative influence on the project. The steps include, but are not limited to, the following:

1. Brainstorm who potential stakeholders might be.
2. Interview potential stakeholders for their interests or concerns they may have about the project.
3. Determine the stakeholder's level of power or influence.
4. Determine the impacts of stakeholders.
5. Develop strategies that will lend support to your projects from these stakeholders.
6. Create a stakeholder map.

Details

A stakeholder analysis is a relatively simple task to do. Keep in mind, however, that key stakeholders may not always be the higher-level managers in an organization. For example, five call centers located in different areas were being moved to a location at least 75 miles away to create a mega-center. The key stakeholders for this project were the call center employees. Their concerns were very high relative to the cost of gas, the increase in time, and day care issues. Most were going to quit. By conducting a stakeholder analysis, their concerns were noted and several steps were taken to make it palatable for these workers to stay with their jobs.

After you brainstorm with your team and others to identify the stakeholders and have interviewed them, the next two steps are relatively simple. Developing strategies can be a little more complicated, but not so much if you did a good job with the previous steps. Table 1.17 shows four elements of the analysis.

TABLE 1.17 Stakeholder Analysis Template

Identify and Interview Potential Stakeholders	Determine Concern or Interest	Impact Assessment	Strategies to Reduce Challenges and Gain Support

For those who have *high power and high concern,* you must get them involved in the stakeholder analysis and make a concerted effort to satisfy their concerns. Before they can be involved, you must be prepared to answer their questions. Here are a few questions that executives might have:

- What is the business need for the project?
- Why are we undertaking it now?
- What is the commercial implication?
- Do we have the right people with the right skills available to do the project?
- Will this affect our market share?
- What is the proposed schedule?
- What are the cost factors?
- Are there any special requirements?
- What would happen if we did not do this project?

For those who have *high power and no concerns,* you should keep them in the loop but not bog them down with details.

For those who have *low power but high concern,* make sure to identify those concerns, and keep them involved in the details of the project. These are the folks who are technically proficient but may not trust that you have all the details needed. They can be a detriment to your project if you ignore them. For example, they might bring up a technical issue that you are not familiar with. If you do not listen to these folks, they may stand back, watch you get in trouble, and say "Well, if you had asked me to help, I would have." Not everyone would do this, but if only one does it, the project can be in peril.

Here are a few questions that people with low power and high concern might have:

- What is the benefit of this project to me?
- Will this project change/eliminate my job?
- Will this project change the way I do my job?
- Will this project create personal conflict for me (start of shift, overtime, day care issues, and so forth)?

For those who have *low power and low interest,* do not send them too much information.

So now we know who the key stakeholders are: those with high power and high concern and those with low power and high concern.

The last step of the analysis is accomplished by creating a stakeholder map. This map (Figure 1.1) allows you to see at a glance how to manage your stakeholders. When creating the map, some people like to color-code the output, for instance, green for positive people plotted on the grid, yellow for neutral, and red for negative.

FIGURE 1.1   Stakeholder map

Low Concern/Interest/Support High Power **Keep Satisfied**	High Concern/Interest/Support High Power **Manage Closely**
Low Concern/Interest/Support Low Power **Normal Monitoring**	High Concern/Interest/Support Low Power **Keep Informed**

Hands-on 1.6: Testing Your Knowledge of the Stakeholder Analysis

1. Complete Table 1.18 to determine the level of power or influence, the impact assessment, and the strategy to leverage or reduce the challenges perceived by these stakeholders.

TABLE 1.18   Stakeholder Analysis

Identify and Interview Potential Stakeholders	Determine Concern or Interest	Impact Assessment	Strategies to Reduce Challenges and Gain Support
Megan Holly			
James Stevens			
Jacob Patrick			
Jordyn Kelly			
Skylar Janes			
Carolyn Lee			
Madison Adams			
Allison Jones			
Darcy Moore			
Louise Rose			
Todd Franks			
Harry Edwards			

2. What are the benefits of interviewing stakeholders and conducting a stakeholder analysis?

3. What other stakeholders may be interested in your project?

4. What other information might you want to know to help understand your stakeholders?

5. How does stakeholder analysis help you to build the support you need?

Hands-on 1.7: Testing Your Knowledge of Stakeholder Mapping

Use Table 1.19 to map the stakeholders that you have analyzed.

TABLE 1.19   Stakeholder mapping exercise

Low Concern/Interest/Support High Power **Keep Satisfied**	High Concern/Interest/Support High Power **Manage Closely**
Low Concern/Interest/Support Low Power **Normal Monitoring**	High Concern/Interest/Support Low Power **Keep Informed**

Task 1.6: Understanding Corporate Strategy

Strategic plans describe the corporate vision for their target markets with the goal of creating customer satisfaction effectively.

Plans that aren't implemented serve no useful purpose. It is imperative that the strategic plan is "in the headlights," so to speak, in order to solve problems and create marketing plans, product development plans, research and development plans, capital improvement plans, and other business plans that may be developed. Optimal decision making is the ultimate result when all plans, problems, and so on are integrated and supported.

Scenario

You have identified stakeholders, analyzed them, and learned a great deal of information. You know that the project must align with corporate strategy, so you have decided that all of your efforts from now on will map to Cimarron's strategic vision.

Scope of Task

Duration

This task could take several hours or days of research, depending on the complexity of the project.

Setup

None.

Caveat

You must have access to information that provides the company's strategic plans, goals, and the like.

Procedure

In this task you will take a look at the items you need in order to understand strategic plans:

- Description of strategic plans
- Elements of a strategic plan
- Project portfolio management
- Business needs

Details

Organizations are always in a state of change because of technological advances, legal requirements, market demand, customer requests, and so on. An organization's strategic plan will also change depending on the rate of change and the organization's ability to manage those changes.

Elements of a Strategic Plan

The elements of a strategic plan typically answer the following questions: Where do we see ourselves going with our business? Is the business and market environment conducive to our success? How do we get there from here?

Project plans should map back to strategic plans. It becomes a tactical plan along with the marketing plan, business plans, and so forth. So it is essential that project managers understand the elements of a strategic plan, which include, in part, these elements:

- Value and vision statement
- Mission statement
- Critical success factors for the business
- What kind of image we want
- What we want to be known for
- Where we want to be in five years
- Key business drivers
- Actions for achievement
- Measurement system for success

Projects should be sanctioned based on their alignment with strategic goals and objectives.

Project Portfolio Management

Project portfolio management is a business process that takes a holistic view of projects and the total investment required of them so that decisions on funding can be prioritized based on corporate strategy and organizational alignment with those strategies as well as resources available, and so on. Investments should not be made based on the political clout of one business unit over another.

For example, most large corporations have business units, and those units have senior managers. The senior managers, with help from their team, forecast which projects will benefit their business unit and budget accordingly. If portfolio management was being used, the business unit leaders would meet with each other and throw all their projects on the table. The team would then prioritize those projects based on what's *best for the business* rather than what's best for the business unit. The benefits are obvious:

- Decisions about funding are more fair.
- Provides an optimal mix of investment risk and reward.

- Facilitates the balance of riskier, higher-reward projects vs. safer, lower-reward ones.
- Categorizes, prioritizes, and monitors new and ongoing investments.
- Better communication between project owners and business leaders.
- Greater understanding and cooperation over funding allocation; everybody sees where the dollars are flowing and why.
- Greater business accountability for investments.
- Portfolio management can be used to assign responsibility to appropriate leaders.
- More-efficient use of human resources. The number of staff and managers allocated to various projects becomes more visible and comparable.
- Exposes redundant and overlapping projects.

There are a few pitfalls to portfolio management, however:

- Some business unit leaders may feel as if their position is in jeopardy if they are not funded for all of their project requests.
- Even in the senior ranks, it is sometimes difficult to change thinking.

It will be up to senior executives to support the process and lead their direct reports through the transition.

Define Business Needs

The business need for the project should tie back to the strategic plan. Typical business needs might be as follows:

- Increase revenue
- Increase market share
- Create better customer satisfaction
- Reduce expenses
- Update technology
- Update infrastructure
- Create new products and services
- Perform capital improvements
- Comply with regulatory or legal mandates

Key business drivers that help create strategic plans may change from year to year depending on the economy or the availability of key personnel. One year the strategic plan might be to reduce expenses by laying off personnel. Another may be to change a capability in order to remain competitive. And there are many others. It is your job to always be able to answer the question, "Why are we doing this?"

Hands-on 1.8: Testing Your Knowledge of Corporate Strategy

1. Why does a project manager have to understand the corporate strategy?

2. List three elements of a strategic plan.

3. Why is portfolio management important?

4. What are the business needs for the Apples and Pears project?

Task 1.7: Creating the Scope Statement

The purpose of creating a scope statement at the beginning of the project is to have a basis upon which to make future project decisions. The project scope statement should give senior management a holistic overview of what to expect throughout the life of the project.

At this stage in the process, you describe what you know. This high-level scope statement then becomes part of the project charter. Further planning steps will progressively elaborate on this initial scope statement, providing additional detail for estimating, assigning, controlling, and finally accepting the project deliverables.

Scenario

Rather than reinvent the wheel, you obtained the original project plans for Cimarron's children's stores; although the plans are outdated, you were able to glean and update what you feel is enough information to develop a scope statement. These facts supplement additional information you have obtained. You learned through your interviews with the stakeholders that not everyone was wild about the project.

You have been privileged to be a part of some strategic planning sessions because your mentor is also your project sponsor. Terri Higgins is a Project Management Professional (PMP®), and hopefully you will become one by the end of December, as this project will give you the required hours needed to sit for the PMP exam. She will be a huge help to you. Thankfully, you know that project management is a key business process and is supported from above. In fact, there is a central project management office (PMO), with a manager of project managers who provides project management services, support, training, and mentoring to their staff. You belong to this group.

You now know that for phase 1 of the project, trial stores will be constructed at a new mall being built in Bellevue, Washington. This is a high-end location, but the company is betting that no matter what their customer's spending habits might be, beautiful clothing that fits and can be purchased at a reasonable price will appeal to most women. The other location will be at Washington Square, just south of Portland, Oregon, where there is a broader range of spending habits.

These stores are to be elegant, with plush carpeting, soft music playing, designer showcasing, private dressing rooms, ambient lighting, as well as displays for jewelry, accessories, and perfume items. There will also be a second-floor bridal gallery.

Senior management initially decided that developing and advertising the brand, hiring personnel, and any IT work would be considered a cost of doing business. You and Ms. Reese have since convinced senior management that the cost for that work will be at least $1,750,000 more than the original estimate and should be included in the project so that real costs can be determined for future use. They agreed to add that amount to the budget.

The project will not include the cost of leasing space at the malls because that is considered a yearly operational cost.

Terri Higgins has advised you that the project has been conditionally approved based on the business case you helped to prepare. The rough order-of-magnitude budget for setting up the two stores is $8,750,000 to be allocated as shown in Table 1.20.

TABLE 1.20   Preliminary Budget

Budget Item	Amount
Advertising	$1,000,000
Space planning	$5,000
Construction	$3,600,000
Noninventoried furnishings	$50,000
Design of clothing	$1,250,000
Hiring and training of personnel	$50,000
Information technology	$700,000
Manufacturing costs	$2,075,000
Delivery and setup	$20,000
Total	$8,750,000

This number will be refined when the details of the project are known. The target date for completion is November 1 of next year for both stores, just in time for the holidays.

Scope of Task

Duration

The duration of this task could take hours or days, depending on the complexities of the project.

Setup

This is not a task you will do alone. You will enlist your team members and others to assist you with this task. Don't forget your sponsor!

Caveat

None.

Procedure

For this task you will build a project scope statement that will include, but is not limited to these factors:

- Project objectives
- Product scope description
- Project deliverables
- Project requirements
- Project boundaries
- Work product acceptance criteria
- Initial project organization

Details

It has been said that a poorly prepared scope statement is often the cause of major cost overruns, schedule delays, poor morale, and ultimately project failure. So where do you get all of the information needed to create the scope statement? You can rely on experts; use templates, forms, and past history; and talk to fellow project managers, who may be your best source if they have managed the same kind of project. You have already conducted a stakeholder analysis, and much of the information you will need comes from that.

A properly prepared baselined project scope statement is comprehensive enough to provide a common understanding of the project objectives and deliverables among all the stakeholders.

After the scope is baselined, it allows for evaluating change requests on additional work to verify whether they are within the boundaries of the originally approved work effort.

Business Goals vs. Project Objectives

Business goals describe *what* you want to accomplish. The business goals should align with corporate strategy. Project objectives describe *how* you are going to accomplish the business goal. The best method to use when writing project objectives is the SMART method, a popular method that has been around for many years. The objectives should be as follows:

Specific The objective tells exactly what, where, and how the problem or need is to be addressed and should be written in a clear, concise, and understandable way.

Measurable Metrics need to be put in place so that you know whether you succeeded.

Accurate The objective should be described precisely so errors do not occur.

Realistic The objective should be a result that can be achieved in the time allowed.

Time-bound The objective must include a specific date for its achievement.

Hands-on 1.9: Testing Your Knowledge of Goals and Objectives

Given what you now know about the Apples and Pears project, write the business goals for this project and the project objectives to achieve them. Use the SMART model (Table 1.21) to assist you.

TABLE 1.21 SMART Goals and Objectives Exercise

SMART	Business Goals (What)	Project Objectives (How)
Specific		
Measurable		
Accurate		
Realistic		
Time-bound		

Product Scope Description

If a project is in-house, the product scope description indicates the characteristics of the end result of the product within the project and should map back to the business goals. Because you will know more as the project progresses, this description will be progressively elaborated.

If the project comes from an external source and will be performed under a signed contract, it is referred to as a *statement of work* or *contractual statement of work*.

This activity should be the driving force for what you want to end up with, so it is imperative that the statement not be confusing. Most elements of the project management plan (which we will discuss later) should map back to this description.

Hands-on 1.10: Testing Your Knowledge of the Product Scope Description

Given what you now know about the Apples and Pears project, use Table 1.22 to write the product scope description for two products.

TABLE 1.22   Product Scope Description

Product Scope Description
1.
2.

Project Deliverables

A task is not considered complete unless the deliverable associated with that task is accepted by predetermined and measurable results. It is vital that the project manager communicate the deliverables and their associated requirements before the project begins. If you do not communicate these items correctly, some people will do just about anything to produce what they think you want.

Deliverables typically include physical properties, content properties (documents or other written artifacts), technical properties, and acceptance criteria. When managing deliverables, follow these steps:

1. Document each deliverable from the client's point of view.

2. Review project objectives, key assumptions, and scope with the client.

3. Review with the client the overall project strategy to ensure that the deliverables can and will be achieved.

4. Define the properties of each deliverable in terms of content and physical properties.

5. Define the acceptance criteria for each deliverable.

6. Establish metrics for each of the acceptance criteria.

Hands-on 1.11: Testing Your Knowledge of Deliverables

Given what you now know about the Apples and Pears project, using your common sense and Table 1.23, describe five deliverables associated with the project. Remember to provide enough detail so there are no questions associated with the deliverables.

TABLE 1.23   Deliverables

Deliverables
1.
2.
3.
4.
5.

High-Level Project Requirements

Project requirements describe the characteristics of the deliverables. The *PMBOK® Guide, 4th ed.*, p. 104, Project Management Institute, 2008 describes requirements as "the quantified and documented expectations of the sponsor, customer and other stakeholder."

Requirements are often not fully known at the onset of a project. A good rule of thumb to follow is to continue to accept requirements until actual work begins. It is much easier to change a document than to perform rework out in the field or when developing software.

So where do we get these requirements? This is something you will never want to do alone. Business process owners, team members, consultants, customers, management staff, and experts are just a few of the people you can enlist to be sure you have all the requirements and only the requirements necessary to fulfill the goals of the project.

A simple approach is to validate the needs and expectations of your customers. You simply take each need and expectation and do the RUMBA! Ask, "Is this requirement...?" Table 1.24 describes the elements of the RUMBA.

TABLE 1.24   The RUMBA

Responsible	You or your organization can meet the requirement (it does not violate company procedures, equipment capability, and so forth).
Understandable	The customers verify that you understand what they require from you.
Measurable	In some way, you can objectively determine the degree or frequency of meeting the requirement.
Believable	Employees will agree to strive for that level of achievement.
Achievable	Can you meet the requirement (is the desired performance level theoretically possible)? If not, you may need to renegotiate as facts and data become available.

For each agreed upon and reasonable expectation, if all answers to the RUMBA questions are yes, then that requirement is valid. Any no answer implies further negotiation until it becomes a yes answer. If it cannot become a yes answer, then the need or reasonable expectation is not a valid requirement and should not be accepted as such.

Hands-on 1.12: Testing Your Knowledge of Requirements

Given what you now know about the Apples and Pears project, use Table 1.25 and the RUMBA to describe and validate five requirements associated with the project.

TABLE 1.25   Requirements

Requirements	R	U	M	B	A
1.					
2.					
3.					
4.					
5.					

Project Boundaries

Describing what is not within the scope of the project will avoid confusion as the project moves along. For instance, if you decide you will be updating equipment for an IT unit, you may decide that it includes only specific equipment and you would name other pieces of equipment that would not be changed. In other words, be very specific with your requirements, and the boundaries will identify themselves. This will help to avoid conflicts as the project continues.

Establishing project boundaries also reduces, or in some cases eliminates, what is called *scope creep,* which are uncontrolled changes to the project. For example, if one of the requirements was to purchase accounting software, you would describe it and point out that you are not going to purchase the payroll software also because the payroll software will be outsourced.

Scope creep often occurs because customers do not really know what they want until the project is well under way. Some client changes can be added to the project as long as appropriate change control measures are followed. We have to learn how to say "no" without saying no. We can do this by saying to the customer, "I would be happy to make that change for you. It will increase the budget by $___ and will extend the schedule until ___ and will increase risk. If you wish to approve these changes with all of the impacts I have identified for you, we can do it." Sometimes they will, but more often then not, they won't. They didn't realize the impacts of their requests.

Remember, if the change comes before actual work begins, then it isn't as risky as making changes in the middle of work.

Hands-on 1.13: Testing Your Knowledge of Project Boundaries

Given what you now know about the Apples and Pears project, use Table 1.26 to describe as many of the project boundaries as you can.

TABLE 1.26   Project Boundaries

Project Boundaries
1.
2.
3.
4.
5.

Product Acceptance Criteria

Product acceptance criteria may include, but are not limited to, the following:

- Quality expectations
- Schedule dates
- Functionality
- Appearance
- Performance levels
- Practicality
- Clarity
- Capacity
- Accuracy
- Availability
- Maintainability
- Reliability
- Flexibility

This should be further developed by identifying particular artifacts, evaluation methods, the required resources, an acceptance schedule, and a problem resolution process.

Hands-on 1.14: Testing Your Knowledge of Product Acceptance Criteria

Given what you now know about the Apples and Pears project, and using the quality measures discussed previously, describe the product acceptance criteria for the clothing that will be designed and manufactured for the stores. Use Table 1.27 to show your answers.

TABLE 1.27   Product Acceptance Criteria

Product Acceptance Criteria	
Schedule Dates	
Functionality	
Appearance	
Performance Levels	
Practicality	
Clarity	
Capacity	
Accuracy	
Availability	
Maintainability	
Reliabiity	
Flexibility	

Initial Project Organization

Understanding the organizational structure(s) that exist within companies will help you manage your project better. At this point, you define authority and accountability issues as well as control issues.

There are several types of organizational structures. First is the *functional organization* (see Figure 1.2). This type of organization is your typical hierarchy; coordination takes place among the functional or line managers. Project managers are rarely assigned, but if they are, they have little or no authority. The people assigned as project managers also have their full-time line job and have not participated in the initiation phase of the project. Their managers will coordinate activities among themselves by using their staff. Staff members do not cut across functional boundaries; their managers do that.

FIGURE 1.2   Functional organizational chart

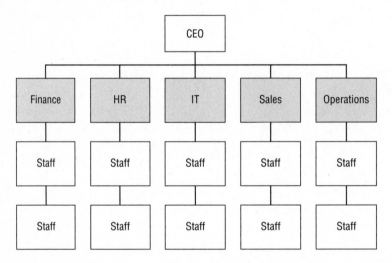

There are advantages and disadvantages of functional organizations. See Table 1.28.

TABLE 1.28   Advantages and Disadvantages of Functional Organizations

Advantages	Disadvantages
Enduring organizational structure.	Project manager has little or no authority.
Clear career path with separation of functions allowing specialty skills to flourish.	Multiple projects compete for limited resources and priority.
Employees have one supervisor with a clear chain of command.	Project team members are loyal to the functional manager.

Projectized organizations have ultimate authority over the project. Figure 1.3 illustrates that the focus of the organization is the project. Staff for the project are focused only on projects and project work—they do not wear more than one hat. Team members are typically colocated, and loyalties are formed to the project, not to a functional manager.

The project manager may hire and fire staff because the project manager is not only a manager of the project, but also a manager of the people.

A *strong matrix environment* is an ideal organizational structure that supports project management (see Figure 1.4). In the figure you can see a director of project management who would be on equal footing with other directors relative to staffing and funding. In this arrangement a project management office is most likely to survive, but project management offices can reside in other organizational structures as well, even if they are not as well supported.

FIGURE 1.3   Projectized organizational chart

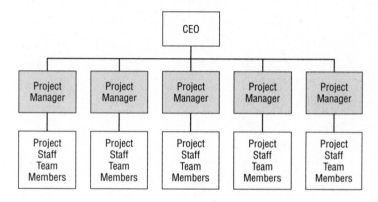

FIGURE 1.4   Strong matrix organizational chart

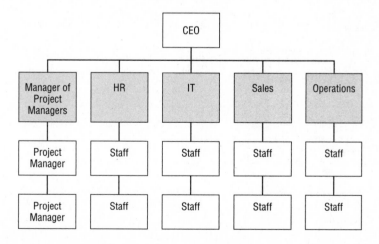

In a *weak* (Figure 1.5) or *balanced matrix* (Figure 1.6) structure, the project management work remains a stepchild to the organization within which it resides. For example, if the budget for marketing is x amount of dollars, you can be sure that only about 5% of that budget will be allocated to project management support. The balanced matrix, however, gives equal power to the project manager and functional manager.

FIGURE 1.5   Weak matrix organizational chart

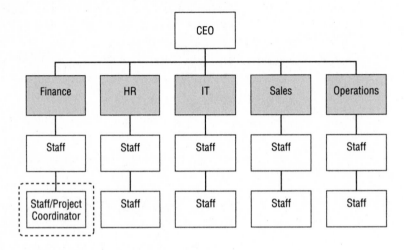

FIGURE 1.6   Balanced matrix organizational chart

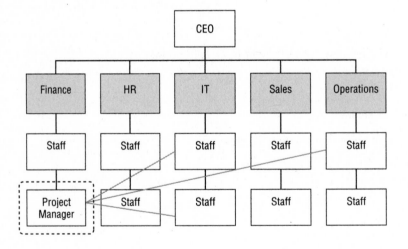

In Table 1.29 you can easily see how project management is viewed in the different organizational structures as well as the power and focus of the project manager.

TABLE 1.29   Comparison of Matrix Organizational Structures

	Weak Matrix	Balanced Matrix	Strong Matrix
Project Manager's Title	Project coordinator, project leader, or project expediter	Project manager	Project manager
Project Manager's Focus	Split focus between project and functional responsibilities	Projects and project work	Projects and project work
Project Manager's Power	Minimal authority and power	Balance of authority and power	Significant authority and power
Project Manager's Time	Part-time on projects	Full-time on projects	Full-time on projects
Organizational Style	Most like functional organization	Blend of both weak and strong matrix	Most like a projectized organization
Project Manager Reports to	Functional manager	A functional manager but shares both power and authority	Manager of project managers

---

Hands-on 1.15: Testing Your Knowledge of Project Organizational Structures

Given what you now know about organizational structures and the Apples and Pears project, answer the following questions:

1. Is Cimarron's organization considered functional, projectized, weak matrix, strong matrix, or balanced matrix?

2. List the characteristics of Cimarron's organization that led you to your answer in question 1.

3. Complete the organizational chart shown here as it relates to your previous answers.

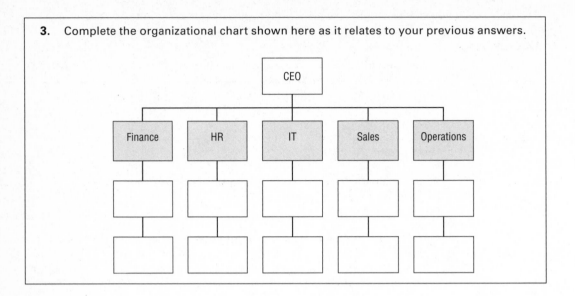

Hands-on 1.16: Testing Your Knowledge of Project Scope Statements

Using Table 1.30, create the high-level Apples and Pears project scope statement with the elements known at this time.

TABLE 1.30   Scope Statement Template

High-Level Scope Statement Template	
Describe business goals	
Describe major objectives of this project	
Describe background for the project	
Describe the unexpected benefits	
List the stakeholders and their role in the project	
Describe the major deliverables	
Describe five high-level requirements	
Describe project boundaries	
Describe product acceptance criteria	
Describe project organization	

Task 1.8: Creating the Project Charter

The project charter formalizes the request from a sponsor for responding to a business need. The project charter is usually a short document that refers to other more-detailed documents such as a new offering request, a request for proposal, or any other perceived business need or client request. The project charter is a created by the sponsor but is signed off by someone external to the project. In reality, you will prepare this document for your sponsor.

Scenario

You have conducted your interviews with stakeholders and created your scope statement but now you find that you are missing a few things. A high-level risk assessment is needed, as well as the assumptions and constraints, scheduled milestones, configuration management, project acceptance, and approval guidelines. You are anxious to complete this part of the project so that it can be formally launched.

Scope of Task

Duration

The duration of this task could take several hours.

Setup

There is no particular setup for this task.

Caveat

None.

Procedure

For this task you will create the project charter, which in addition to the high-level project scope statement includes the following:

- Summary of milestones (preliminary)
- Summary of costs (preliminary)
- A description of the project's risks
- Configuration management requirements
- Environmental, organizational, and external assumptions
- Environmental, organizational, and external constraints
- Project approval requirements
- Project acceptance criteria

Details

The purpose of the project charter is to

- Acknowledge the existence of the project
- Name the project manager who will lead the project
- Provide the project manager with the authority to utilize corporate resources
- Failure to write a charter may lead to
- Ambiguity about the project objectives
- Ambiguity concerning the solution to a business need or client request
- Missing an important stakeholder for the project

You have determined the rationale for the project and written the high-level initial scope statement, but you still need additional information.

Scheduled Milestones

Milestones are significant events in a project, for example, the completion of deliverables. You can add additional milestones as the project planning progresses. Senior managers are not usually interested in all of the project details, but they will be interested in key milestone information. They simply want to know whether a scheduled milestone was completed as scheduled or if it was not, why not.

Hands-on 1.17: Testing Your Knowledge of Milestones

Given what you now know about the Apples and Pears project, use Table 1.31 to list the milestones for this project. You may use your imagination to indicate specific dates.

TABLE 1.31 Project Milestones

Milestones	Date

Estimated Budget Costs

We will spend more time on this subject in Phase 2. For now, we are talking about high-level estimates based on what is known now. Estimated time and costs should validate the proposed high-level budget and include at least the following:

- High-level estimates for the proposed project
- Requirements for out-of-the-ordinary funding, if needed
- Ongoing costs
- Major arguments that support time and cost elements

Hands-On 1.18: Testing Your Knowledge of an Estimated Budget

Given what you now know about the Apples and Pears project, and using your common sense, list any additional costs you feel have been left out and insert them into Table 1.32.

TABLE 1.32   Estimated Budget

Item	Amount

High-Level Project Risks

High-level project risks help you to decide whether the project should be approved or denied. You want to be able to answer questions that senior management may have regarding risks, such as the following:

- What is the probability of success?
- Will expectations be met?
- Is the scope statement understood by all?
- Is there a project champion for this project?
- Is there any known opposition to the project and if so, from where?
- Is the base budget reasonable?
- Is the schedule reasonable?
- Will resources be available when needed?
- What are the assumptions and constraints for this project?

- Are there marketing risks to this project?
- Are we aware of external project dependencies?
- Do we have the capability for support after launch?

Most folks look at risks as being negative, but opportunities also exist when defining risk. Suppose you are trying to solve a problem regarding some sort of risk. Your solution not only solves the risk, but can be used in daily operations and therefore becomes an opportunity as well.

We will discuss risk response strategies in Phase 2.

Hands-on 1.19: Testing Your Knowledge of High-Level Project Risks

Given what you now know about the Apples and Pears project, and using your common sense, list any high-level risks or opportunities at this stage of the project in Table 1.33.

TABLE 1.33   High-Level Risks

High-Level Risks and Opportunities
1.
2.
3.
4.
5.

Configuration Management Requirements

This is not a subject to take lightly. In the *PMP: Project Management Professional Exam Study Guide, Deluxe Edition,* 2nd edition, (Sybex, 2007), configuration management is described as consisting "of documented procedures that describe how to submit change requests and how to manage change requests. Configuration management tracks the status of change requests and defines the level of authority needed to approve changes. It describes the characteristics of the product of the project and ensures that the description is accurate and complete. Configuration management controls changes to the characteristics of an item and tracks the changes made or requested and their status." It is especially important for IT.

The project charter should describe a brief narrative of the change control process that will be used. (We will discuss change control in Phases 2, 3, and 4.)

Environmental, Organizational, and External Assumptions and Constraints

False assumptions and unknown constraints can bring your project to its knees. You may think you have your bases covered, but then find you are scrambling to overcome challenges due to false assumptions and unknown constraints. Although we discussed assumptions and constraints earlier in this phase, we will revisit them in greater detail here.

ASSUMPTIONS

Assumptions are those things we believe are true or take for granted. There are many elements that we don't know about the project, so we make assumptions. You might assume that Connie in IT will be the individual who manages testing. She is the only one that knows the new test environment. Then you find out that when you need her to perform her task, she is out on maternity leave. This assumption now becomes a risk.

You can find these assumptions by communicating with your stakeholders—all of them. Ask them to provide you with their assumptions. Document them. There will be redundancies, which means that others believe the assumptions are true also.

If an assumption turns out not to be true, then you have a risk—maybe even a major one. Try to validate any assumptions that are unclear and be sure to test them frequently by asking, "Is this assumption still true?"

CONSTRAINTS

Constraints are limitations or barriers that may or may not be obvious at the beginning of a project. Some will surface as the project progresses. Constraints can break a project if they are not managed. There are two major steps that can help manage constraints:

1. Identify constraints such as time, budget, quality, schedule, technology, and directives from management, legal, political, skill sets and attitudes, and geographical perspectives.

2. Develop a response strategy for those that can be managed. For instance, if management says there is to be no overtime, allow longer durations for a task if that is appropriate. If you are dependent on external factors such as delivery of products, allow a longer lead time.

There are also enterprise environmental factors and organizational process assets that may help you to define assumptions and constraints. The *PMBOK® Guide, 4th ed.*, p. 14 describes enterprise environmental factors as follows:

- Organizational or company culture and structure
- Governmental or industry standards
- Infrastructure (including IT)
- Human resources
- Personnel administration
- The organization's work authorization system
- Marketplace conditions
- Stakeholder risk tolerance
- Commercial databases (referring to industry-specific information, risk databases, and so forth)
- Project management information systems

The *PMBOK® Guide, 4th ed.*, p. 32, describes organizational process assets as follows:

- Organizational standard policies
- Guidelines, procedures, and plans
- Approaches or standards for conducting work
- Templates
- Communication requirements
- Project closure guidelines
- Financial control procedures
- Quality management procedures
- Change control procedures
- Risk control procedures
- Approval and work authorization procedures

Hands-on 1.20: Testing Your Knowledge of Project Assumptions

Given what you now know about the Apples and Pears project, use Table 1.34 to list three assumptions that you know are true and three assumptions that you are not sure about.

TABLE 1.34   Project Assumptions

Project Assumptions	
1.	True
2.	True
3.	True
4.	Not Sure
5.	Not Sure
6.	Not Sure

Hands-on 1.21: Testing Your Knowledge of Project Constraints

Given what you now know about the Apples and Pears project, list three constraints in Table 1.35 and determine a response strategy for them.

TABLE 1.35 Constraints and Response Strategies

Constraint	Response Strategy
1.	
2.	
3.	

Project Approval Requirements

Project approval should be aligned with the progressive business case at the *project charter scorecard* level (Table 1.36). You know that you can proceed if the summary scores are at least those shown back in Table 1.13. Remember, the project charter will be signed by someone external to the project. You need to provide the signatories a level of confidence that those scores are valid, so be prepared to defend your project brilliantly!

TABLE 1.36 Project Charter Summary Scorecard

	Minimum Score	Actual Score	Difference
Program Assessment	85		
Financials	8		
Internal Issues	38		
Alternatives and Recommendations	10		
Milestones	5		
Totals	146		

Project Acceptance Criteria

Project acceptance criteria vary according to the type of project, but most follow these general acceptance criteria:

- All work has been inspected.

- All deliverables have been accepted.

- Training of staff has been completed.

- Manuals and procedures have been provided.

- As-built drawings have been received and approved.

- Punch list items are completed and approved.

- Supplier contracts and agreements have been closed out.

- Contractors have received final payment.

It's important to list these criteria in the project charter so you don't lose sight of them down the road. This will be an important element when you create your project acceptance plan.

Hands-on 1.22: Testing Your Knowledge of Putting It All Together

Just as you did for the project scope statement, fill out the template (Table 1.37) to complete the project charter.

TABLE 1.37   The Project Charter

The Project Charter	
Summary of Milestones	
Summary of Costs	
High-Level Risks	
Configuration Management	
Assumptions	
Constraints	
Project Approvals	
Project Acceptance Criteria	

Believe us when we say that it will be worth doing all of these steps. Some will be redundant (go ahead and cut and paste), but no matter how it's put together, completing the initiation phase will give new meaning to the saying, "We have bonded!" You will be intimately involved with your project, which is where you want to be. We are not talking about micromanaging here, but being this informed will keep the meddling managers off your back because they will have a higher level of confidence that you really know what's going on and have the ball moving in the right direction.

Phase 2

Planning Process

Planning a project can be as simple or elaborate as you make it. Some folks spend more time planning and creating forms and documents than they do managing the project. But no matter what, proper planning will decide the fate of your project.

Planning should not be done alone, although some project managers feel that they *can* create the project plan on their own. They have the technical expertise and feel they are professional practitioners and, therefore, do not need any help. This could be true. But even if you *could* do all of the project planning, it is simply wrong to do so! A team of one is not a team. When you allow some of your stakeholders to participate in the planning process, you take the first step in developing your team as well as creating a more robust and realistic project plan.

Sometimes you are brought into the project after it has begun. Maybe you don't believe you have the right support or have enough time to plan. Are you implementing someone else's plan? And how accountable do you feel when you are asked to simply implement someone else's plan? You may feel defeated before you begin. Or that someone else is running the show! Do you have the authority necessary to manage this project?

You may believe that these things will hinder your ability to create a good plan. But fear not! You *can* make the project work in spite of those things. *Believe in your own abilities and make it happen*—because in this phase, we are going to show you what good project planning is all about. You will come out smelling like a rose!

Planning is not a substitute for thinking. It requires every step of the project to be thought out more fully than ever before. It also requires wholehearted support of all management—upper, middle, and peer levels.

The project manager and staff must be a part of the effort. A common mistake is to turn items such as network development or scheduling over to a staff "expert" or outside consultant and hope for the best.

You must use the plan throughout the project to monitor and control. The old saying, "plan the work and work the plan," applies here. The plan only provides information. It is up to the project manager to keep the project on schedule and within budget. This process includes the following:

- Identifying team members
- Defining roles and responsibilities in this phase
- Creating a project organization structure
- Developing a communications plan

- Creating the work breakdown structure (WBS)
- Creating subsidiary plans
- Determining project risks
- Creating the master project management plan
- Obtaining plan approval
- Developing a change management plan

Abraham Lincoln once said, "If I had six hours to chop down a tree, I would spend the first four hours sharpening the ax." He knew that advance planning is essential for successful outcomes.

Task 2.1: Identifying Team Members

Should you define the tasks first and then identify who will do the work? Or identify team members and decide what the work is? In reality, it's both. You inherently know who some of the team members are. You may have worked with them before on a project; some folks, such as IT, are on all of your projects because they play a key role. Because we already know the high-level scope of the project, refining that scope will identify others.

Scenario

You, Carrie MacIntyre, have been designated in the project charter as the official project manager. Now that Cimarron's project charter has been approved and you have intimately bonded with your project, it is time to identify your team members. Some of them worked with you on the charter, but new people may be coming into the project as it moves along. You have already determined the high-level scope of the project. Now you have to identify, estimate, and schedule the work to be performed, among other things—but first you need to identify your team.

Scope of Task

Duration

This task should not take more than a day or two, depending on the size of the project.

Setup

None.

Caveat

Be sure to include geographically dispersed team members. The duration of tasks may be affected, particularly if team members live in other countries or time zones.

Procedure

This task will describe the characteristics needed to staff a project with the right people who have the right skills and are available when needed for the right duration and within the planned budget.

Details

When we identified our team members, they advised us if there were others that needed to be on the team. There are also ways to obtain team members depending on your company's organizational structure.

Projectized Organization

In this organization, the project manager can hire team members who are suited to the tasks. The project manager may have a set of core individuals who work on all projects (such as construction). These people remain on the project payroll as long as their services are needed. Others are hired for a one-time-only event. They may be consultants, subject matter experts, or the like.

Matrix Organization

In this organization, the project manager may have to *negotiate* with a functional manager for a specific individual. This can be a problem because that person may not be available to work on your project. Project managers also tend to tell the functional manager how much time they have to complete tasks. The functional manager (who is often a peer) feels like the project manager is telling them how and when to do their job. We really don't know what functional managers have on their plate. Here's what you can do instead:

- Discuss the known task(s) with the functional manager.
- Ask how long the task will take.
- Ask for a time commitment to finish the task.

When the functional manager is approached this way, an element of trust is achieved. The functional manager will usually become a trusted ally and send one of their staff personnel to be a team member on your project.

The conversation may end with something like this: "I know that it's your place to manage your workload with the folks you have available. I also know you will finish the task as agreed; however, I would appreciate a commitment from you that you will not change that resource if at all possible. If you must change the resource, please let me know as far in advance as possible. That will give me a chance to make adjustments."

Functional Organization

In this organization, the functional manager determines who will work on a project task. You already know the people from the project charter work who will be team members; some will be full-time and others will be ad hoc. In this case, the project manager is typically the functional manager as well.

Now that you have identified your team, you are ready to place their responsibilities and accountabilities into the responsibility assignment matrix that we discussed in Phase 1.

Hands-on 2.1: Testing Your Knowledge of Identifying Team Members

Using Table 2.1 as a model, create the responsibility assignment matrix for Cimarron's Apples and Pears project. Add as many rows as needed.

TABLE 2.1   RAM for Cimarron Apples and Pears Project

Tasks	Project Manager	PMO	Team Members	Line Managers	Dept Manager	Sponsor	Senior Management
Project management							
Advertising							
Space planning							
Construction							
Noninventoried furnishings							
Design of clothing							
Hiring and training of personnel							
Information technology							
Manufacturing							

R	Responsible
A	Accountable
S	Support
C	Contributor
I	Information

Step 1   List the tasks.

Step 2   Use the letters of RASCI for each task as it corresponds to the title of the person listed above.

Step 3   Make sure there is only one accountable individual.

Task 2.2: Assigning Responsibilities in the Planning Phase

Creating a project plan is like creating a road map. You want your team members to know exactly where they are going and which road to take to get there. In the event a team member is unclear about their role, they may take off down the wrong path (with all good intentions, of course). You are not trying to tell them *how* to perform their work—they already know that. What you do want is for each team member to have precise and unambiguous role and responsibility assignments.

When the work is done by the right person at the right time, it helps the project manager ensure that tasks don't fall by the wayside.

Scenario

James Stevens has agreed to be the project sponsor, even though he is still concerned about the cost and the economy. This role will give him a firsthand look at the budget and costs that are incurred.

Jocelyn Greer is a new person you met on a conference call. She is Cimarron's liaison in Europe for clothing design. She has been a clothing designer for 20 years and is up on all of the latest fashions. She will coordinate the European and stateside people who will be designing the clothing for the Apples and Pears project.

Jocelyn is excited that the project is to include wedding and formal apparel; she will work with her partner Jeness Hopkins to design some of the apparel and search for other designs to bring into the wardrobe. Jeness is a buyer of formal wear, and so this partnership should work out well. Jeness and her team of buyers will be responsible for purchasing clothing that will not be made in the manufacturing plant.

Eric Nash is the manufacturing director. He will oversee the construction at the manufacturing plant of the clothing Jocelyn and Jeness will design.

Michelle Price will coordinate the flow between designers and manufacturing.

You believe you have identified the proper team for the project. All of your team members have a great reputation as individuals, but you know that it takes a bit of time to "synch up" as a team.

Scope of Task

Duration

This task may take hours or minutes, depending on how robust your project management methodology is. It may take hours because your organization is new at formal project management or minutes because the roles and responsibilities have been predefined in a mature project management methodology.

Setup

None.

Caveat

None.

Procedure

In this task you will assign roles and responsibilities to identified team members.

Details

Team members of a project sometimes perform different work during the different phases of a project. Table 2.2 represents the roles and responsibilities of those who participate in the *planning* phase.

TABLE 2.2   Roles and Responsibilities for Planning

Team Member	Role	Responsibility/Accountability
Project sponsor	Takes part in planning the project	Ensures that the project plan is sufficient to actualize the project
Project manager	Guides the planning process	Creates a master plan that can be successfully deployed
Functional (line) manager(s)	Provide estimates for work to be performed by their groups and communicate availability of the staff that will be assigned to the project	Accountable to the project manager and sponsor regarding performance of their parts of the project
Suppliers	Plan the work to be performed by their groups and the availability of the staff that has been assigned to the project	Supplier managers are accountable to the project manager and sponsor regarding performance of their parts of the project
Clients	Owners of the project	Have significant authority regarding scope definition and whether the project should be initiated and/or continued
Individual contributors	Perform project work	To ensure the work is in compliance with the PM plan as well as any industry standards pertaining to their work

TABLE 2.2   Roles and Responsibilities for Planning *(continued)*

Team Member	Role	Responsibility/Accountability
Project management office	Facilitates and supports project management	Performs administrative activities, methodology coaching, training and enforcement, providing portfolio tracking, and so forth
Subject matter experts	Individual performers with expertise in their process	To provide expertise as needed on either technical or business issues
Key decision makers	Anyone with the responsibility to make major decisions regarding the project	Make major decisions regarding the project such as to stop the project or allow it to continue

Hands-on 2.2: Testing Your Knowledge of Roles and Responsibilities in the Planning Phase

Using Table 2.3, define the specific roles, responsibilities, and authority levels of your identified team members for the Apples and Pears project. Be sure to include any new members.

TABLE 2.3   Roles and Responsibilities for Planning

Team Member	Role	Responsibility/Accountability

Task 2.3: Creating the Project Organizational Structure

A project's organization is influenced by the characteristics of the project. This is not to be confused with hierarchical organizational structures such as the matrix and projectized structures we looked at earlier. However, the project organizational structure *is* created through hierarchical, organizational *relationships*. In fact, most of these relationships live in a matrix or other organizational structures.

You can build a hierarchical project structure in terms of rank, but there are benefits to building a flat structure instead. Consider managing projects on a horizontal plane—that is, there is no rank. That does not mean that everyone on the team runs the project—the project manager is accountable for the project and should be the single point of contact for all team members. The project manager simply has a different role to play than the members of the team. Everyone comes to the table with something of value to lend to the process. Having said that, be sure, as project manager, not to sit at the head of the table!

The project organizational structure must also support the skills and abilities of the staff. Some team members are provided a "developmental opportunity" that may be beyond their skills and capacities.

Organizational project planning facilitates communication between functional groups and project team members by defining roles and responsibilities and defines specific staffing requirements to ensure that the performers have the desired skill levels and competencies to perform project activities.

Scenario

You have defined the roles and responsibilities of your team members. Now you want to create a project organizational structure that provides a visual of who the team is and what their accountabilities are. You have managed many projects in the past, but have not used a formal methodology because your previous projects have been small compared to this one.

Ms. Reese named you as the project manager in the project charter. She also sent a companywide memo announcing your position. Hopefully, this will help gain support of all the stakeholders.

You were a functional manager in the past, and those who reported directly to you respected you. You were able to accomplish many good things, so you are confident that you can manage this project and the people taking part in it.

Scope of Task

Duration

This task may take one day or a few hours, depending on the size of the project.

Setup

None.

Caveat

This task depends on the following:

- The size of the project
- The degree of uniqueness
- The degree of managerial complexity
- The degree of technical complexity
- Organizational factors

Procedure

In this task you will create a project organizational chart.

Details

The line (or functional) manager, the product manager, the project manager, and the project sponsor are part of a *core* team. They usually participate for the duration of the project.

Primary performers working in a matrix organization have a *dotted line* relationship to the project manager; that is, as long as they are on the project, they report their work to the project manager. The functional manager (their regular boss) assigned them to the project and still manages their administrative issues or concerns. These performers come and go as phases are completed and new work commences.

Think of functional managers as subcontractors on the project. They have their own piece of the action to fulfill as contributors to the project. A partnership should develop between project managers and functional managers because they are often peers. Having a partnership attitude makes all the stakeholders have an investment (money or otherwise) in the project, and all parties in the partnership will benefit when the project comes to fruition as planned.

So what about the steering committee and the project sponsor? Shouldn't they be at the top? If you are operating flat, they are equal members of the team. They have different accountabilities and authorities but they are "in it to win it" just like everyone else. So don't get hung up on rank. Senior managers are quite often very likable and approachable.

Project Organizational Chart

The purpose of a project organizational chart is to help communicate the reporting relationships within the project team, and to explain how the project team relates to or reports to the larger organization.

In the example shown in Figure 2.1, the project sponsor has a dotted line relationship with the steering committee, and a dotted line relationship with the project manager, as well as directly reporting to the VP. Notice that the arrow goes both ways between the project manager and sponsor, making this a horizontal instead of a vertical, or hierarchical, relationship.

The project organizational chart maps how the project is structured and provides stakeholders with a view of who is involved in the project. It is a good idea to keep the project organizational chart up-to-date as project members come and go.

The functional managers also have a two-way dotted line relationship with the project manager and directly report to the director. The performers report directly to functional managers but also have a dotted line relationship with the project manager.

Group leaders, contractors, and leaderless teams all have a dotted line relationship with the project manager. This type of project organizational structure facilitates teamwork and communications; an open door policy is clearly the goal.

FIGURE 2.1   Horizontal project organizational chart

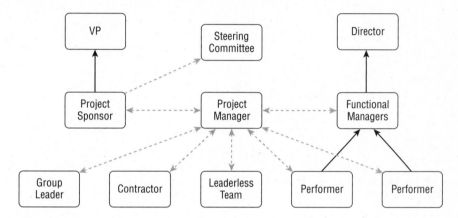

Project Interfaces

You need to be in constant communications with your project interfaces. It is essential that each team member is performing the right work at the right time in accordance with the manner needed by the project or by contractual agreement. They may be formal or informal reporting relationships, and generally fall into one of three categories:

- *Organizational interfaces* exist internally among different departments, business units, or specialized organizational units or between a company and external contractors.

- *Technical interfaces* are the formal or informal relationships that exist among different technical disciplines, such as between sales and IT.

- *Interpersonal interfaces* exist among different individuals who are working on the project.

Limiting Factors

The project manager and team will encounter factors that can limit their options in the organizational planning process. We looked at constraints earlier. If we don't address constraints, they can become hindrances to the project. Here are some examples:

- The project manager doesn't have the authority needed.

- Labor unions will dictate what work individuals may do.

- The experience level of individuals determines how closely they must be supervised.

- The people who are eventually assigned to the project may be geographically dispersed.

- Functional managers may have other demands that affect their ability to provide resources when you need them.
- The organization may have policies that restrict the use of outside contractors or temporary help.

You can overcome all of these constraints through good project communication. We will discuss this in detail in the next task.

Hands-on 2.3: Testing Your Knowledge of Project Organizational Structures

Answer questions 1–3 and follow the instructions for item 4:

1. What challenges are associated with working in a horizontal reporting structure?

2. What are two challenges associated with managing a project within a vertical structure?

3. How can you overcome the challenges of working in a horizontal reporting structure?

4. Create a vertical hierarchy project organizational structure.

Task 2.4: Developing a Communication Plan

Some projects may involve many teams and large numbers of people. When there is an extensive undertaking, communication of information and coordination of efforts across teams are critical success factors. The objective is to ensure accurate, consistent, and timely communication of information to the business teams, project teams, and management.

The project manager will be engaged in many types of project communications including, but not limited to, the following:

- Project plans (schedules, budgets, risk plans, resource plans, and so forth)
- Project meetings
- Status reporting
- Organizational charts
- Requirements
- Contracts
- Presentations
- Decision memoranda
- Policies and procedures
- Historical records

To be able to do all of this effectively, you must create a communications plan.

Scenario

You have identified your team members; defined roles, responsibilities, and accountabilities; and created a project organizational chart. That has really helped you to see your team as a whole. But now you want to be able to communicate with your team members in an effective manner.

You have been on projects where everyone on the team receives the same information at the same time. Some of it is pertinent—but often it is not. You are determined that your team will receive the information identified by your stakeholders as information they want, when they want it, and in the right format.

Scope of Task

Duration

This task may take a few hours or days, depending on the size of your project.

Setup

None.

Caveat

None.

Procedure

This task will show you what is to be included in a communications plan.

Details

The project manager should be the focal point for the flow of communications in a project environment. Let's take a look at three common scenarios:

Between the project manager and the customer   The project manager receives the project goals from the customer. The project manager reports back to the customer regarding the performance of the project relative to these goals.

Between the project manager and the sponsor   The project manager receives the project priority from the sponsor. The project manager sends performance information such as budget and schedule results to the sponsor.

Between the project manager and the project team   The project manager provides the project standards to the project team and receives performance results from the project team.

To be successful with these communications, you need to determine the communication needs of stakeholders.

Determine the Needs of Stakeholders

You interviewed your stakeholders in Phase 1 to determine their issues and concerns, and whether they supported the project. Now you want to establish *communication objectives* for each of the stakeholders. For example:

- A communication objective for the project sponsor is to keep the project manager in the loop regarding strategic changes to the business.

- A communication objective of the project manager is to keep the team informed of what is going on and to provide credit and recognition when it is due.

- You must include the project team, sponsor, suppliers, and the delivery and performing organizations' management and others who may need information regarding the project.

The information needs of the various stakeholders should be carefully analyzed to determine how information will be provided and the sources of that information. Here are two examples:

- Know the official or formal communication channels in your company.

- Interview stakeholders to understand their information needs and informal communication channels.

Table 2.4 identifies some of the key stakeholders and the type of information they may require.

TABLE 2.4   Stakeholders' Information Needs

Business Stakeholder	Key Knowledge Need	PM Communication Approach
Senior management	<ul><li>Information to understand business impact of business initiatives</li><li>Consistent, cross-discipline information</li><li>Planned vs. actual</li><li>Progress</li><li>Cost</li></ul>	<ul><li>Gather necessary information from project teams</li><li>Present cross-team information in management information format</li><li>Meet cross-enterprise requirements for project information</li></ul>
Project manager	<ul><li>Information to support decision making</li><li>Defined plans to assess progress</li><li>Budget/actual financial information</li></ul>	<ul><li>Define cross-team standards</li><li>Gather, review, and integrate information</li></ul>

TABLE 2.4   Stakeholders' Information Needs *(continued)*

Business Stakeholder	Key Knowledge Need	PM Communication Approach
Other business communities	• Information on business projects • Forum for discussion on issues • Background on business initiatives • Information on issues requiring management direction	• Disseminate information broadly • Provide database for information access and update capability • Present information for management assessment/decision making
Core and extended project teams	• Standards and templates • Forum for discussion of commitments and issues • Support for planning and administration	• Define templates and examples as required • Define and implement standard processes • Host inter-team meetings • Provide project planning and support.

What Should You Communicate?

Communication that is designed to support the information needs of each stakeholder and to support the flow of information between stakeholders is critical for project success. Key information is gathered, reviewed, consolidated, and reported to stakeholders based on their particular requirements. Here are several elements that should be communicated to stakeholders, based on their needs:

Progress reports   Highlight progress from the previous report.

Status reports   Provide project details for management review. The information is gathered in a standard format from each team in a predetermined time frame and reviewed with the project team prior to providing status to other stakeholders. There should be no surprises when information is given to any who have a need to know. The reports provide the communication vehicle to summarize the overall status of each project.

Forecast reports   Forecast project outcomes. You don't have to make three separate reports; they can be combined into one as long as progress, current status, and estimated future outcomes are included.

Report cards   Provide a management summary of each project. The report cards can also be consolidated and submitted to the quality assurance office for review.

Project issues   Highlight critical items affecting projects. The issues and action items should be maintained in a data repository; the results are consolidated and reports provided to the project manager.

Budget/actual   Provides the project budget and actual expense information. Actual expenses are consolidated and compared to the budget; the results are published for those stakeholders with a need to know.

Project changes   Highlight changes affecting project scope, vendor agreements, overall project plans, or deviations from the project. The changes are reported to the project manager, who in turn advises all stakeholders with a need to know.

Vendor's information   Identifies and tracks those vendors supporting projects. Updates to the vendor information will be presented to the project manager as changes occur.

Consolidated work plans   Consolidate all project plans to produce an extract of significant project deliverables. The deliverables list is reviewed on a biweekly basis with those who have a need to know.

When Should You Communicate?

Each stakeholder group may have different needs for receiving information. It is useful then to create a communications matrix. Table 2.5 shows an example of a communications matrix.

TABLE 2.5   Communications Matrix

Legend					Reported To					
		Project sponsor	Project managers	Functional manager	Team performers	Clients	Suppliers	Individual contributros	Subject matter experts	Key decision-makers
Daily	D									
Weekly	W									
Biweekly	BW									
Monthly	M									
As needed	AN									
Initiated From										
Project sponsor		▨								
Project manager			▨							
Functional manager				▨						
Team performers					▨					
Clients						▨				
Suppliers							▨			
Individual contributors								▨		
Subject matter experts									▨	
Key decision-makers										▨

Communications Deliverable Template

A table similar to Table 2.6 can be used to identify and control the development and delivery of each communications deliverable.

TABLE 2.6 Communications Deliverable Template

Audience	Messages	Media	Responsible Party	Date	Owner

Deliverable	Approved?	
	Yes	No
Project description	☐	☐
Audiences	☐	☐
Key messages	☐	☐
Communication timing	☐	☐
Communication vehicles	☐	☐
Feedback mechanism	☐	☐
Advance notification	☐	☐
Communication sign-offs	☐	☐

Communication Tools	Definition
Status web page	Provides anyone access to a project web page. Show web link.
General announcements	Announcements that go to everyone on the project. Show web link.
Global email	Allows for targeted email to predefined databases and responsibilities. Show global access telephone number.
Emergency numbers	List of specific numbers to an individual assigned as an emergency contact.
Voice mail	Used to send broadcast messages to all voice mail recipients. Show local telephone access number.
Executive status report line	At specific milestones executives receive an hourly update as to the completion of that milestone. Provide this status number *only* to executives.

The *audience* could be team members, customers, business partners, managers, executives, and/or professionals who need to understand what deliverables are being developed and when they will be available.

The *messages* column is defined by the specific communication this audience needs to be informed of at the appropriate time (prior to the completion of development or after delivery of the product).

The *media* column indicates the type of communication (web, one-on-one, one-on-group, presentation, phone, email, and so on) that would go out to the specific audience.

The *responsible party* column identifies the person or organization that will develop the deliverable. If it is a group, the individual leader of the group should be identified by name.

The *date* column defines the timing of each communication. Delivery of these messages on a timely basis is necessary for the success of the project.

The *owner* column identifies the person who will provide direction and approve the finished product. This person will sign off on the communications plan before distribution. This individual approves draft communications before they are released.

The following represents a template that includes the elements for a project communications management plan:

Section 1: Organizational Chart

- Insert your project organizational chart.

Section 2: Team Directory

- Name
- Address
- Telephone
- Cell phone
- Fax number
- Email

Section 3: Information Needs of Stakeholders

- Senior management
- Project sponsor
- Project manager
- Team members
- Vendors and suppliers
- Consultants

Section 4: Information to Be Collected and Distributed

- Status reports
- Report cards
- Project issues

- Performance results
- Vendor information

Section 5: Filing Structures

- Intranet
- Team rooms

Section 6: Communications Matrix

- Insert your communications matrix here.

Section 7: Communications Deliverables

- Project description
- Audiences
- Key messages
- Communication timing
- Communication vehicles
- Feedback mechanism
- Advance notification
- Communication sign-offs

Section 8: Communications Tools

- General announcements
- Global and local email
- Emergency numbers
- Voicemail
- Executive status report phone line
- Voicemail and associated distribution lists
- Audio conferencing
- Video conferencing
- Websites
- Electronic workroom or other databases such as IBM's Lotus Notes or Microsoft's Outlook Express
- Online meetings

Section 9: Controlled Information

- Access to buildings
- Passwords

Section 10: Communications Schedule

- Table 2.7 represents a communications schedule.

TABLE 2.7 Section 10—Communications Schedule

Communications Schedule															
Conference Calls				Video Conference				Face-to-Face Meetings			
Date	Time	Location	Subject	Date	Time	Location	Subject	Date	Time	Location	Subject

20 Questions

The communications plan is the ultimate goal of the communications planning process. Let's walk through the questions that, when answered, will ensure that you have created a robust project communications plan:

1. Have you reviewed memos from the sponsor, formal or informal agreements, and the project organizational structure in order to determine the requirements for reporting and meetings imposed by the sponsor, the project definition statement, or other sources?

2. Have you reviewed supplier agreements to determine requirements for reporting performance and meetings?

3. Have you reviewed the project procedures to understand the specific project policies and procedures regarding status reporting and status meetings?

4. Have you determined whether there are any external media communication requirements? (Identify key messages, announcements, and/or marketing that needs to be delivered and can or should be included with routine or recurring communications. You may have to consult with your public relations group prior to committing to provide information.)

5. Have you determined how the information needs of each stakeholder will be satisfied?

6. Have you identified and reviewed the communication technology media available within the project infrastructure?

7. Have you defined formal reports that will be produced to satisfy stakeholder requirements?

8. Have you defined the levels and project organizational units within the project structure for which the reports will be built?

9. Have you defined the types of reports that will be produced for various levels and project organizational units?

10. Have you defined the project meetings that will occur?

11. Have you defined the information retrieval and distribution strategy that will be used to share information among your project team members?

12. Have you assigned responsibilities for creating and delivering the various types of communications?

13. Have you identified key events, milestones, and deliverable dates that will initiate communications?

14. Have you defined a process for handling ad hoc inquiries the project is likely to encounter?

15. Have you developed a library of project information and assigned responsibilities for its maintenance?

16. Have you created internal and external feedback loops to help evaluate the effectiveness of communications?

17. Have you scheduled the work of communications and related triggers into the project schedule to ensure they are part of the overall plan?

18. Have you defined a process for updating or changing the communications management plan?

19. Have you documented the approval process needed for any of the communications?

20. Have you finalized the plan by reviewing it with your project team?

At this stage of the project, you don't have all the answers to these questions. As the project progresses, however, you will want to review these questions again to be sure you have covered them and include them in your communications plan. It has been said that 90% of a project manager's job is communications. Now you know why!

Hands-on 2.4: Testing Your Knowledge of Communications

Answer the following questions:

1. The information needs of the various stakeholders should be carefully analyzed to determine the information that will be provided and the sources of that information. What can you do to acquire this information?

2. What factors may influence the selection of communications technology?

3. What sort of metrics could you put in place that would measure the efficacy of your communications?

Task 2.5: Creating the Work Breakdown Structure

The work breakdown structure (WBS) is at the heart of the project. In fact, if you don't create one, the project will skip a beat or two or a hundred and could die a quick death.

The WBS provides the foundation so that the responsibility assignments for each deliverable can be established, estimated costs and budgets can be determined, and planning can be performed. The total project can be described as a summation of subdivided deliverables.

If done well, the WBS prevents omitted deliverables, gains commitment of project personnel, enables the development of a basic project plan, ensures the deliverable's visibility, and reduces risk

By definition, according to the *PMBOK® Guide, 4th ed.* p. 444, glossary, the WBS is a "deliverable-oriented hierarchical decomposition of the work to be executed by the project team to accomplish the project objectives and create required deliverables. It organizes and defines the total scope of the project." The scope statement that is created with the project charter creates only a high-level picture of a project. The WBS adds details (tasks and activities) that comprise the overall project scope. In this task you will learn how to create a WBS.

Scenario

During the process of creating the project charter, you also determined the project scope statement—at least at a high level. Now you need to break it down into smaller, more-manageable chunks of work that will be performed by a live body or group. You have reviewed the scope statement and decided that these are the high-level elements of the project:

- Advertising
- Hiring and training
- Space planning
- Construction
- Furnishings
- Design of clothing
- Information technology
- Manufacturing of clothing
- Delivery and setup

You are ready to list the tasks in the project and have set up a team meeting with those you feel will participate in this effort with you and are ready to get started.

Scope of Task

Duration

This task may take hours or days, depending on the size and complexity of the task.

Setup

None.

Caveat

Be sure to include geographically dispersed team members.

Procedure

In this task you will create a partial WBS that involves four steps:

1. Create the list of work that results in producing your previously identified deliverables.
2. Organize the work.
3. Review and adjust with the team.
4. Verify that the WBS is correct and complete.

Details

Work that is not in the WBS is not part of the scope of the project! A WBS is *not* just an extensive list of work. It is a thorough categorization of project scope.

Some folks believe that the WBS *is* the project plan. Although it is at the heart of the project, it is part of the scope plan, a subsidiary of the master project management plan. The WBS is commonly used at the beginning of a project for further *defining project scope, organizing schedules,* and *estimating costs.* It is a living document throughout the project, and the project schedule can be used for reporting project costs, as well as managing risks.

On larger projects, the WBS may be used throughout the project to identify and track work packages, to organize data for earned value management (EVM) reporting, for tracking deliverables, and so on. We will discuss these items later.

The good news is that there are no formal rules on how to create a WBS. The key thing to remember is that the WBS must fully cover the scope of the project. Following the four steps helps ensure that all the scope and only the scope is successfully and completely decomposed in the work breakdown structure.

Before we move further, let's look at some important definitions.

PMBOK® Guide Glossary Definitions

WBS dictionary (p. 445)   "A document that describes each component in the work breakdown structure (WBS). For each WBS component, the WBS dictionary includes a brief definition of the scope or statement of work, defined deliverable(s), a list of associated activities, and a list of milestones. Other information may include responsible organization start and end dates, resources required, an estimate of cost, charge number, contract information, quality requirements, and technical references to facilitate performance of the work."

Work package (p. 445)   "A deliverable or project work component at the lowest level of each branch of the work breakdown structure."

Control account (p. 422)   "A management control point where scope, budget (resource plans), actual cost, and schedule are integrated and compared to earned value for performance measurement." We will discuss more about this in Phase 4.

Let's go through the steps we defined earlier.

Step 1: Create the List of Work

When you are meeting with your team for this work, describe the scope of work and what is to be delivered so the team won't get off track. Remember, we discussed that this is a horizontal project structure, so please, participate as a peer.

It will be helpful to start by using command verbs. Table 2.8 shows several useful command verbs. Then brainstorm the rest of the work to be done and compile the list of work. Decide whether adequate costs and durations can be developed at the level of detail you have identified.

TABLE 2.8   Command Verbs

Assessment	Review, research, collect, analyze, assess, determine, identify
Requirements	Define, describe, design, develop, choose, obtain, prepare, approve
Construction	Construct, build, write, obtain, create
Validation	Validate, pilot, check, test
Implementation	Implement, move, train, replace, evaluate

Hands-on 2.5: Testing Your Knowledge of Creating a List of Work

You have been charged with defining the tasks associated with furnishings as they relate to the Apples and Pears project.

Decompose the higher element "Determine the furnishings required" (found in the high level WBS below) until you believe you have accomplished the deliverable "Furnishings identified."

1. Obtain copy of space planning results.

2. Determine the furnishings required.

3. Order furnishings.

4. Set up furnishings.

Step 2: Organize the Work

Now it's time to create logical groupings. You can do this by phase, by geography, by organization, by key work products, chronologically, or any other way that your team feels will accomplish this task.

Hands-on 2.6: Testing Your Knowledge of Organizing Tasks into Logical Groupings

You have worked with your team on and have made a list of tasks associated with advertising, training of sales and marketing staff, and printing of brochures and manuals for the Apples and Pears project.

1. Place the following tasks into four logical groupings: training of sales, training of marketing, preparation of advertising, and printing brochure and manual:

    - Familiarize sales with the brochure and manual.

    - Return sales to territories.

    - Consolidate specific marketing training.

    - Draft and approve the brochure.

    - Design the layout of the brochure.

    - Design the customer instruction manual.

    - Select marketing personnel for training.

    - Distribute advertising to the proper media.

    - Prepare an article for a professional journal.

    - Train marketing personnel.

    - Send sales personnel to training.

    - Proceed with familiarization course.

    - Select sales personnel.

    - Print brochures.

    - Print customer instruction manuals.

    - Return marketing to territories.

    - Publish the article in the professional journal.

    - Bring marketing personnel to the home office.

    - Prepare phase 1 of training.

- Prepare phase 2 of training.

- Prepare regional advertising.

- Release and carry regional advertising.

- Consolidate advertising plans.

- Determine a general marketing approach.

- Approve regional advertising.

- Approve the customer instruction manual.

- Conduct phase 1 training.

- Conduct phase 2 training.

- Send manuals to the training center.

2.   What challenges would you have if you did not create a WBS?

Step 3: Review and Adjust the WBS with the Team

Because your team helped to create the WBS, you will want to review it and make adjustments as needed. This sort of team involvement cements the plan for your team members. Your review should include the following:

- Show the team what has been done so far.

- Go through the WBS and fix and/or confirm groupings.

- Adjust task and activity names, if necessary.

- Change wording, if necessary, to make it more clear but do *not* adjust intent.

Hands-on 2.7: Testing Your Knowledge of Reviewing and Adjusting a WBS

You have worked with your team and created work lists, placed them into logical groupings, and decomposed the tasks and activities until a deliverable was produced. Review the following construction WBS and review and adjust groupings if necessary. Add tasks or activities if needed until you feel you can produce appropriate deliverables. Make sure command verbs are used.

- Work plans

- Submit plans

- Permits

- Stake the corners and offsets

- Establish a monument (set pin) for points of reference

- Dirt work
    - Dig out foundation
    - Sell or save the dirt
    - Bring in utilities
- Inspect dirt work for grade to set pins
- Order materials per plan
- Foundation
    - Forms
    - Rebar
    - Pour concrete
    - Pour test cylinders
    - Strip and clean forms
    - Allow concrete to cure
    - Analyze test cylinders
    - Inspection
- Framing
- Rough in electrical and plumbing
- Set up material delivery in back of building
- Set up sidewalks, walkways, and blacktop
- Rafters
- Sheet the roof
- Create traces for wiring
- Electrical/plumbing to roof
- Put up roofing
- Pull wire
- Inspect wiring
- Insulation
- Sheetrock
- Install cabinets

- Tile and linoleum
- Finish carpentry
- Finish plumbing
- Finish electrical
- Finish heating
- Cleaning service
- Install carpeting

Step 4: Verify That WBS Is Correct and Complete

The best way to verify completeness and correctness is to ask the question at the lowest level, "Will these tasks fully complete the required deliverable?" If you have prefaced your tasks with command verbs, you should be able to associate a deliverable with the tasks.

Common Obstacles

Even though you are acting as a peer on this process, your facilitation skills will be needed if you encounter any of these obstacles:

- Discussing or adding new requirements
- Talking about the solution rather than the work
- Wanting to establish dependencies too early
- Wanting to assign resources too early
- Being overly detailed such that you spend more time creating the WBS than managing it
- Levels of a WBS:
    - Commonly a WBS has between five and seven levels.
    - It may take only three or four levels to create a budget-level deliverable.
    - If you have seven or more levels, typically this would then become a subproject or a program with multiple subprojects.

Levels of Detail in a Work Package

You know you have broken the scope of the project down far enough when you feel that the work package:

- Can be realistically and confidently estimated
- Cannot be logically subdivided further
- Can be completed quickly
- Has a meaningful conclusion and is deliverable
- Can be completed without interruption (without the need for more information)
- Will be outsourced or contracted out

Task 2.6: Creating Subsidiary Plans

As we said before, the master project management plan is not just a list of tasks. To really have a handle on the project, you must consider all aspects of the project. In this task, we will detail the other plans that may be found in the master plan.

Scenario

You now have a partial WBS that you are still working on, but you realize that other plans have to be created as well. This is not a linear process—pieces and parts will eventually populate the master project plan. Based on your WBS, you don't have enough information yet to validate the initial budget spelled out in the project charter, but wish to start the subsidiary plans and update them as more information is known.

Scope of Task

Duration

This task may take hours or days, depending on the size and complexity of the task.

Setup

None.

Caveat

None.

Procedure

We will explore the following additional plans to be included in the master project management plan:

- Resource and staffing plan
- Schedule plan
- Finance/cost plan
- Quality plan
- Procurement plan

Details

The project manager must determine the resources needed to complete the full scope of the project. You already have a team put together, but they are not the only resources that will be used on the project. You must also work with functional managers and possibly your Human Resources (HR) department to gain commitment of needed resources.

Develop a Staffing Plan

Steps needed to create a resource and staffing plan include the following:

1. Determine human and nonlabor resources.
2. Determine resource skill sets.
3. Create a resource calendar.
4. Determine resource assumptions.
5. Determine resource risks and mitigation strategies.

STEP 1: DETERMINE HUMAN AND NONLABOR RESOURCES

After you complete the WBS, you will know what the deliverables are so you can determine specific human resources needed. To define the required human resources needed for the project, you will want to consider these factors:

- The deliverable
- The type and quantity of resources needed
- The source of the resource
- Their cost assumptions
- Special needs
- Training needs
- Material needs

STEP 2: DETERMINE RESOURCE SKILL SETS

Most of the time, a project manager doesn't get to choose their team members. You use those people who are assigned by others. So how do you know whether the individual has the skill sets needed for your project? You have a discussion with the manager providing the resource. You will want to know if the resources are:

- Expert
- Highly competent
- Competent
- Novice

Knowing competency levels will help you understand how much supervision will be needed and make adjustments for learning curves as well.

STEP 3: CREATE A RESOURCE CALENDAR

A resource calendar lets you know how many resources you need as well as when you need them. When you are planning a project of significant duration, a functional manager may commit to resources for six months from now. In six months, they probably won't remember what they committed to. So, a resource plan includes a process for reminding the resource suppliers well in advance that they made the commitment to your project and the amount of time that was committed.

STEP 4: DETERMINE RESOURCE ASSUMPTIONS

We spoke of project assumptions earlier. Resource assumptions work the same way. An assumption is something you believe to be true. If it turns out not to be true, it becomes a risk. Here are some typical resource assumptions:

- The sole-source resource will be available when needed.
- Suppliers will provide correct materials when needed.
- Resources will not be overburdened.
- Resources will have the skill sets you need.
- Resources will be available when you need them.

Now that you have identified these assumptions, what do you do if the assumption turns out not to be true? You determine resource risks and strategies to overcome them.

STEP 5: DETERMINE RESOURCE RISKS AND MITIGATION STRATEGIES

Resource risks happen when your assumptions about them are not true. You should create a staffing risk list that describes the risk associated with each resource and then define a strategy to overcome the risk.

Planning ahead for determining all resources needed and appropriate staffing will also assist in developing the finance/cost plan. You want to know as much as possible about your resources now in order to have more-accurate resource costs.

The following is a template that includes the elements of a resource and staffing management plan:

Section 1: Human Resources

- Quantity
- Cost assumptions
- Dates needed
- Date released
- Special needs
- Special skills
- Training needs
- Office and material requirements

Section 2: Nonlabor Resources

You will want to list the type of resource, the source of the resource, the quantity, and the cost of each resource.

- Training
- Facilities, such as floor space furniture and moving costs
- Dates needed
- IT hardware such as computers, printers, and the like
- IT software for administrators, end users, and technical support
- Publishing items such as binders, reproduction expenses, and office supplies
- Environmental needs such as asbestos, soil preparation, site work, and so on
- Construction material and equipment

Section 3: Resource Knowledge, Skills, and Abilities

- Task name
- Type of resource
- Quantity of resources needed for tasks
- Skills
- Experience level
  - Expert
  - Highly competent
  - Competent
  - Novice

Section 4: Resource Calendar

- Insert your resource calendar in this section.

Section 5: Resource Assumptions

- Insert your documented assumptions in this section.

Section 6: Resource and Staffing Risks

- Resource
- Risk
- Mitigation strategy

Hands-on 2.8: Testing Your Knowledge of Staffing Risks

You have already determined that the resources may be a source of risk in staffing your project. Use Table 2.9 to describe the potential risks and the strategy you might use to overcome these risks.

TABLE 2.9   Resource Risks and Strategies

Resource	Risk	Strategy
Sole-source human resource		
Sole-source supplier in your geographic area		
Internal resources		

Develop a Scheduling Plan

A good scheduling plan maximizes the productivity of resources on project activities. You know by looking at your schedule who is to do what, and when.

The project manager is responsible for the schedule. If there are a huge number of tasks, for example on a megaproject, it may be beneficial to hire a project scheduler.

The following represents the processes necessary to create and understand a project:

- Define scheduling activities.
- Determine activity sequencing.
- Estimate resources.
- Determine activity durations.
- Develop the schedule.

DEFINE SCHEDULING ACTIVITIES

The WBS we described earlier shows only the major tasks within logical groupings. What you want to do now is further define those tasks into subtasks (if appropriate) and activities that can be scheduled and are associated with deliverables.

Name the tasks and subtasks. At this point you will want to have some sort of numbering convention, such as in Figure 2.2. Finally, name the activities that create a work package. These activities are also called *schedule activities* because you can assign a resource to the activity.

Figure 2.2 shows us a partial WBS with tasks, subtasks, and activities needed to install a lawn sprinkler system.

FIGURE 2.2   Tasks, subtasks, and activities

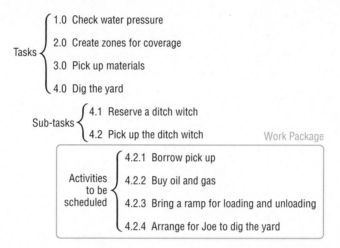

The work package fully accomplished the subtask "Pick up the ditch witch" and the subtasks fully accomplished the task "Dig up the yard." Notice the numbering convention—outlining is common. At the lowest level of a WBS you can now schedule activities.

DETERMINE ACTIVITY SEQUENCING

Activity sequencing establishes logical relationships (dependencies) between the project activities. Project teams work together to identify the dependencies between tasks. You have to know the type of dependencies first. There are three types of dependencies:

Mandatory   Mandatory dependencies use *hard logic* (that is, task A must be completed before task B).

Discretionary   Discretionary dependencies use *soft logic* or *preferred logic*. For example, using soft or preferred logic, you typically would paint the walls before you would lay carpet; however, if the painter is running late on another project, you can, at your discretion, choose to install the carpeting first (with plastic to cover it) and have the painting done later. Anytime you bypass preferred logic, you must also account for risk that is being added to the task that was done, in this case by covering the carpet with plastic.

External   External dependencies determine when some activities can be scheduled. For example, say you have to cross a street underground to lay in fiber. The gas company is also doing an underground street crossing in the same location. The city won't give you a permit for a second underground street crossing. You would have to coordinate your efforts with the gas company.

The result of sequencing tasks is a network diagram. Two types of diagramming techniques can be used. One is the arrow diagramming method (ADM), shown in Figure 2.3, and the other is the precedence diagramming method (PDM), shown in Figure 2.4.

Arrow diagramming method (ADM)

- Activity identified on the arrow (AOA)
- Circles represent the start or finish of an activity
- Uses only finish-to-start relationships
- Can use multiple time estimates to determine durations
- May need dummy activities to complete the logic (shown with dashed line) that are used to show only complex precedence activities such as finish to start

FIGURE 2.3 ADM network diagram

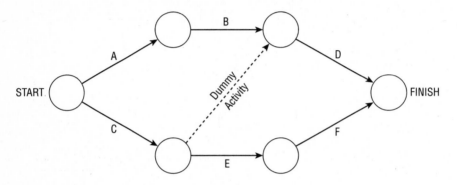

Precedence diagramming method (PDM)

- Activity identified on the node (AON)
- Can use four precedence relationships
- Finish to start
- Start to finish
- Finish to finish
- Start to start
- Uses only one duration
- Other project information can be displayed on the node

FIGURE 2.4 PDM network diagram

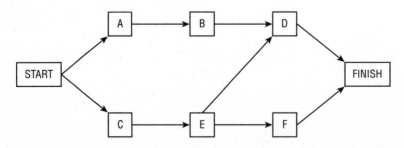

Precedence relationships simply show how tasks relate to each other based on how the network diagram was built, specifically the dependencies between tasks. In most cases, one activity cannot start until another activity has finished. This is referred to as a finish-to-start relationship, and it is the most common form. However, there are four ways, listed in Table 2.10, that one or more activities can be related to each other.

TABLE 2.10   Four Activity Relationships

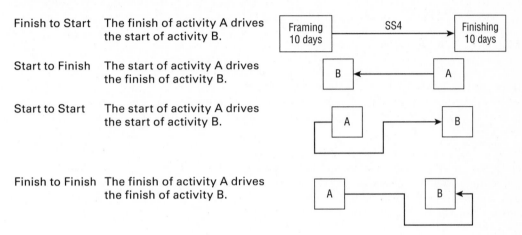

Finish to Start	The finish of activity A drives the start of activity B.
Start to Finish	The start of activity A drives the finish of activity B.
Start to Start	The start of activity A drives the start of activity B.
Finish to Finish	The finish of activity A drives the finish of activity B.

To illustrate how precedence relationships work, consider the initial plan of a project in ADM mode with a duration of 20 days (see Figure 2.5).

FIGURE 2.5   ADM with finish-to-start relationship

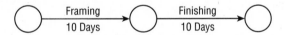

Assume you have to reduce the duration of this project by starting the finishing activity four days after you start the framing activity. In Figure 2.6, we have modified the plan and shortened the duration to 14 days. Notice the "dummy" activity that completes the logic.

FIGURE 2.6   ADM with reduced duration

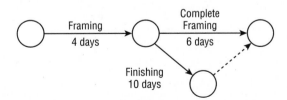

You can see in the less complicated PDM diagram, Figure 2.7, that four days after you start the framing activity, you will start the finishing activity by using a start-to-start relationship of four. Four days after framing has started, you can start the finishing activity by using a start-to-start dependency relationship. The default relationship is always a start-to-finish dependency relationship, which in this case would be 20 days.

FIGURE 2.7 PDM with reduced duration

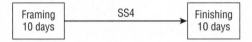

When using precedence relationships, you sometimes may want to use lead and lag times. They enable you to further describe what is happening with a task.

Lead is a modification of a logical relationship that allows an *acceleration* of the *successor* task. For example, in a finish-to-start dependency with a 10-day lead (see Figure 2.8), the successor activity can start two days before the predecessor has finished. Perhaps you have framers putting up interior walls on a multistory, street-of-dreams private mansion. The electricians have to wait until the walls are up before they can start running the electrical wiring. That does not necessary mean they have to wait until all the walls are up; they could, if you schedule it properly, lead into the electrical wiring after a certain percentage of the predecessors' task is complete or a specific number of days prior to completion of the predecessors' task.

FIGURE 2.8 Lead dependency

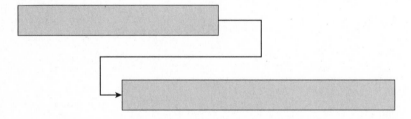

Lag is a modification of a logical relationship that directs a *delay* in the *successor* task. For example, in a finish-to-start dependency with a five-day lag (see Figure 2.9), the successor activity cannot start until five days after the predecessor has finished. For example, you have poured concrete, and the next task is to frame the building. The lag time tells us to wait five days and does not use any resources. You don't need to put into your plan a task called "watch the concrete cure"!

FIGURE 2.9 Lag dependency

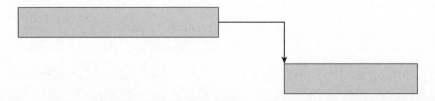

ESTIMATE RESOURCES

Your resource plan helped you determine the resources you need, but now you have to estimate what these resources will cost. The project manager works with the resources assigned to do the work to first estimate the time needed for activities.

Most resource managers tend to estimate with their known constraints. They have full plates and give a duration based on their own situation. Ask them to give you an unconstrained estimate instead; that is, if it were a perfect world, how many hours would it take an average performer to complete the task? Think of these estimates as billable hours. What we are talking about, of course, is effort vs. duration. If it should take only 40 hours, don't accept an effort estimate of three weeks. It may take three weeks to get it done, but you should bill only around 40 hours.

You should also express estimates in ranges and communicate assumptions that you validate and revise as a normal part of project control. If you have a very long project, estimate it in phases. Estimate the first phase or two with a bottom-up approach and the rest with a top-down approach. Variance is greater in longer-range estimates and greater still when there is no history.

There is no need to pad estimates. You can apply other factors. Table 2.11 lists factors that help bring reality to the estimate. You should consider productivity as well. As you can see, many items could affect an estimate. After all, the production time or utilization rate of an eight-hour shift is rarely, if ever, eight hours. The utilization rate for an oil field employee in winter conditions, for example, may be only three hours in an eight-hour shift. Safety considerations may require warming breaks after so much exposure time to the elements. Suiting up once at the site with appropriate protective apparel is required but not considered productive time.

TABLE 2.11   Factors That Bring Reality to the Estimate

Productivity	Other Factors
Number of effective work hours	Size of team
Tools and techniques	Number of clients
Skill level	Client availability
Motivation	Understanding of objectives
Working environment	Project complexity
Leadership and direction	Experience of team
Time spent on rework	Time on other work
Number of tasks involved	Availability of historical data

DETERMINE ACTIVITY DURATIONS

You now know the scope of each activity. The Associated General Contractors of America uses productivity rates to determine activity durations. It considers the productivity rate as it relates to the work quantity and then divides the work quantity by the production rate to determine an estimate of the activity duration.

activity duration = work quantity / production rate

You have everything you need to put together correct durations for the advertising, brochure, and training pieces of the WBS. You should now add durations to your Microsoft Project or other scheduling software file.

DEVELOP A SCHEDULE

You understand the concept of dependencies as well as lead and lag time. Now we will cover other essentials that will help you develop a schedule:

- Critical path
- Float and float
- Forward and backward pass logic

Creating the network diagram is easy, but you should understand the logic that is used in project management software so you can make changes to your network diagram and understand what the results of your changes are. But first you need to understand the critical path method (CPM). CPM calculates a single, deterministic, early and late start and finish date for each activity based on specified, sequential network logic and a single duration estimated. The focus of CPM is calculating float to determine which activities have the least scheduling flexibility.

A *forward pass* is performed, calculated from the early start and early finish dates of all network activities. Then a *backward pass* is performed, calculated from the latest start and latest finish dates of all network activities. Any task that has no float is considered *critical*.

Understanding the logic of CPM and float helps you make schedule trade-offs and is useful in individual task control as well as total schedule control. Critical path tasks have no float or slack in them. That's why they are critical. Without float, if a task on the critical path takes longer than expected, it will delay the end of the project.

Free float or *free slack* is the amount of time an activity can be delayed without delaying the early start of any immediately following activities. *Total float* or *total slack* is the amount of time an activity may be delayed from its early start without delaying the planned project finish date.

The word *float* is used interchangeably with the word *slack*. It is a mathematical calculation and can change as the project progresses and changes are made to the project plan.

late start – early start = slack

The main thing to remember is this: Do *not* let your team members know what their float is. Parkinson's law is alive and well here—work expands to fill the time. What your team members usually do not know is that the float they think they have for their task can be cumulative for the entire path. So if Joe sees that he has one-week float on his task and uses it up, the rest of the members on the path suddenly may not have any float at all. In fact, after the float is used up, you now have another critical path!

Sequencing activities is only part of the action you need to build a schedule. The software that you choose utilizes the forward pass and the backward pass. These functions are performed automatically as you build your network, but again, it is useful for you to understand this built-in logic that determines the amount of float you have for a task or an entire path. When you make changes to the durations or dependencies between tasks, float and critical path could change.

We are now going to determine dependencies, perform a forward pass, perform a backward pass, and then determine the critical path and float time.

Figure 2.10 shows an example of determining the dependencies between tasks. Figure 2.11 performs the forward pass. Tasks that have no predecessor begin the early start with the 0 (see A7, C6, D8, and F6). The forward pass is noted on the top of the box or node. Starting with 0 as the early start of the first task, add the duration; this becomes the early finish date. The early finish date follows the arrow(s) to the next node(s) and becomes that node's early start.

FIGURE 2.10   Determining dependencies

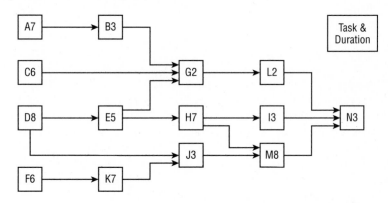

FIGURE 2.11   Performing a forward pass

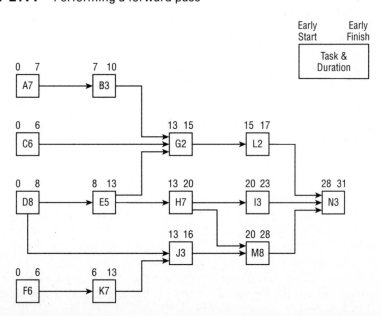

Proceed to the end of the project, keeping in mind that when several arrows from different nodes land into just one node, the forward pass rule is to use the largest early finish date.

Figure 2.12 performs the backward pass. Doing the backward pass is a little trickier than the forward pass. It's just a matter of watching how many arrows flow into and out of the nodes.

FIGURE 2.12   Performing a backward pass

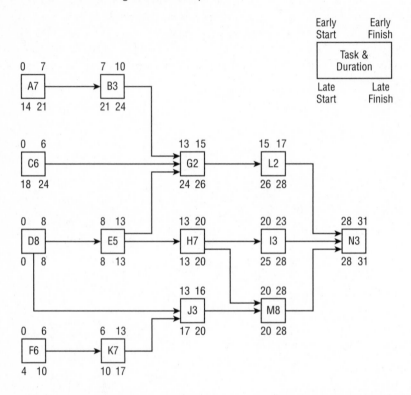

Begin with the last node in the project. Place the late start and late finish dates at the bottom of the node. On the last node this will always be the same as the early start and early finish. Now the fun begins.

Notice how many arrows are flowing into the last node. Follow those arrows to their originating node. The late start of the last node becomes the late finish of the preceding nodes.

Subtract the duration of the current node, and this becomes the late start of that node.

Notice again how many arrows are flowing into these nodes. If there is more than one, take the smaller of the late starts and proceed backward until you reach the beginning of the project.

Figure 2.13 shows how to determine float and the critical path. Float is determined by simply subtracting the early start from the late start, or the early finish from the late finish. If you have done your calculations correctly, both of the answers on each node will be the same.

FIGURE 2.13   Determining float and critical path

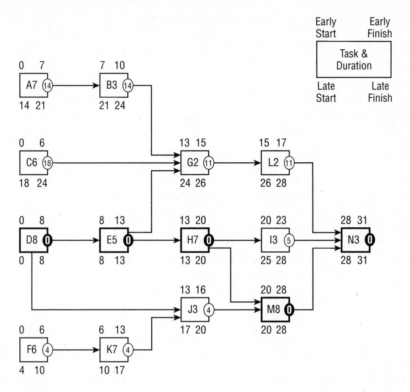

Now you know this:

1. The critical path is D8, E5, H7, M8, and N3 because these tasks have no float.

2. Total float for path A, B, G, L, N = 14. Tasks A and B have a free float of 3 that can be shared between the two tasks without impacting the rest of the path, which is 11.

3. Total float for path C, G, L, N = 18. Task C has a free float of 7 before impacting the rest of the path, which has 11.

4. Total float for path D, E, G, L, N = 11. There is no free float for an individual task—they must share 11.

5. Total float for path D, E, H, I, N = 5. Only task 1 can use this float because the remainder of the tasks are on the critical path.

6. Total float for path F, K, J, M = 4. The float is shared so there is no free float.

So you know the duration of the project, which is also the critical path. You also know how much float is available for noncritical tasks. You now have everything you need to develop your schedule.

Hands-on 2.9: Testing Your Knowledge of Network Logic

You have just determined the following major activities required for the implementation of a new telephone system:

A	Conduct station reviews (3): Predecessor none
B	Obtain network requirements (2): Predecessor none
C	Create station designs (2): Predecessor A
D	Create network cable design (4): Predecessor B
E	Build out switch room (8): Predecessor B
F	Install patch panel in switch room (2): Predecessors D, E
G	Install hardware (3): Predecessor E
H	Install cable (2): Predecessors D, E
I	Tie down cable to patch panel (3): Predecessors F, H
J	Install, program, and test stations (2): Predecessors C, G, I
K	Conduct continuity tests (3): Predecessors J, I
L	Test software (1): Predecessor K

1. Using the precedence diagramming technique, draw the network diagram for this project and calculate the ES, EF, LS, and LF of each of its activities.

2. Show all float activities starting at their early start. Show these activities starting and ending at the most appropriate times.

3. Determine the critical path.

USE GANTT CHARTS

Gantt charts are named for Henry L. Gantt. Gantt worked in a ship building facility during World War I and decided to use a two-dimensional relationship between task and time to better serve those activities. The process was very successful and is widely used today.

Most project management software builds this timeline for you when you sequence your tasks. When tasks are "rolled up" into milestones, the Gantt chart can provide management with a quick view of the status of the project. Figure 2.14 is a Gantt chart provided through Microsoft Project with the details of your advertising, hiring, and training tasks.

DETERMINE PROJECT SCHEDULING IN THE FACE OF UNCERTAINTY

For very large-scale, one-time, complex, nonroutine projects, you can use a process referred to as *program evaluation and review technique (PERT)*. PERT is used when there is uncertainty and when uncertainty hinders decision making.

Booz Allen Hamilton developed this process during the *Sputnik* crisis. This consulting firm was engaged by the U.S. Department of Defense's U.S. Navy Special Projects Office in 1958 as part of the *Polaris* mobile submarine–launched ballistic missile project.

PERT was used to simplify planning of large projects that have outcomes that are unknown. Whereas CPM uses only one duration, PERT uses three:

Optimistic (t_o) Activity time if everything progresses in an ideal manner

Most likely (t_m) Activity time under normal conditions

Pessimistic (t_p) Activity time if major problems are encountered

PERT calculates the average or expected time (t_e) of each activity as follows:

$$(t_e) = \frac{(t_o + 4(t_m) + t_p)}{6}$$

The variance of each activity (v) is calculated as shown in the following equation:

$$v = \left(\frac{t_o \quad t_p}{6}\right)^2$$

The *total* variance of the project is equal to the sum of the variances of the critical path activities. The standard deviation (SD) of a project's duration is equal to the square root of its total variance.

Finally, the PERT assumption that the distribution of the project's completion time (T) is a normal (bell-shaped) distribution enables you to compute the probability of meeting a specified project completion date.

Consider the project in Figure 2.15. All numbers are in days. The first number is the activity's optimistic time. The second number is the activity's most probable time. The third number is the activity's pessimistic time.

FIGURE 2.15 Three time estimates per task

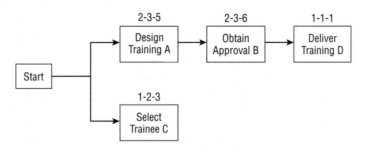

FIGURE 2.14   A Gantt chart

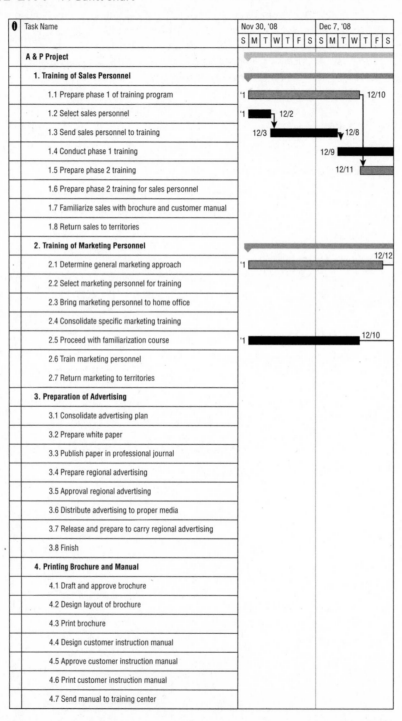

FIGURE 2.14   *(continued)*

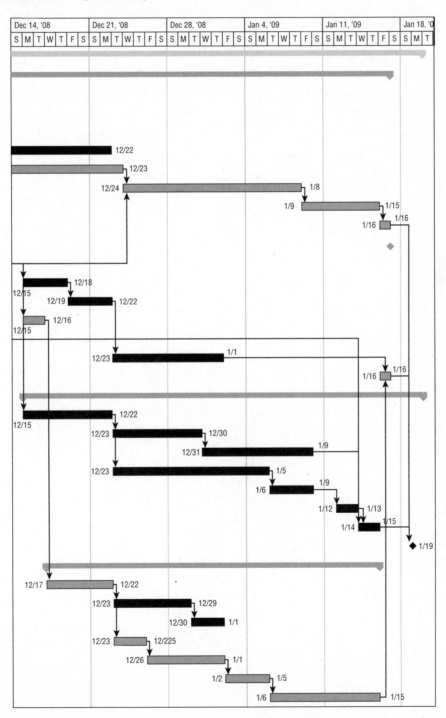

The duration of this project (T) is equal to the sum of the expected times of its critical activities (A, B, D):

$T = t_{eA} + t_{eB} + t_{eD} = 3.17 + 3.33 + 1.00 = 7.50$

Table 2.12 shows the expected time (t_e) and the variance (v) of each activity on the critical path of the training project, using two decimal places in the calculation.

TABLE 2.12   Expected Time and Variance

Activity	Optimistic	Most Likely	Pessimistic	Expected Time $O + (4M) + P/6$	Variance $v = \left(\dfrac{t_0 \cdot t_p}{6}\right)^2$
A	2	3	5	3.17	0.25
B	2	3	6	3.33	0.45
D	1	1	1	1.00	0.00
			Total	7.50	0.70

Using two decimal places, the sum of each variance of the project is 0.70. The standard deviation (SD) of the project is 0.837:

$(SD = \sqrt{70} = 0.837)$

Let's take a closer look at standard deviation. *Standard deviation* is a measure of how spread out your data is. The center line in Figure 2.16 is the mean. On either side of the mean are (plus or minus) one, two, or three standard deviations (sigma noted as σ).

FIGURE 2.16   Standard deviation model

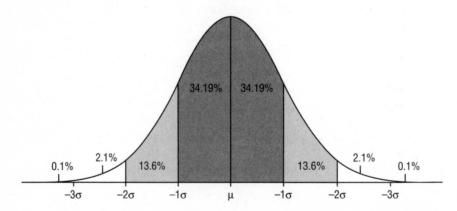

For 68.3% of the time, the project will be completed plus or minus one standard deviation from the expected time. For 95.4% of the time, it will be completed plus or minus two standard deviations from the expected time, and 99.7% of the time it will be completed plus or minus three standard deviations from the expected time.

If you want to know the probability that your project would complete at 68.3%, you would perform the following calculation:

$$\frac{(100\% - 68.3\%)}{2} = 15.85$$

The difference between 50% (on the plus side) and 15.85% is equal to 34.15%, which equals the probability that your project would *not* come in on time. You would perform the same calculations at 2σ and 3σ.

There are 11 steps to follow when using PERT:

1. Build the network diagram.
2. Determine the duration for each task.
3. Do a forward pass.
4. Do a backward pass.
5. Determine the critical path.
6. Draw a standard deviation diagram.
7. Determine the mean.
8. Determine the variance for each task on the critical path.
9. Sum the variances for each critical task to determine the total project variance.
10. Determine the standard deviation for the project.
11. Add the standard deviation to the mean, and to each sigma.

REDUCE THE SCHEDULE

Earlier we suggested that you estimate durations based on the best-case scenario. The reason for that is simple—it makes the schedule realistic. Most of us estimate our durations based on constraints. We are told, "The project must be completed by this date." So what do we do? Regardless of the constraint presented, ask your team to provide unconstrained estimates for more-realistic outcomes. This may require renegotiations with the source imposing the constraint, but then you will have the required data to defend that information brilliantly and facilitate reasonable project time frames for all involved.

For example, let's say management wants this project completed by October 15. You present the schedule that says the project will most likely complete on November 30. Sometimes management will simply approve that. They gave you perhaps an arbitrary date and need ammunition to support any other date. You have given them the ammunition (rationale) so they can defend the date if needed to others who may question the date.

Hands-on 2.10: Testing Your Knowledge of PERT

Table 2.13 contains information you have developed for a project.

TABLE 2.13 PERT Exercise

Activity	Predeccesor	Successor	Optimistic	Most Likely	Pessimistic	PERT Duration	Critical Tasks	Variance of Critical Tasks
A	None	B, D, E	6	7	14			
B	A	C	8	10	12			
C	B, D	G	3	4	5			
D	A	C	6	7	8			
E	A	F	5	5.5	9			
F	E	G	2	3	4			
G	C, F	None	1	2	3			
					Totals			

1. Create the network diagram.

2. Determine the critical path.

3. Determine the variation for each task on the critical path.

4. What is the total variation for the project?

5. What is the standard deviation of this project?

6. What is the probability that the project will be completed at 1 sigma?

7. What is the probability that the project will be completed at 2 sigma?

8. What is the probability that the project will be completed at 3 sigma?

9. Using the standard deviation of question 5, what is the number of weeks for the project at 1 sigma?

10. Using the standard deviation of question 5, what is the number of weeks for the project at 2 sigma?

11. Using the standard deviation of question 5, what is the number of weeks for the project at 3 sigma?

Other times, of course, the date is cast in stone for whatever reason. So in the preceding example you would have to reduce the schedule by six weeks. Most folks simply ask everyone in the project to shorten their durations. You do not need to do this. Now that you know how CPM works, you know that you only have to reduce the critical path. There is danger in creating more than one critical path, however. Here are some suggestions for reducing the project duration:

1. Crashing the project by reducing the duration of activities located on the critical path:

   - When faced with the choice of reducing an upstream vs. a downstream activity, reduce the upstream activity.

   - Determine the cost to reduce by one unit of time each activity on the critical path.

   - Reduce the least costly activity first.

   - Reduce the duration of the critical path until it becomes equal to the longest non-critical path.

   - Now there are two critical paths, and both paths must be reduced to further compress the duration of the project.

   - In reaching the final decision regarding which activity to reduce, consider quality, cost, and all other appropriate factors.

   - Figure slope to defend yourself brilliantly!

2. Fast-track the project. Fast-tracking is simply doing things in parallel that normal logic suggest you do in series. You introduce risk during fast-tracking, but it is an effective way to reduce the project duration.

3. Calculate slope. The calculation of slope, shown Figure 2.17, shows the cost per day of crashing the project.

   - Negative slope indicates that as the time required for a project decreases, the cost increases.

   - If costs and times are the same regardless of whether they are crashed or normal, the activity cannot be expedited.

FIGURE 2.17   Slope formula

$$\text{Slope} = \frac{(\text{Crash Cost} - \text{Normal Cost})}{(\text{Crash Time} - \text{Normal Time})}$$

Another thing to consider when you are reducing the duration of a project is that your resources may be limited. If that is the case, then do the following:

- Schedule the project within the time limit if the end date is fixed, but resources may have to be added to meet the date.

- When scheduling the project within the resource limit, plan to complete the project as soon as possible without using more than the available resources. The project end date could be extended in order to avoid scheduling more resources than are available.

Additionally:

- Move from the start to the end of the project.
- Do not violate your original logic.
- Do not exceed the available resources.
- If you have a choice, schedule the shortest activity first.

MANAGE YOUR RESOURCES

It is important to make sure that your resources don't get "burned out." When they are assigned more hours than they can handle, they become overburdened. It is up to the project manager to ensure that resources are available when you need them, considering the commitments they may have to other projects or work. There are two processes you can use to ensure this:

Resource loading is the process of allocating resources to tasks. Sometimes it is referred to as *resource allocation*. The loading begins when the task-level estimates are being made. Remember, in order to estimate the effort and duration of a task, you must assume a certain number of resources at an assumed skill level (for human resources).

Resource leveling is the process of ensuring that resources are not overburdened and that resource use on the project is relatively smooth. There will be peaks and valleys within a project in terms of resource usage, and you should be prepared to spread the work around if you can, given the ability of another person to handle the same work as someone who is overallocated.

The following represents a template that includes the elements of a project schedule management plan:

Section 1: WBS

Insert a copy of your WBS that includes these items:

- Task name
- Duration of task
- Resource assigned to the task
- Deliverable associated with the task, including work packages

Section 2: Gantt Chart

Include your Gantt chart or describe where the daily updated Gantt chart is located.

Section 3: Network Diagram (optional)

Include your network diagram or describe where the daily network diagram is located.

Section 4: Monitoring the Schedule

- Describe how you plan to monitor your schedule.
- Describe how status will be received and posted to the schedule.

Section 5: Controlling the Schedule

- Describe how you will use resource leveling and resource loading.
- Describe the process you will use to compare actual results with planned results.
- Describe how preventive and corrective actions will be done.

Hands-on 2.11: Testing Your Knowledge of Reducing a Project's Duration

You prepared a proposal for Cimarron to do a portion of the manufacturing of wedding clothing. Unfortunately, because of a typing error, the proposal promised that the project would be completed five weeks following a purchase order from one of your vendors. The original length of the project is eleven weeks, and you discover the error as soon as the purchase order is received. There is also a penalty of $3,000 for each week of delay in completing the project beyond the end of the fifth week. The fifth week for this task actually starts six weeks after the project begins. You quickly prepare the information in Table 2.14.

TABLE 2.14   Crashing Exercise

Activity	Predeccesor	Successor	Normal Time	Normal Cost	Crash Time	Crash Cost
A	None	B	4	$3,200	2	$5,200
B	A	E	3	$6,000	1	$12,000
C	None	D	5	$5,000	2	$9,500
D	C	E	3	$3,000	1	$5,400
E	B and D	None	3	$1,200	1	$2,200

1. Create the PDM network diagram.
2. Determine the critical path.
3. What is the crash cost to reduce the project to eight weeks?

Develop a Finance/Cost Plan

After resource and staffing planning has taken place, the project manager can develop an estimate of resource costs. A finance plan (or as it is sometimes called, a *cost plan*) should be credible enough that there will be sufficient budget in place before work begins, particularly when you are dealing with projects that require several subcontractors, vendors, and so on.

A financial management system should be in place for receiving, approving, and paying suppliers and subcontractors. The invoices you receive should map back to purchase orders, contracts, and receipts of materials or work that has been completed and accepted. The finance plan should also possess a process for the final audit of the contract (where present) and closeout of that contract.

You should include contingency reserves in the baseline budget. Management reserves that are approved are also included as part the cost plan, but are not part of the baseline budget.

This is not a plan that you can create and forget about. Like all project plans, it should be iteratively refined. You want to be able to validate the capabilities of the financial controls you have in place. Elements of a cost plan include cost estimating, cost budgeting, and cost control.

COST ESTIMATING

You know what the high-level estimate was when the project charter was signed, but now you need to "true it up." You now know more than you did when you started, so the costs should be more realistic. Let's take a closer look at estimating types:

Parametric modeling is considered "top down." It uses project characteristics (parameters) in a mathematical model to predict project costs. For example, if you are going to build a commercial building in a certain city, information is available that you can use (for example, cost of materials, land values, and so forth). But that information averages all types of buildings, from a local fast-food restaurant to a high rise, and the average cost of commercial land. As a result, the difference in accuracy can be anywhere from −25% to +75%. By the way, consider this about averages: If you are standing with one foot in a bucket of boiling water and the other foot frozen in a block of ice, on "average" you are considered comfortable!

Analogy estimating is another top-down estimating method, but the accuracy improves the more similar your analogy is to your current project. You use the actual cost of a previous, similar project as the basis for estimating the cost of the current project. The difference in accuracy may be −10% to +25% when the current project is very similar to the analogous project. The variance could be greater if this is an early estimate. For example, some organizations apply T-shirt sizes to their analogies. In other words, without spending a lot of time or looking at too much detail, an analogy may simply put a project into a small, medium, or large label on a project for consideration prior to acceptance of a project into a portfolio. This may be all the detail required to advance an internal enhancement type of project. Remember, you learn more and will be more accurate with your estimates as the project progresses.

Definitive estimating often has a −5% to +10% level of accuracy. You estimate the cost of individual work items so that when you summarize, or roll up, the individual estimates, you can get a project total. This type of estimating is considered bottom up.

When preparing the base project budget, you must consider the realistic availability of resources, which is about 75%. Then determine the loss factors associated with the project, such as errors, interruptions, rework, and so on. This will give you the effort estimate for cost. Next you consider nonproject loss factors such as training, vacations, sick time, holidays, and the like, and this gives you your effort estimate for the schedule.

COST BUDGETING

The total effort required to perform the project is determined in the estimating and scheduling process. Until the final schedule has been agreed upon, estimating isn't complete because as you schedule you may reassign resources, which may change effort estimates for individual tasks.

The effort is multiplied by the hourly rate(s) for the resources to obtain human resource costs. These are allocated over the project duration based on where in the schedule the resources are expected to expend their effort.

Then, capital costs or costs that are associated with nonhuman resource elements, such as equipment purchase, software license costs, and the like, are added. You also have to add in the costs of supplies and facilities directly charged to the project. You then add overhead to get the total cost estimate. This total cost estimate is spread across the project duration, based on when the expenditures are expected to be made, to form the budget for the project.

The budget must be reassessed from time to time and changed if variances (differences between the budget and actual expenditures) are significant enough to warrant it. Usually, as you move from phase to phase in the project, you have an acceptable range of budget that must be met before moving on to the next phase. For example, your organization may allow a 10% overage to move forward but will stop the project if costs exceed the range. After you know who does what and when and their loaded rate (including benefits and overhead), you can create a report showing the budget (see Table 2.15).

TABLE 2.15 Human Resource Cost Budget

Activity	Resource	Est. Effort	Loaded Rate	Budget	Actual Effort	Actual Cost
A	Michelle	80 h	$85	$6,800		
B	Jeness	40 h	$85	$3,400		
C	Carrie	1,800 h	$60	$108,000		
D	Jocelyn	120 h	$100	$12,000		
E	Todd	480 h	$35	$16,800		
		Estimated Budget		$147,000		

The estimated resource budget (in this abbreviated example) plus nonlabor costs (excluding contingency and management reserves) becomes your baseline cost budget. We will discuss contingency and management reserves in "Task 2.7: Managing Project Risks."

COST CONTROL

According to a study from the Standish Group, cost overruns average about 56% of original budgets! Cost control entails monitoring actual cost performance to identify and act on cost variances. It also includes vigorous control of changes to the project scope to prevent unnecessary cost increases. Finally, it includes communicating cost performance and variances to applicable stakeholders and working with them to define plans to keep the project within its approved scope. We will look at ways to control cost in the monitoring and controlling phase.

The following is a cost management plan template that may be useful when you create your cost plan:

Section 1: Estimates

- Describe how you derived your estimates.
- Describe the estimates derived from human resources.
- Describe estimates required for nonlabor resources.
- Describe estimates from contingency funds associated with known risk events.
- Describe the estimate of the management reserve that may be needed.

Section 2: Cost Budgeting

- Allocate costs per work package.
- Allocate costs to time elements such as months, quarters, or years.
- Define spending plans to answer, "Will the project partially fund itself?" For example, if a project is launched to upgrade the infrastructure for cable TV, as soon as the upgrade is complete in an area, customers begin to pay to use the new service; as a result, some of those profits can fund the continuing project.

Section 3: Cost Control

- Document procedures for retrieving cost information.
- Use earned value to determine whether funds are adequate within predetermined ranges.
- Compare planned costs to actual costs.
- Establish cost-control procedures.

Section 4: Establish a Cost History

- Build a WBS with actual costs of activities so as to establish cost history for similar projects.
- Utilize or create a historical database to capture cost information.

Hands-on 2.12: Testing Your Knowledge of Cost Budgeting

1. Who should perform activity estimating? Why?

2. We discussed top-down and bottom-up estimating. Is there a place for both types in a project? Why or why not?

3. Provide two scenarios in which a human resource estimate might change the budget.

Develop a Quality Plan

Quality of a project is measured by whether the project meets or exceeds customer expectations. The expectations, of course, are the product (deliverables), service, or result the customer will receive throughout the project.

A *project quality plan* is simply a set of actions defined at the onset of the project that will produce quality results during the execution of the project. How do you create this? You work with the client, owner, and others to establish *acceptance criteria* for each of the deliverables you produce. You can complete a deliverable, but until the client accepts the deliverable, the task is not complete.

For example, you order 36″ × 36″ acoustical tiles that will be used for the flooring in a television studio. The vendor purchases and installs 12″ × 12″ tiles of the same material. The client does not accept the flooring. The reason the client wanted the bigger tiles is to reduce jitter when cameras roll across the floor. The jitter is undetectable in the larger tiles but would be noticeable with the smaller tiles. If complete acceptance criteria were identified in the first place, this might not have happened (although you could spell out the acceptance criteria and the vendor might still decide to order the smaller tiles to save money).

A project *quality plan* identifies the standards that will be used on the project. It includes performing quality actions such as peer reviews by using various quality resources (templates, standards, checklists) available within your organization.

There are nine basic steps in the quality planning process:

1. Review the documents for quality language.
2. Identify a quality team and leader.
3. Identify plan components and owners.
4. Negotiate specific quality assurance (QA) requirements.
5. Plan the QA and quality control (QC) steps for the project.
6. Educate the project team on QA/QC guidelines.
7. Incorporate QA/QC tasks into the project plan.
8. Get client sign-off.
9. Collect and report QA/QC data and replan if necessary.

COLLECT THE RIGHT DATA

The development of the quality plan *document* begins with the collection of all the information needed for the project. The data to collect will depend on what product, service, or result is being delivered, and might include the following:

- Customer quality characteristics or product description
- Attribute description
- Technical specifications with tolerance ranges
- Blueprint drawings
- Configuration diagrams

- Legal documents
- Standards documents
- Calendar
- Measurement devices
- Any other relevant information from the scope statement or other project documents to get started

This information as well as additional information is then used in the elements of the quality plan.

VALID REQUIREMENTS

How do you know whether you are meeting your customer's needs? Indicators help you determine whether your processes are capable of meeting your customer's needs. An *indicator* is defined as a measure of meeting valid requirements. Indicators are used to monitor both the effectiveness or condition of a part of the work process (process indicators) and the quality of the output or outcome of the process (quality indicators).

No matter what type, all indicators should have the following characteristics:

Measurable   They can be expressed quantitatively (in time, dollars, customer specifications, and so forth).

Verifiable   Multiple, independent observers of the process should be able to agree on the results obtained from measuring the process. Accurate records should be kept so the measurements can be tracked over time.

Cost-effective   Indicators must be chosen with economy of time and cost in mind. Ideally, data for indicators will be available from existing sources and/or management information systems. In any case, common sense tells us that the benefits gained from using an indicator should exceed the costs associated with tracking it.

QUALITY MANAGEMENT PLAN

The quality management plan describes how the project management team will execute the project while complying with policies, standards, or legal requirements. The following represents a quality plan template that you may find useful:

Section 1: Quality Control Activities

- Describe the planned approach for verifying that the required quality has been obtained.

Section 2: Project Management Quality Activities

- Describe activities such as compliance reviews, templates, checklists, and so on.

Section 3: Quality Assurance Checkpoints

- Describe points in the project when checks will be made to verify that the quality control activities and project procedures have been implemented effectively.

Section 4: Quality Roles and Responsibilities

- Define the quality roles of all participating in the project—for example, the functional manager delivers the work product as described in the acceptance criteria pertaining to that work product.

Section 5: Work Products and Quality Characteristics

- Describe the work products for each deliverable and the set of attributes assigned to them.

Section 6: Quality Criteria

- Describe the measurable properties of work products that must be implemented to ensure that the level of quality for a particular quality characteristic will be met.

Section 7: Quality Contributors

- Include project elements such as skills, standards, tools, methods, and procedures that when applied will contribute to achieving specified quality criteria and customer satisfaction.

Section 8: Quality Standards

- When appropriate, include a mapping of quality contributors and project procedures to required quality standards such as the International Organization for Standardization (ISO) or the American National Standards Institute (ANSI).

Section 9: Technical Specifications

- These may be separate documents, but include them in the quality plan.

Section 10: Project Schedule

- Attach a Gantt chart that shows the activities and time scales necessary to implement quality tasks.

Section 11: Assumptions

- Define important assumptions on which the quality plan is based.

Section 12: Dependencies

- Describe any external dependencies on which the plan depends.

Section 13: Risks

- Describe the risks that will affect quality.

Section 14: Costs

- Define the costs associated with implementing this project quality plan, not including costs accounted for elsewhere in the project management master plan.

Section 15: Corrective Actions

- Describe the procedures for taking corrective actions for the problems encountered during project execution.

Hands-on 2.13: Testing Your Knowledge of Quality Planning

1. Using your common sense, what conditions must be met for team members to make maximum contributions to the project?

2. What are the differences between product results and project results?

3. In Phase 1 you identified many quality attributes associated with the quality of clothing in Cimarron's Apples and Pears project. What quality attributes do you want to see associated with the construction of the stores?

Develop a Procurement Plan

The procurement management process consists of six separate processes and related activities involved in procuring goods and services needed for the project from external sources.

PROCUREMENT PLANNING

This is the process of determining what part of the total project scope to outsource. It includes the make-or-buy analysis, one of the key decisions in procurement management. After the make-or-buy analysis is completed, the project manager or designee writes the *statement(s) of work* to enable the procurement process to begin.

When you develop a contractual statement of work (CSOW), essentially you are preparing the document that will provide potential vendors detailed requirements so they can determine whether they are a good fit for your needs, and if so, provide enough information so they can prepare an appropriate bid for your contract work. The more-complete and accurate the CSOW is, the less heartburn, grief, and rework you will encounter later. The vendor is interested in the same things you are. They want to make money and produce a quality work product. To do that, you need to set your vendors up to succeed. A good CSOW helps you do that. The elements of a CSOW include, but are not limited to the following:

- Clear roles and responsibilities
- Location of work

- Security issues if necessary, such as access to proprietary information, key codes, building access codes, and so on
- Milestones and deliverables with acceptance criteria
- Clear description of quantities, technical specifications, and quality expectations
- Progress reports
- Payments
- Change control

Procurement planning entails writing the various procurement documents needed to support steps engaged in during conduct procurement and developing evaluation criteria that will be used to select the best-value suppliers.

Knowing the estimated dollar value of the procurement will help you determine what procurement solicitation process you will choose. The dollar values are determined within your organization. Let's look at the differences among several types of proposals:

Preferred vendors or general marketplace   Reasonable and adequate competition exists, so there is no need to send out proposals—a preferred vendor list or a solicitation to the general marketplace can be used. A suggested dollar value for this type of proposal is $0–$5,000.

Requests for quotes   These are similar to requests for proposals (RFPs), but are generally used for goods or materials rather than services, solutions, or procurements that will be running a portion of your project or the entire project. If you need to purchase 200 hammers, all you really need to know is the product specification and the price for that quantity and variety. Getting three or more responses increases the probability of getting fair market prices for the materials or goods you seek.

Requests for information   Requests for information (RFIs) are generally used when the buyer may not know what options are available in the marketplace or when open to various solutions rather than a specific result. RFIs ask vendors what they would offer to solve a particular problem or opportunity and usually do not require any pricing information at that point. RFIs may also be used to better understand the options, narrow the field to those suggestions you like, and then issue an RFP to the narrowed group of competitors.

Requests for proposals   Requests for proposals are generally used when both the solution and the pricing are under consideration. RFPs may be supplemented with an oral presentation or product demonstrations for those making it through the initial screening.

The final procurement document should have a legal review. Only when the review is completed and is acceptable should the documents be distributed.

Requesting seller responses is considered part of the conduct procurements process in the *PMBOK® Guide, 4th ed*. We will discuss that process along with source selection in Phase 3. Contract administration will be discussed in Phase 4. The closed contract process will be discussed in Phase 5.

TYPES OF CONTRACTS

There are several types of contracts you could use. The following contract types are typically found in the project world:

Firm fixed price A *firm fixed price (FFP)* contract is used most often. Another name for this contract is *lump sum*. In this type of contract, the contractor agrees to furnish supplies or services at a specified price that is not subject to adjustment because of performance costs. This type of contract is best suited when reasonably definite production specifications are available and costs are relatively certain. The seller bears the greatest degree of risk in this contract type and may therefore pad their price for contingencies that may occur during the project. In this situation, the seller is motivated to decrease costs by producing efficiently because regardless of what the costs are, the seller receives the agreed-upon amount. As a consequence, the seller should place emphasis on controlling costs.

Fixed-price incentive A *fixed-price incentive (FPI)* contract is composed of a target cost, target profit, target price, ceiling price, and share ratio. This contract type is probably the most complex.

Example: Based on a ceiling price of $120,000, a target cost of $100,000, a target profit of $10,000, a target price of $110,000, and a share ratio of 70/30, for every dollar the seller can reduce costs below $100,000, the savings will be shared by the buyer and seller based on the negotiated sharing formula, which reflects the degree of uncertainty faced by each party. Assuming the seller tries to maximize profits, it is provided an incentive to reduce its costs by producing more efficiently.

When a ceiling price is agreed to up front, the seller assumes all overruns above the ceiling; but if costs exceed the target cost of $100,000, regardless of the costs incurred by the seller, both the buyer and seller share the risk up to the ceiling. This incentive-type contract is usually used when contracts are for a substantial sum and involve a long production time. This enables the seller to develop production efficiencies during the performance of the contract.

Cost plus incentive fee A *cost plus incentive fee (CPIF)* is a cost-reimbursement contract. The CPIF means the seller is paid for allowable performance costs along with a predetermined fee and an incentive bonus. If the final cost is less than the expected cost, both the buyer and seller benefit by the cost savings based on a prenegotiated sharing formula. This sharing formula is an agreed-upon percentage reflecting the degree of uncertainty each party will bear.

Example: Say that the expected cost is $100,000, the fee to the seller is $10,000, and there is a sharing formula of 85/15. Under this contract, the buyer absorbs 85% of the uncertainty, and the seller absorbs 15% of the risk. If the final price is $80,000, resulting in a cost savings of $20,000, the seller's compensation includes the final cost and the fee, plus an incentive of $3,000 (15% of $20,000), for a total reimbursement of $93,000.

Cost plus fixed fee A *cost plus fixed fee (CPFF)* contract provides that the seller be reimbursed for allowable costs of performing the contract, and in addition the seller receives as profit a fee payment, usually based on a percentage of estimated costs. This fixed fee does not vary with actual costs unless the scope of work is changed.

Example: If the estimated cost for performance is $100,000, and a profit fee of $10,000 is agreed upon, even if the cost for performance rises to $110,000, the fee remains $10,000.

Cost plus award fee   *Cost plus award fee (CPAF)* contracts include an estimated cost and potential awards paid based on periodic subjective evaluations of contractor performance.

Example: The estimated cost for a project is $500,000, to be completed in six months. The project was completed five weeks early and 10% under budget. The buyer decided that because the project came in early and under budget, the award would be formulated as follows:

Base award = 2% of the original budget, or $10,000.

Cost award = $10,000 for every 5% under budget. In this case the cost award is $20,000.

Schedule award = $5,000 for every week the project comes in early from the original time estimate. In this case the schedule award is $25,000.

The total award is $55,000.

Time and materials   *Time and materials (T&M)* contracts have fixed-unit arrangements but are open-ended. The *PMBOK® Guide, 4th ed.*, p. 324, describes time and materials contracts as a "hybrid type of contractual arrangement that contains aspects of both cost-reimbursable and fixed-price arrangements."

T&M contracts resemble *cost-type arrangements* in that they are open-ended, because the full value of the arrangement is not defined at the time of the award. Thus T&M contracts can grow in contract value as if they were cost-reimbursable arrangements.

Conversely, T&M arrangements can also resemble *fixed-unit arrangements*, when, for example, the unit rates are preset by the buyer and seller, as when both parties agree on the rates for a specialty resource (for example, senior engineer). This contract type is often used for staff augmentation agreements rather than project completion contracts.

Cost plus percentage of cost   A *cost plus percentage of cost (CPPC)* provides for reimbursement to the contractor for allowable costs of contract performance. Additionally, the contractor receives an agreed-upon percentage of the estimated cost as profit.

Example: If the estimated cost is $100,000 and the agreed-upon percentage is 10%, the estimated total price is $110,000. If the seller increases costs to $110,000, the total price would be $121,000, which will result in an *increase in profit* of $1,100.

RESPONSIBILITIES

Although the project manager has overall responsibility for procurement and contract management, on large projects a contract manager is usually assigned who will perform many of the duties described in this plan. The project manager works closely with the contract manager to define requirements, write a statement of work, help recommend sources, and so on.

For example, your project may require ergonomic seating for a service center. The procurement contact (manager, agent) will do the leg work of finding these chairs for you and ask you to select the chair from a list of choices. This person already knows who is on the preferred vendor list and has done this many times before. The contact may not even offer you a choice of chairs. As long as the chairs meet the product acceptance criteria, the contact's choice should be fine.

Most organizations have definite policies and procedures regarding procurement (or acquisitions, purchasing, and so forth). Be sure you are aware of them. Consult with your purchasing or procurement department. Evaluate the standard processes to see whether they serve the purposes required for your project.

SUBCONTRACTORS

A *subcontractor* is a group or individual providing products or services to the project. Commonly, subcontractors are considered vendors (see the following section). However, there is a growing understanding that any internal group that provides products or services (for example, an internal technical writing department) is a subcontractor to the project manager. Of course, in this broader usage, the agreement between the parties is not a legally binding contract, but it is a contract nonetheless.

VENDORS

A *vendor* is an external organization or individual providing products or services under contract to the client or to the project performance group. Vendors are also referred to as outside contractors or subcontractors.

SUMMARY

Acquisition is a timely process. Allow sufficient lead time in the project plan to properly perform the work of describing the product/services needed, getting bids from qualified vendors, selecting the right one, awarding the contract, getting feedback and approval from the participants in the procurement process, kicking off the engagement, managing the supplier during the engagement, and wrapping up.

The following represents a template that can be used to create your project procurement plan:

Section 1: Specifications

- Design specifications
- Performance specifications
- Functional specifications

Section 2: Source Selection Package

- Bid documents (usually standardized)
- List of qualified vendors (expected to bid)
- Proposal evaluation criteria
- Bidder conferences and schedules

- How change requests will be managed
- Supplier payment plan

Section 3: Procurement Actions

- What procurement actions the project team is authorized to execute on its own without reference to the procurement department
- What status reports the project team will require from the procurement department on outsourced items
- How multiple providers will be managed
- How procurement will be coordinated with other aspects of the project
- Purchasing decisions (including authority to commit)
- Make-or-buy decisions with supporting data

Section 4: Procurement Documents

- Request for quotes
- Requests for information (RFIs)
- Requests for proposals (RFPs)

Section 5: Types of Contracts

- Firm fixed price (FFP)
- Fixed-price incentive (FPI)
- Cost plus fixed fee (CPFF)
- Cost plus incentive fee (CPIF)
- Cost plus percentage of cost (CPPC)
- Cost plus award fee (CPAF)
- Time and materials (T&M)

Section 6: Contract Administration

- Change management
- Specification interpretation
- Adherence to quality
- Warranties
- Subcontractor management
- Production surveillance
- Waivers
- Contract breach

Hands-on 2.14: Testing Your Knowledge of Contract Types

1. What should the project manager monitor when managing a CPIF contract?

2. Under a CPFF contract, the project manager assumes what type of risk?

3. What should the project manager monitor when managing a CPFF contract?

4. From the buyer's standpoint, a CPPC is the most undesirable type of contract. Why?

5. What should the project manager monitor when managing a CPPC contract?

6. What should the seller monitor on an FFP contract?

Hands-on 2.15: Testing Your Knowledge of Contract Calculations

Cimarron has just completed a two-story expansion of one of their children's stores located at the Mall of America in Bloomington, Minnesota. As with most projects at Cimarron, Olivia Ross was anxious to see the lessons learned.

Ms. Ross initially wanted to receive just FFP bids, but after speaking with her procurement director, Harry Edwards, it was agreed that other types of contract offers would also be considered.

Several contractors submitted FFP bids:

- Contractor A bid $825,000.

- Contractor B bid $795,000.

- Contractor C bid $850,000.

- Contractor D bid $790,000.

- Contractor E bid $800,000.

Details of the contracts are as follows:

- Contractor A submitted a CPPC contract with a percentage of 4 percent.

- Contractor B submitted only an FFP bid.

- Contractor C submitted a CPIF contract with a target cost of $725,000 and an 80/20 share ratio.

- Contractor D also submitted a CPIF bid, with the incentive of $25,000 for every month that was completed early.

- Contractor E offered an alternative FPIF, which indicated receiving 10% of the total cost per month for completing the project early and 10% for every $10,000 below the fixed price.

Mr. Edwards had originally chosen contractor D because of its FFP bid. As part of a contract audit performed by A-Z Audits Plus, an independent auditing company, contractor D willingly revealed the costs associated with the project, which were $720,000, and the project was completed one month early.

1. If contractor A's cost was $720,000, what would have been the cost for contractor A's CPPC bid?

2. What would be the cost of the contract if Olivia chose contractor D's CPIF bid?

3. What is the cost of contractor C's CPIF contract if its cost was $700,000 and the cost-sharing ratio was 80% for the client and 20% for the seller?

4. What is the profit of contractor E's contract if the target cost is $720,000, target profit is $10,000, target price is $730,000, ceiling price is $750,000, and actual cost was $700,000?

Task 2.7: Managing Project Risks

Risk is often thought of as something negative, something that should be avoided. Depending on whether one is a risk seeker or opposed to risk, opinions will often lead to very different results. Within project management, risk is looked at both ways—as a potential problem and as a potential opportunity. Regardless, risk always involves something that will occur in the future. It will involve some sort of change, as well as an element of personal choice.

Managing risk includes identifying elements of risk, quantifying risks by assessing their probabilities of occurrence, analyzing financial and nonfinancial factors, mitigating their potential negative effects or enhancing the opportunities that may occur, and controlling risk, should it occur. In any case, managing risk:

- Increases the understanding of the project

- Identifies the alternatives available in delivery and methods

- Ensures that uncertainties and risks are adequately considered in a structured and systematic way that enables them to be incorporated into planning and project development processes

- Establishes the implications of these on all other aspects of the project

Scenario

You have been overwhelmed in the past while managing projects, and as you thought about the reasons for being overwhelmed, you realized that all you were doing was responding to risks and performing "brute force coordination." It seemed you were constantly putting out fires. And although you were able to work through most of them, you are determined that with this project you are going to be proactive about risk.

Scope of Task

Duration

This task may take a few hours or a few days, depending on the complexity of your project.

Setup

None.

Caveat

None.

Procedure

In this task you will do the following:

- Understand the differences among certainty, uncertainty, and choice
- Understand the rules of probability
- Understand stakeholder risk tolerance
- Learn the process of risk identification
- Learn how to categorize risk
- Learn the process of qualitative risk assessment
- Understand the benefits of using a risk register
- Learn the process of quantitative risk analysis
- Determine the expected value of a risk event
- Learn the elements of a risk-response plan
- Understand the difference between contingency reserves and management reserves
- Learn the elements of a risk management plan

Details

In reality, human beings do their best work during a crisis. They tend to support each other regardless of personal circumstances. Observe the behavior that occurs during a natural catastrophe to see that this is true. But the question begs to be asked: At what cost? Substantial savings can occur if risk mitigation strategies are developed ahead of time. Planning for risk is simply good business and provides clients with a sense of confidence in the potential project outcome. Risk management should always be used when uncertainty hinders decision making.

Uncertainty, Choice, and Certainty

Uncertainty exists when there is a complete absence of information. Nothing is known about the possible outcomes, and no probability distributions (based on experience) can be developed. Project managers typically do not deal in areas of total uncertainty.

Choice, on the other hand, negates the existence of risk. If there is no choice, there is no risk, even if there is a loss. If a person making a decision can take actions to increase or decrease the chance or magnitude of the loss or gain, then risk exists.

Certainty implies that all information to make a decision about a situation is known ahead of time and there is a certainty of occurrence. There are three ways to encounter a risk:

- Placing yourself at risk

- Being put into a risk situation by another

- Acts of nature (contracts may also refer to this as *acts of God*)

You can also be placed at risk without recognizing that it exists, and perceived risks are as important as real risks. Not choosing is considered a choice.

Some folks also believe that *issues* are the same as risk, but there is a difference between an issue and a risk. All issues need to be acknowledged, documented, assigned an owner, and continuously monitored for resolution.

A risk event may or may not occur. Some risks have higher priorities than others. The project manager makes sure that a risk response is developed for each risk. Part of the risk-response strategy is to create a contingency fund for risks that have high impact and high probability of occurrence.

Understanding Probability Theory

Risk analysis is rooted in the use of probabilities. In the absence of known facts, probabilities are used to help find ways to look at future events. Before we can truly qualify or quantify risks, we must understand probability theory and the notion of randomness.

The mathematical study of randomness, called *probability theory*, is used to assign relative frequencies to each of the possible outcomes of an event. Randomness exists where individual outcomes are uncertain but there is a regular distribution of frequencies when a large number of repetitions occur. For example, when throwing a pair of standard six-sided dice, we know that 36 combinations exist and that the probability of throwing a 10 is 3/36 or 0.0833 percent.

Understanding probability theory will help the project team create a probability/impact risk-rating matrix that enables scoring interpretations based on risk event value. There are three simple rules of probability:

- The probability of an event occurring plus the probability of an event not occurring always equals 1. The event either happens or it doesn't, which can be split on the continuum infinitely, such as a 50-50, 70-30, or 60-40 split.

- The probability of two events happening simultaneously is the *product* of the probabilities. If you have a 60% chance of using one process and a 40% chance of using it in conjunction with another, then the probability of using both together is 24%.

- The probability of two independent and mutually exclusive events is the *sum* of probabilities of all possible outcomes of an event and is equal to 1. When there are more than two possible outcomes, the sum of the probabilities is still equal to 1. For example, suppose a high school consists of 25% juniors, 15% seniors, and the remaining 60% are students of other grades. The relative frequency of students who are either juniors or seniors is 40%. We can add the relative frequencies of juniors and seniors because no student can be both a junior and a senior.

Understanding Stakeholder Risk Tolerance

Risk cannot be objective based on a given individual's perspective; sometimes there are winners and sometimes there is only a chance for a loss. What determines whether risk is acceptable depends entirely on the tolerance for risk by the individual risk taker. Individuals may be one of the following:

Risk Averse   Prefer outcomes that do not have the highest monetary downside value, which usually translates to lower potential upside as well

Risk Neutral   Indifferent to outcomes of the risk event

Risk Seeker   More willing to take a chance

Most people think of themselves as more risk-taking than they really are. Decisions change from situation to situation. Very few people are totally averse to risk. Stakeholders may be risk averse, risk neutral (indifferent) to outcomes of the risk event, or risk seeking (more willing to take a chance).

Accepting a sure loss is admitting defeat and is not an easy thing to do, but at times you might have to choose to cut your losses and move on—lose the battle so you can win the war. Honor your risk takers by rewarding good tries as well as successes.

Risk Identification

Identifying risk events is a major part of the up-front planning process. It should be incorporated into the planning process *before* implementation occurs. Having said that, you must also acknowledge that the risk management process is highly iterative and may occur whenever there are changes to the original plan.

Initial risk discovery incorporates historical data and interviews with experts or those folks in the trenches who have previously been exposed to or had to respond to specific risk events. In other words, you need to "blow holes in the plan" by considering what could possibly go wrong. Risk identification must occur as early in the project as possible, but is typically the last of the subsidiary plans to be created before the overall project plan is finalized. You want to know as much as you possibly can about the project, and so your first steps involve best case, logical parameters. Once you believe that your plan makes sense, it's time to establish categories where the plan can go wrong or be further enhanced.

These tools can be used for risk identification:

- Documentation reviews
- Information-gathering techniques:
    - Brainstorming
    - Delphi technique—another way of obtaining group input for ideas and problem-solving. A question is posed and sent out for answers. When the answers are returned, the results get distributed to all who participated by a facilitator who sent out the original questions. There may be voting involved, but in any case, anonymity is the key with this process.
    - Interviewing
    - Root cause analysis
- Checklists analysis
- Assumptions analysis
- Diagramming techniques, such as cause and effect or flow charting
- SWOT (strengths, weaknesses, opportunities, and threats) analysis

Risks that may affect the project for better or worse can be more effectively managed if they are organized into risk categories. The *PMBOK® Guide, 4th ed.*, p. 280, identifies four broad categories, but others can be used that make sense to the project team. They should reflect common sources for the industry or application area of the project. Let's take a closer look.

RISK CATEGORIES

You are fairly adept at identifying *technical risks*. They may include such items as relying on unproven technology, unrealistic performance goals, or changes in the state-of-the art or industry standards. There may be complex requirements, a difficult operating environment, integration or interface problems, and perhaps severe reliability issues.

In reality, you may not always consider *project management risks*. They can cause severe issues if not addressed and may include poor allocation of time and resources, inadequate quality of the project plan, or poor use of the project management discipline. The project manager or team members may be on a learning curve. There may be unrealistic schedule and cost estimates, poor communication, short planning time, no change control procedures, and unmanaged project assumptions.

Organizational risks include cost, time, and scope objectives that are internally inconsistent; lack of prioritization of projects; insecure funding; and resource competition. Field inexperience and changing or untimely decisions can also cause risk.

External risks could include a shifting legal or regulatory environment; labor issues; country risk; weather; unavailability of raw materials; permitting difficulties; postulated events such as vandalism, terrorism, or sabotage; or social and environmental issues. Additionally, you may want to consider fluctuating currencies, political unrest, failure of a supporting infrastructure due to others, or failure of design, execution, or suppliers due to bankruptcy. This list could go on forever.

Other risks include the following:

- Personnel
- Human resource management
- Financial
- Operational
- Natural and man-made disasters
- Political
- Economic cycle/marketing
- Contractual/legal
- Requirements changes
- Design changes
- Task omissions
- Estimating and scheduling errors
- Technical errors
- Staff turnover, illness or death, unplanned vacations and leaves of absence
- Late delivery of external deliverables
- Priority changes that result in loss of resources, including support work
- Late approvals and acceptances
- Extended learning curves
- Unavailable or unreliable tools and methods
- Assumptions that turn out not to be true

Risk events and their impact to the project change throughout the life of the project. There are three elements to risk:

- The risk event
- The probability of the risk occurring
- The impact of the event on the project

The categories of potential risk events can help you identify specific risks that fall into those categories. Some project managers would prefer to brainstorm the risks and then place them into categories. It really doesn't matter which method you use.

Perform Qualitative Risk Assessment

After you have identified the risks, the next process for risk management is qualitative analysis. In this process, you want to determine the likelihood of occurrence and the impact of the risk if it does occur.

SIZING THE PROBABILITIES OF RISK LIKELIHOOD

Project stakeholders must agree on the break points between severity descriptors and percentages associated with them in order to be consistent in their assessment regarding the likelihood that a risk event will occur:

- *Very low* may indicate a 5% likelihood of occurrence or that the risk event *hasn't* happened within the past five years.

- *Low* may indicate a 20% likelihood of occurrence *or* that the risk event *has* happened within the past five years.

- *Medium* may indicate a 40% likelihood of occurrence *or* that the risk event has happened once or twice within the past 24 months.

- *High* may indicate a 60% likelihood of occurrence *or* that the risk event has happened once within the past 12 months.

- *Very high* may indicate an 80% likelihood of occurrence *or* that the risk event has happened on a regular basis over the past 24 months.

SIZING THE IMPACT OF RISK EVENTS OR THE AMOUNT AT STAKE

Impacts, or consequences associated with risk, are examined to assess the consequences to project objectives. Project stakeholders describe and agree on severity descriptors in order to be consistent in their assessment regarding the impact or amount at stake that a risk event may inflict.

The following are examples of using severity descriptors:

- *Very low* may mean having insignificant impact on the project objectives (for example, 5–10% slippage on the schedule and/or budget).

- *Low* may mean having minor outcomes that are unlikely to have a permanent or significant effect on the project objectives (for example, 20% chance that materials won't arrive when planned).

- *Medium* may mean having a potentially serious impact that can be managed without major impact to the project objectives (for example, 40% chance that training will be delayed by one month).

- *High* may mean having a potentially significant effect on the project objectives that will require major effort to resolve (for example, 60% chance that manufacturing won't finish on time).

- *Very high* may mean having significant risk that could totally jeopardize the objectives of the project (for example, 80% chance that your labor pool will go on strike during the time you need them).

PROBABILITY AND IMPACT MATRIX

Many people want things to be certain and unambiguous. But as it has been said by that famous philosopher, Mick Jagger, "You can't always get what you want." Give them what they need—a realistic assessment of risk and uncertainty.

Table 2.16 shows a probability and impact matrix with varying shades of gray. The darker gray represents risk averse, the lighter gray represents risk seeking, and the lightest gray represents risk neutral. Your organization may look differently at risk—whereas this table shows a slightly more risk-averse culture, your organization may be more risk-seeking. When you multiply the probability by the impact, you can obtain a defendable rating to the degree that your data are accurate.

TABLE 2.16   Probability and Impact Matrix

Probability	Risk = Probability X Impact				
0.90	0.09	0.27	0.45	0.63	0.81
0.70	0.07	0.21	0.35	0.49	0.63
0.50	0.05	0.15	0.25	0.35	0.45
0.30	0.03	0.09	0.15	0.21	0.27
0.10	0.01	0.03	0.05	0.07	0.09
	0.10	0.30	0.50	0.70	0.90

Impact

You can identify and qualify risks in six steps:

1. Send a blank risk event worksheet (Table 2.17) to each person whom you believe will be able to identify risk events for the project. Ask them to consider all risks that could affect the objectives of the project in their area of support. For example, if your team member is from IT, they should identify those items that could be risks in IT.

2. Ask them to fill out the worksheet(s) completely, one for each risk, and return it to you in whatever time frame is needed—typically no longer than one week.

3. Collect the filled-out worksheets (via whatever tools the team agrees on—typically email) and sort by probability, impact, category, and risk response. There will probably be duplicates. This will eliminate many hours of brainstorming or trying to collect all of the risks at one sitting.

4. Set up a meeting with your team and show them the risk events that were identified, what their probabilities and impacts are, and their categories. This can be done via conference call and meeting software or face-to-face.

TABLE 2.17   Risk Event Worksheet

Risk Event Worksheet				
Risk				
Probability	Impact	Category	Risk Response	Triggers
Very Low ☐	Very Low ☐	Technical ☐	Avoid ☐	
Low ☐	Low ☐	Project Management ☐	Transfer ☐	
Medium ☐	Medium ☐	Organizational ☐	Mitigate (reduce) ☐	
High ☐	High ☐	External ☐	Accept ☐	
Very High ☐	Very High ☐	Other ☐		
Describe your risk response strategy				

5. As a team, reach agreement on the probability of the risk, the impact to the project objectives, the categories, and the risk responses.

6. You, as project manager, will facilitate this discussion and add the completed information to the risk register.

TRIGGERS

Triggers are symptoms and warning signs that a risk event is likely to occur. Using one of our qualifying risk examples, hearing the news that contract negotiations have broken down is a trigger that your labor pool may go on strike.

After you have identified and qualified your risk events, place them in a risk register such as the sample found in Table 2.18.

Hands-on 2.16: Testing Your Knowledge of Identifying and Qualifying Risk Events

1. Identify two risk events that could occur on the Apples and Pears project in each of the following categories:

- Organizational

- Project management

- External

2. Decide the probability of occurrence, the impact of occurrence, and your risk response for the risk events identified in question 1, and place your answers in the blank risk register found in Table 2.19.

TABLE 2.18 Risk Register Sample

RISK #	RISK EVENT DESCRIPTION	PROBABILITY Low	PROBABILITY Med.	PROBABILITY High	DESCRIBE IMPACT ON PROJECT	IMPACT Low	IMPACT Med.	IMPACT High	MITIGATION STRATEGY	Owner	Status
1.	Technical Obsolescence		▓		Future use of stations may require external equipment and complex testing.	▓			Absorb risk: workarounds for test station usage already exist.	Jeff	Not started
2.	Audit failures			▓	May require unplanned revisions to department test practices.	▓			Control: prepare summary of operational differences.	Terri	Not started
3.	Inadequate funding			▓	May cause reductions in scope and technical capabilities.			▓	Avoid: fight for adequate funding. Deflect: Capital Acquisitions has contingency funds.	Lin	Not started
4.	Inadequate schedule			▓	May result in inadequate test capacity and use of alternative test methods.			▓	Avoid: create schedule contingency.	Lin	Not started
5.	Micromanagement			▓	May consume inordinate amounts of resources, schedule, and budget.		▓		Avoid: negotiate protection with sponsor and management in advance.	Diane	Not started
6.	Internal customer confidence			▓	Continued proliferation of alternate test methods and equipment.		▓		Control: communicate with and solicit participation of internal customers.	Julie	Not started
7.	External customer confidence		▓		External specification of manufacturing test equipment and subcontracting test work.		▓		Control: communicate and address concerns with external customers.	Julie	Not started

TABLE 2.19 Blank Project Risk Register

Risk Register

RISK #	RISK EVENT DESCRIPTION	PROBABILITY			DESCRIBE IMPACT ON PROJECT	IMPACT			MITIGATION STRATEGY	Owner	Status
		Low	Med.	High		Low	Med.	High			

Perform Quantitative Risk Analysis

The value of quantitative risk analysis depends on the accuracy of the data used to perform this task. When you multiply the potential loss ($) by the probability of that loss occurring, you can use the results to rank the risks and to make decisions based on those results.

The results of your *qualitative* analysis determine which risks you will use in this process. Normally you would work on risks that were qualified as high impact and high probability of occurrence. Or, if your organization is more risk-averse, you may choose to quantify those in the medium/high range. In any case, there are tools you can use to assist you in this process.

INTERVIEWING

Follow these steps to conduct a successful data collection interview:

1. Interview project stakeholders and subject matter experts in order to quantify the probability and consequences of risk on the project objectives. The information needed depends on the type of probability distributions that will be used.

2. The project manager must then define the benefits and boundaries of the project and document the rationale of the risk ranges discovered during the risk qualification process.

3. The project manager must prepare for the risk interview by performing triage on key risk elements in order to establish risk ranking.

4. Set up a meeting with the subject matter experts and those who planned and who will manage the work.

5. Conduct the interview. Everyone's views are valuable but do challenge the ranges they may give you. There may be motivational biases or a lack of understanding that may result in underestimates.

PROBABILITY DISTRIBUTIONS

Continuous probability distributions are used to model random data. Data are captured and turned into a model such as a histogram. The veracity of the model depends on the accuracy of the data collected. If the model is based on observed (physical) data, the model will be equally accurate. Errors account for skews in the distribution.

Beta distributions are continuous distribution models and are frequently used in quantitative risk analysis; however, they are constrained to a finite interval of possible outcomes.

Triangular distributions have three possible outcomes, all of which are equally likely. The mean is calculated in the same way as a beta distribution and is what you use in PERT calculations: that is, the mean is equal to:

$$\frac{O + (4M) + P}{6}$$

SENSITIVITY ANALYSIS

Sensitivity analysis is a simple tool that investigates how estimated performance varies with changes in the pre-identified key assumptions that are based on the project objectives. This process can help the project team discover which risk events have the greatest impact on the project objectives.

Sensitivity analysis uses the data gathered in the interviewing process to "examine the extent to which the uncertainty of each project element affects the objective being examined when all other uncertain elements are held at their baseline values" (*PMBOK® Guide*, *4th ed.*, p. 298, glossary). If a small change in a parameter results in relatively large changes in the outcomes, the outcomes are said to be *sensitive* to that parameter.

Generally, there are five steps involved in creating a sensitivity analysis:

1. Design the experiment.
2. Assign ranges of variation to input factors.
3. Generate the input vectors through the design.
4. Create the corresponding output distribution.
5. Assess the relative importance of inputs.

EXPECTED MONETARY VALUE ANALYSIS USING DECISION TREES

Decision trees provide a highly effective, visual structure within which the project team can display options and further explore the possible outcomes of choosing those options. Decision trees help form a balanced picture of the risks and rewards associated with each possible course of action. Let's create a decision tree one step at a time. There are three steps to this process:

1. Determine what decision you wish to make.
2. Apply probabilities based on collected data.
3. Apply monetary value and analyze the data.

The decision tree in Figure 2.18 shows step 1, which is to determine which machine combination will be the most cost-effective: machine A with machine B, machine A with machine D, machine B with machine C, or machine B with machine D.

FIGURE 2.18   Step 1: What machine combination is least expensive?

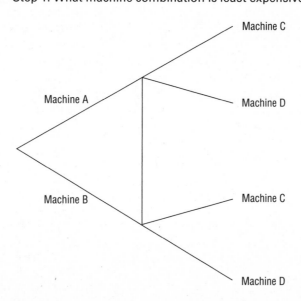

Next you determine the probabilities, given the data you have available. When you multiply the probabilities, you can determine a more realistic probability. Each grouping should be equal to 100, as shown in Figure 2.19.

Figure 2.20 shows that on the AC and AD branches, AD passes. On the BC and BD branches, BD passes. Between the two passes, BD is the least expensive choice.

FIGURE 2.19   Step 2: What are the probabilities?

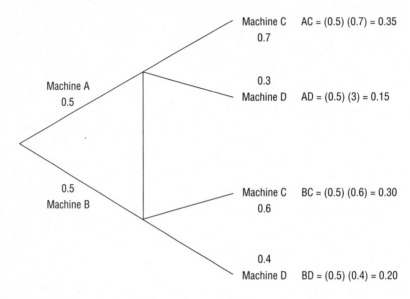

FIGURE 2.20   Step 3: Apply monetary values.

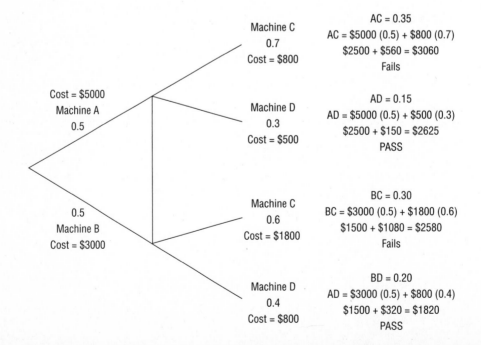

Hands-on 2.17: Testing Your Knowledge of Decision Trees and NPV

A proposed project will have an initial outlay of $1,500. At the end of one year, there is a 0.3% probability of a $100 loss and a 0.7% probability of $2,000 revenue. At the end of the second year, there is a 0.4% probability of a $200 loss and a 0.6% probability of $5,000 revenue.

Assuming an interest rate of 10% compounded annually, which of the following is the expected net present value of the project? Is this a project to pursue?

A. $3,254

B. $2,158

C. $450

D. –$200

E. –$2,042

F. None of the above

Show your work and all calculations. (Hint: Use a decision tree for a two-year period and round to the nearest dollar.)

SIMULATION

Monte Carlo simulation received its name when the process was used in casinos in Monte Carlo, Monaco, to determine probabilities and outcomes of various gambling scenarios. This process is useful in most scenarios using probabilities.

Monte Carlo simulation requires the generation of random numbers between 0.00 and 1.0. The fraction is then converted to an equivalent sample based on the distribution of interest.

We will now explore the process steps used to create a Monte Carlo simulation:

1. During a single trial, a computer program randomly selects a value from the defined possibilities and assesses the range for the variables to determine the probability distribution (the range and shape of the distribution) for each uncertain variable.

2. The simulation then selects variable values (such as optimistic, most likely, and pessimistic) at random to simulate a model that translates uncertainties specified at a detailed level into their potential impact on project objectives.

3. The simulation then conducts a deterministic analysis on the effect of varying inputs on outputs of the modeled system.

4. It then calculates multiple scenarios of a model by repeatedly sampling values from the probability distributions for the uncertain variables (usually a minimum of 2,500 iterations).

Plan Risk Responses

Risk-response planning is the process of developing responses to the risks identified and analyzed in the previous steps. Possible responses to any risk include avoidance, transference, mitigation (reducing the probability and/or impact), and acceptance. After responses are developed, they should be recorded on the risk register.

Project risks diminish naturally as the life cycle of the project unfolds, and the project is completed. The purpose of risk management is to drive risk as low as possible before the amount at stake gets too high. You can see that *total project risk decreases* as you move toward project completion, but the *amount at stake increases* toward the end of the project life cycle.

Keeping that in mind, create the risk-response plan so that appropriate and timely strategies can be established. For example, if you know a key resource may not be available when their work is needed, actions should be taken to backfill that person should that situation arise. If you wait until later in the project to find a replacement, it may be more costly to train someone with a learning curve, or in the absence of someone in-house, costly outsourcing may be necessary.

ELEMENTS OF THE RISK-RESPONSE PLAN

The risk-response plan must be documented at a level of detail at which action will be taken. The *PMBOK® Guide, 4th ed.*, pp. 305–306, suggests the inclusion of some or all of the following:

- Identified risks, their descriptions, the areas(s) of the project or WBS element affected, their causes, and how they may affect project objectives

- Risk owners and their responsibilities

- Results from the qualitative and quantitative risk analysis process

- Agreed-on responses including avoid, transfer, mitigate, accept, exploit, share, or enhance for each risk in the risk-response plan

- The level of residual risk expected to remain after the strategy is implemented

- Secondary risks that may arise because of implementation of suggested strategies

- Specific actions to implement the chosen response strategy

- Budget and times for responses

- Contingency plans and fallback plans

The following questions should be asked as you plan your mitigation strategies:

- How could this risk be avoided?
- Can this risk be reduced?
- Can the risk be shared or transferred?
- Should we face the risk (and if so, should schedule and financial allowances be made)?
- Can we contain the risk?
- Will this risk response be funded?

 Be careful to limit your responses to only those items that affect your project. It is far too easy to examine the ills of the entire company when exploring risk events. You are hoping to mitigate risk on a specific project. You are *not* trying to solve world hunger.

In answering these questions, you must determine which risks are likely to affect the project and document their characteristics. This is most easily done by classifying them according to their cause and then ranking them according to your ability as a project team to effectively manage the responses. Ultimately, the responsibility to manage risk events rests with the project owner. The risk-response plan becomes a part of the overall risk management plan.

Contingency Plans

Contingency plans are created in advance and are applied to risk events that arise during the project. They reduce the cost of an action. An example of engaging a contingency plan would be when a milestone is missed, additional resources that were identified and estimated in your contingency plan are added to a specific task to get back on track.

The contingency plan will be implemented if certain trigger points or previously agreed-upon metrics occur. These triggers could include missed milestones, failed inspections, or the inability to get good people or supplies delivered in a timely way.

Contingency Reserves vs. Management Reserves

Cost is associated with each risk-response strategy identified in the risk-response plan, and these costs become line items in the project budget. These are *known* risks, with *known* recovery costs. According to the *PMBOK® Guide, 4th ed.,* p. 177, contingency reserves are allowances for unplanned but potentially required changes that can result from realized risks in the risk register.

Management reserves, on the other hand, include those budgets set aside for "unknown unknowns" that may cause changes to the project scope and cost. These costs are also placed in the project budget and are typically a percentage of the total project budget. Management may have to approve access to these funds. By the way, they are not included in earned value calculations—more about that later.

Take Corrective Action

The best-laid plans still require estimates, and no one is able to predict the future with total accuracy. Changes occur regularly, resources do not always complete their work according to their estimates, and so corrective action needs to take place. Project managers should set expectations with project performers: if the performers cannot meet their commitments to the project, a recovery plan must be defined and enacted to get back on track. There may be performance issues to face and any of a variety of challenges. The corrective action must be immediate and monitored for its efficacy.

Choose Alternative Strategies

Using an alternative strategy for the project or any piece of it assumes that the alternative was well thought out to begin with in regard to when it should be employed, with what approvals, and under what conditions. An alternative strategy is almost always more costly to the project, as you are discarding the initial strategy (or parts of it) and must "shift gears," so to speak; additional planning may be needed.

Update the Risk-Response Plan

Implementation of risk controls may reduce the probability or impact of identified risks. Risk rankings must be reassessed so that new, important risks may be properly controlled. Risks that do not occur should be documented and closed in the risk-response plan.

Whenever a workaround happens or a change request is implemented, the affected project plans (including the risk management plan and the risk-response plan) may need to be updated following the project's integrated change control process.

Create a Risk Management Plan

Now you have everything you need to put together an entire risk management plan. This is how we recommend it should be put together:

1. Describe the risk methodology you used. This includes your risk assumptions, roles and responsibilities, time frames, rating and scoring techniques, risk communications, and a risk tracking process. You also want to include how you identified and categorized risk, your means of determining risk impacts and probabilities, and how you prioritized them.

2. Include your risk-response plan.

3. Describe how you will track or monitor your risks.

We have included a simple risk management template to use if this is the first time you have had to create one:

Section 1: Management Strategy

Describe the risk methodology you used for the following:

- Risk identification
- Risk categories
- Risk probability and impact
- Risk priorities
- Risk assumptions

Section 2: Risk-Response Plan

- Describe your response strategies (mitigation, sharing, transference, and so forth) for each risk.
- Document the detailed response for each risk and whether it is cost-/schedule-effective.
- Describe what will happen if the risk event occurs.
- Describe triggers including time frames.
- Assign a responsible person for each risk response.

Section 3: Risk Monitoring

- Describe what dates and actions were taken to mitigate risk.
- Document whether those mitigation strategies were successful. (Was there a contingency plan and was it sufficient as planned?)
- Describe successive actions needed to overcome or reduce the risk.
- Establish a review schedule.
- Validate assumptions.
- Review the risks (see Figure 2.21).

Section 4: Risk Control

- Confirm that risk strategies are still valid.
- Take corrective action when risk events occur that are outlined in the risk-response plan.
- Assess actual impacts in terms of time, cost, and quality.
- Ensure that the master project management and risk plan is being followed.
- Ensure that the change control plan is being followed.
- Make revisions as needed.

The flow chart in Figure 2.21 shows how you might review risk events.

FIGURE 2.21 Risk review flow chart

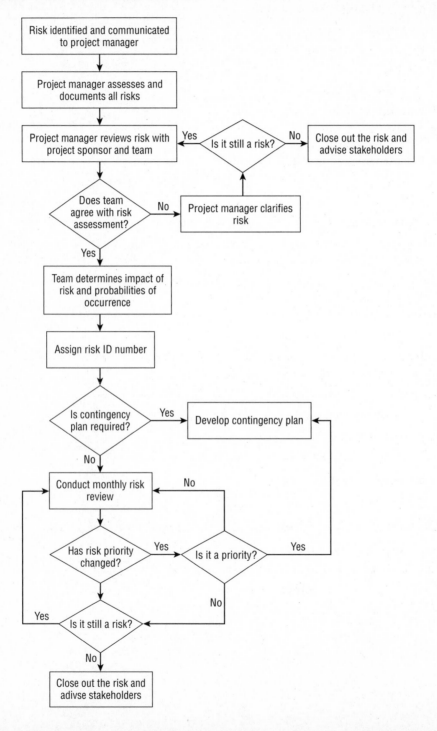

Task 2.8: Creating the Master Project Management Plan

The master project management plan is the culmination of the many days and hours that have been spent to ensure that the project will be a success. The master project management plan is like a pattern or a template. You probably wouldn't create a wedding dress without a pattern, or an Adirondack chair without a template if you are new at making furniture. But if you have a pattern or template with good directions, it will turn out just right.

Your project management plan becomes your project control book. As we said earlier, plan the work, now work the plan. However, it is also a known fact that your first plan is your worst plan. There will be many iterations of the project plans as you "go forth and do," so the project plans will be refined periodically.

Scenario

Wow! You have spent many days with your team creating documents that have provided you and your team a better understanding of the Apples and Pears project. You have done some additional research and have the perfect template to put it all together.

Scope of Task

Duration

This should take hours to a few days, depending on the size and complexity of the project.

Setup

None.

Caveat

None.

Procedure

In this task you create the master project management plan.

Details

The master project management plan has many parts. You are not going to reinvent the wheel. You have determined, however, that you will include all items necessary to ensure that you are very clear as to what you will be doing on the project.

Consolidate Subsidiary Plans

First you will consolidate all of the plans you have put together thus far:

- Resource and staffing plan
- Communication plan
- Schedule plan
- Finance/cost plan
- Quality plan
- Procurement plan
- Risk management plan

Next, you will create a milestone list.

Create a Milestone List

A *milestone* is considered the end of a series of tasks, the completion of work packages or even phases. It could also reference key decision points or mark the end of reviews. At key decision points, a milestone might signal how far you have come or where you wish to go next.

You typically use milestones in your schedule plan to determine whether you are where you want to be at a given place in time. Although milestones quite often are used to measure progress, do not be fooled. You may pull resources from some tasks and put them on critical activities but you may be left with neglected tasks. A true measure of progress is shown through earned value calculations, which you will study in Phase 4.

Management really isn't interested in seeing the minutiae that go along with plans, especially lengthy ones. They would rather see a dashboard view of the happenings in a project. You can create a task milestone list within your schedule plan and a risk milestone list in your risk plan. There may be financial milestones as well.

After you have completed your subsidiary plans, you can establish project baselines.

Establish Project Baselines

You use baselines as a starting point from which you can begin to measure progress by comparing the actual results to planned results.

Project baselines include, but are not limited to, the following:

- Scope baseline
- Schedule baseline
- Cost baseline
- Quality baseline

As you know, all of these baselines are the result of the planning process. We said earlier that your first plan is your worst plan. All of the plans created thus far are iterative. But you have to start measuring results when you begin the execution phase of the project. The baselines are typically not changed unless there is an *approved* change order that modifies the scope, schedule, cost, or quality of the project. If scope, schedule, cost, and quality changes are *not* approved, you, as project manager, are not doing your job.

If, however, the estimates were all high level, you have an inexperienced team, or you are inexperienced, you may not be able to stay within the original estimates. It is very demoralizing to work on objectives that cannot be reached. At this point you should speak to the sponsor and the change review board and ask for a baseline change to make your project more realistic.

Create a Resource Calendar

You looked at resource calendars earlier. When you get to this stage of planning, you will have created your schedule plan. If you use project management software and load resource data into your plan, this calendar will automatically be created for you.

Insert the Risk Register

You looked at a sample risk register in Table 2.18. You will want to insert it here.

Configuration Management

Configuration management was developed by the U.S. Department of Defense as a technical management system. It takes a holistic view of products, hardware, software, and so on, so if there are any changes to the product, hardware, or software, you can be aware of the impacts that those changes may have. For example, in a software configuration management process you would visit such topics as these:

- Documentation
- Logical access controls
- Change control
- System testing
- Input/output controls
- Records management
- Reports

The way this applies to a project management plan is by simply taking the big picture view and assessing what a change may do to the rest of the project. For example, a scope change has been approved. You now need to look at all of your subsidiary plans to see whether the change impacts any of those plans. Does it affect the schedule, resources, budget, quality, procurement, and so on? If it does, you need to make changes to the plan. Usually configuration management rests with a change control board that will approve or disapprove the change.

Management Review Process

It has taken a bit of time to produce your project management plan. Now it is time to have your plan reviewed. The review typically takes place at a number of levels. The project sponsor will want to review it, as well as functional managers and workers. These folks are usually invited to a meeting, and the project manager conducts a presentation highlighting all the elements of the plan. Here is where you can make changes *before* the work begins.

Task 2.9: Obtaining Plan Approval

You have completed the daunting task of planning your project. You want to get this plan approved so you can conduct a stakeholder kickoff meeting and actually begin executing the project.

Scenario

You have managed projects before, but they have always been "brute force" coordination activities. You can see now that much time and grief could have been avoided if you had been proactive instead of reactive in managing projects. The proactive master project management plan should now be approved by the sponsor and other senior managers that may have a keen interest in the project, as well as by the client.

Scope of Task

Duration

This task may take a few hours to a few days, depending on the availability of signatories.

Setup

None.

Caveat

None.

Procedure

In this task you will learn how to establish approvals for the project.

Details

Obtaining approval should be easy at this point, as long as you have kept your stakeholders in the loop and have created a plan that provides management and customers, as well as your team, a level of confidence that the project will be successful if the plan is followed. Following approvals, a kickoff meeting is conducted and further meetings can begin.

Obtain Approval from Management

If management has participated in the management review you conducted, and all of their questions and concerns have been answered, they will typically approve the plan. You need to know what your internal approval processes are. There may be people whom you have never heard of that need to approve and sign off on the plan. Your sponsor should be able to tell you exactly who needs to approve and sign the plan.

Obtain Approval from the Customer

You also need to have your customer approve the plan. You have identified the true scope of the project and given the customer everything they need to approve the plan. These customers may be internal or external, but are treated the same. Someone needs something that you will deliver. By sharing plans with the customer, you eliminate surprises and know what your anticipated result will be.

Conduct a Kickoff Meeting

Now that your plan is approved, you need to conduct a kickoff meeting. You have spent a lot of time preparing the plan, and you want this meeting to showcase the efforts of those plans. You want your team to come away from this meeting with the following:

- A unified team spirit
- A mutual understanding on how the project will be managed
- A complete understanding of individual roles and responsibilities
- The project goals and objectives
- Project assumptions
- Key success factors
- How and when status meetings will occur
- How information should be distributed and received
- An agreement of expectations between the project manager and the team and vice versa

Each team member has participated in the planning and has a copy of the approved plan. This is also the time to answer any questions that may arise.

To be effective, you have to plan this meeting well. Table 2.20 provides a template to help you prepare for your meeting.

You also want to have a feedback mechanism to evaluate your meeting after it is conducted. See Table 2.21. You will be conducting many meetings from now until the project is finished. This feedback loop will give you information regarding what was good about your meeting as well as suggestions for improvement.

TABLE 2.20   Meeting Characteristics and Preparation Template

	Kickoff	Status	Steering	News	Issues	Decision
Intent						
Purpose						
Subject						
Participants						
Size of Meeting						
Roles						
Frequency						
Agenda						
Prep Steps						

TABLE 2.21   Meeting Evaluation

Meeting Evaluation								
Date:			Subject:					
Instructions: Indicate on the scales that follow (1 low, 7 high) your assessment of the meeting.								

1. Purpose of the Meeting

Totally unclear as to the purpose or objective of the meeting. | 1 | 2 | 3 | 4 | 5 | 6 | 7 | The purpose or objective of the meeting was well defined.

2. Decided What We Wanted to Achieve

By the end of the meeting, we still had no idea of what we wanted to achieve. | 1 | 2 | 3 | 4 | 5 | 6 | 7 | We decided what we wanted to achieve by the end of the meeting.

3. Meeting Preparation

We were totally unprepared for this meeting. | 1 | 2 | 3 | 4 | 5 | 6 | 7 | We were sufficiently prepared for this meeting.

4. Meeting Effectiveness

Disconnected information and tangent discussions. | 1 | 2 | 3 | 4 | 5 | 6 | 7 | Crisp & focused presentation and discussion. Good flow of information.

5. Team Participation

Little team participation in discussions. | 1 | 2 | 3 | 4 | 5 | 6 | 7 | Team participated actively in the meeting.

6. Ground Rules

We violated many of our rules during the meeting. | 1 | 2 | 3 | 4 | 5 | 6 | 7 | It was evident that we were living by our rules.

7. Meeting Process

Meeting started/finished late. | 1 | 2 | 3 | 4 | 5 | 6 | 7 | Meeting started & finished on time with consistent attendance.

8. Time Allocation

Agenda items continually ran over allotted times. | 1 | 2 | 3 | 4 | 5 | 6 | 7 | Agenda items addressed per the allotted times.

9. Meeting Usefulness

A complete waste of time. | 1 | 2 | 3 | 4 | 5 | 6 | 7 | The meeting was an effective use of my time.

10. Team Building

The meeting was a chore. | 1 | 2 | 3 | 4 | 5 | 6 | 7 | We had fun.

Please Provide Any Additional Comments Below:

1. If you have answered any of the above questions with a response of 1 or 2, please identify why you have given that question(s) such a low rating, and offer your suggestions for making an improvement.

2. If you have answered any of the above questions with a response of 7, please identify why you have given that question(s) such a high rating.

Task 2.10: Developing a Change Management Plan

Change is inevitable. Just when you think the project plan is cast in stone, a change pops up. You want to be able to do the following:

- Manage each request for change, in order to ensure that any new scope, cost, and/or schedule of the project remains under control and has full traceability
- Make sure each request for change is assessed by all affected functional areas
- Make sure each assessed change request has a decision made (accepted, rejected, or deferred) by the appropriate authority

The project manager drives the decision-making process and ensures that all the stakeholders who might be impacted by the change are fully involved.

The change management process includes subprocesses to briefly assess each proposed change, to analyze the potential impact of the proposed change on the project as a whole, to decide how to proceed with a change request (CR) after its impact has been analyzed, and to monitor the progress of approved changes until they are complete.

Additionally, a change review board (CRB) should be engaged if the changes affect the project scope, the original schedule, and/or costs beyond the authority level delegated to the project manager. The CRB provides advice and counsel on whether the CR should proceed to the funding board for review and request for approval.

Scenario

Many changes have occurred during plan preparation. You have decided that it is essential to have a robust change management plan in place to keep track of these changes—especially because you are about to enter the execution phase.

Scope of Task

Setup

None.

Caveat

None.

Procedure

This task is accomplished by documenting the change request process in five steps:

1. Submit, receive, and review the change request.

2. Analyze the impact.

3. Make a decision on the change request.

4. Escalate to the CRB or funding board, if necessary.

5. Manage the change orders.

Details

A *change request* is a request to change some aspect of the project after it has been approved and committed. Change requests may affect one or several of the following:

- Work to be done or work in progress, with regard to schedule, solution definition, deliverables, and so on

- Business plans or procedures, including project costs or acceptable risk levels

- Obligations within a statement of work, or other formal agreements with customers or vendors

Change Request Process

The change request procedure is launched when a change is requested after specific deliverables are approved, and anytime after exiting the planning phase if the change would affect the project's schedule, scope, or costs. The end result of the procedure is one of the following:

- The change is accepted and will be implemented.

- The change is rejected.

- The change is deferred.

STEP 1: SUBMIT, RECEIVE, AND REVIEW THE CHANGE REQUEST

In this step a change request is submitted and assigned a number. The change request documents the need and rationale for the proposed change. Table 2.22 is a sample of the change request form.

To avoid any confusion, Table 2.23 provides directions on filling out the change request form. When you receive the CR form, log it into the CR log found in Table 2.24. Figure 2.22 represents a flow chart of step 1.

TABLE 2.22   Change Order Request Form

Change Request Identification	
Project Name:	Date Raised to Project Team:
CR Number:	Status:
Submitter:	Change Type:
Priority with Supporting Rationale:	1. Additions, Changes or Deletion to Requirements 2. Change in Technical Assumptions 3. Resources Unavailable 4. Other (briefly describe)
Change Request Description	
Detailed Description:	
Accepted for Assessment On:	Analysis Assigned To:
Small Change: Y/N	Assigned Date:
Change Request Impact Analysis	
☐ Schedule Impact: ☐ Scope Impact: ☐ Cost Impact: ☐ Other:	
Solutions Considered:	
Effort Estimate:	Cost Estimate:
Impact Level:	Resources:
Estimates Validated On:	Estimates Validated By:
Analyzed By:	Analysis Completed On:
Change Request Implementation	
CR Decision:	
Decision Date:	Decision Made By:
Approved Effort:	Approved Cost:
Approved Start Date:	Target Completion Date:
Impact on Plans	
Incorporated Into Plans On:	Incorporated Into Plans On:
Plans Changed:	
Completion Criteria:	
Change Order ID(s):	
Date Closed:	Date Implementation Completed:

TABLE 2.23   Change Order Request Form Instructions

Form Entry	Definition
Changes Request Identification	
Project Name:	Program and release name — what it was called at the Planning Gate exit
CR Number:	This sequence number assigned to the CR.
Priority:	One priority for this CR should be selected, from High, Medium, or Low.
Submitter:	Enter name of person submitting CR.
Date Raised to Client:	The date CR is first submitted to the project team.
Status:	Enter status, from In Progress, Accepted, Rejected, or Deferred.
Priority with Suporting Rationale:	One priority for this CR should be selected, from High, Medium, or Low, and reasons from the submitter's perspective for assigning this priority.
Change Type:	Enter the type of change according to the following: **1. Addition/Changes/Deletion to Requirements** This section would be checked when the Change Request is based on DOCUMENTED requirements being added to, changed, or deleted. If the original requirement isn't documented, the PM may have a difficult time getting CRB and FB approvals, which are required for Scope changes. **2. Change in Technical Assumptions** This section would be checked when the Change Request is based on DOCUMENTED technical assumption changing. Usually these assumptions will be found in an Analysis or Design document, Statement of Work, or Project Definition Report. If the original assumption isn't documented, the PM may have a difficult time getting CRB and FB approvals, which are required for Scope changes. **3. Resources Unavailable** This section would be checked when the Change Request is based on a critical set of resources (people, envrionmental, systems, etc.) not being available when needed and scheduled per the approved and DOCUMENTED Project Plan. It may also trigger a follow-up set of CRs to reflect related scope, schedule or costs changes as workaround or program resets occur. **4. Other (briefly describe)** This section would be checked when the Change Request is based on anything not covered above. Example: The Change Request is based on changing the committed schedule or staffing levels of the project. This might occur if the sponsor or customer asks to get the project done sooner or to delay the implementation date, either of which might involve adding or removing resources from the project.
Changes Request Description	
Detailed Description:	A description of the change that is being proposed and assessed. The altered or affected baselined requirements should be indicated.
Accepted for Assessment On:	This is the date that the project team determined that the CR needed additional impact analysis prior to a vote, and approved it for assessment.
Small Change Y/N:	If it is determined that the project team can make the decision concerning the CR without conducting an impact analysis of the change, this would be "Y".
Assigned Date:	The date the Change Request was assigned to the person/team doing the analysis of the CR.
Assigned for Analysis To:	This is the name of the person or lead for the team that will perform the analysis of the CR.

TABLE 2.23   Change Order Request Form Instructions *(continued)*

Change Request Impact Analysis	
Impact Analysis — Schedule, Scope, Cost, Other:	Enter details on the results of the analysis of the CR, showing what type of impact(s) will occur as a result of implementing the CR.
Solutions Considered:	Describe the intended solution for the change request, and, where applicable, any alternatives considered can be described along with their reasons for not being chosen. This information is especially useful if the CR gets regected or deferred, and has to be referenced or revisited in the future.
Effort Estimate:	Estimate of the effort needed to implement the solution for the CR, preferably in hours.
Cost Estimate:	Estimate of the cost, in dollars or appropriate currency, to implement the solution, if any.
Impact Level:	If the CR is approved or recommended for approval, then an impact level of High, Medium or Low should be assigned and noted here.
Resources:	This is the number of resources, and their associated functional areas, required to implement the solution for the CR.
Estimates Validated On:	The date that the estimate to implement the solution for the CR was validated.
Estimates Validated By:	Person's name who validated the estimates to implement the CR.
Analyzed By:	Person's name who conducted the analysis of the CR.
Analysis Completed On:	The date of the completion of the analysis.
Changes Request Implementation	
CR Decisions:	Possible entries: 1) Approved; proceed to implement the solution; 2) Rejected; do not start or continue work effort, or 3) Defer the CR and rationale for deferral; if applicable, identify any future target release that should consider including the CR.
Decision Date:	The date that the final approval authority made the decision. If this is NOT the client, then the dates should show the review sequence — dates of client recommendation, CRB recommendation, and FB decisions.
Decision Made By:	Indicate final authority level — whether project team, CRB, or FB decision.
Approved Effort:	Amount of effort approved to implement the solution for the CR, preferably in hours.
Approved Cost:	The approved cost, in dollars or appropriate currency, to implement the solution is entered here, if any.
Approved Start Date:	Enter date that has been approved to start the implemtation of the CR.
Target Completion Date:	Enter a target date if there is uncertainty about whether the implementation can be started on the approved date.
Impact on Plans	
Incorporated Into Plans On:	The date that CR and its impact were incorporated into the project plans.
Incorporated Into Plans By:	The person's name that incorporated the CR and its impact into the project plans. This is usually the PM.
Plans Changed:	Describe how the plans changed as a result of implementing the CR. Also, include any changes to other work products.
Completion Criteria:	Describe the criteria that signal that the solution has been successfully implemented.
Change Order ID(s):	The sequence number(s) given to the change order which is the approval document that directs the PM/project team to implement the CR.
Date Closed:	Date that the CR is closed.
Date Implementation Completed:	The date that the CR was successfully implemented.

TABLE 2.24 Change Request Log

CHANGE REQUEST LOG

CR#	Change Type	Description of Change	Scope	Date Submitted	Investigation Authorized		Implementation		Status	Status Date	Schedule Impact N, or Y with new date
					Start	Finish	Date Auth	Effort Auth			

FIGURE 2.22   Flow chart for submitting, receiving, and reviewing the change request

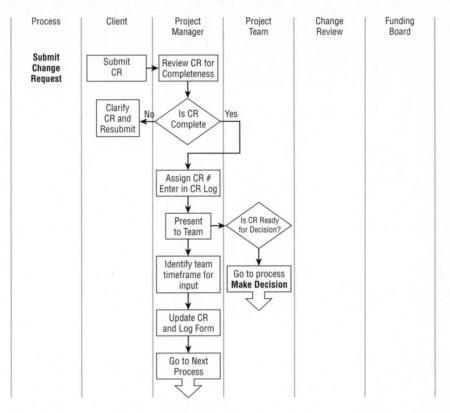

STEP 2: CONDUCT AN IMPACT ANALYSIS

Develop an estimate of the effort needed to assess the requested change. The purpose of this subprocess is to provide the approving body with the detailed information it needs to decide whether to implement a proposed change. Impact analysis involves determining what would need to be done to implement the change and then estimating how it would affect the baseline of the project, including the schedule, costs, and benefits.

Figure 2.23 represents a flow chart of step 2.

STEP 3: MAKE A DECISION ON THE CHANGE REQUEST

The purpose of this step is to describe how to proceed with a CR after impact analysis has been completed. For a small change request, a decision may be made almost immediately after being presented to the project team, whereas for a larger one it will be after a more detailed impact analysis has been completed. Based on the projected impact of the change, the request may also need to be reviewed by the change review board and then go to the funding board for final approval. In all cases, it is the project manager's responsibility to ensure that the decision is made in a timely manner.

Figure 2.24 represents a flow chart of step 3.

FIGURE 2.23   Flow chart for the impact analysis

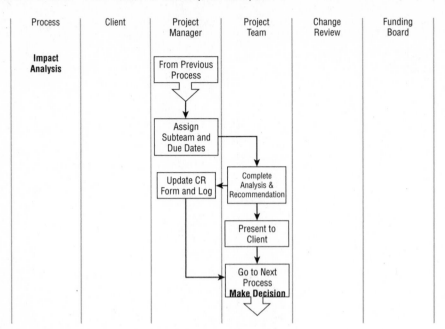

STEP 4: FOLLOW ESCALATION PROCEDURES

The purpose of this subprocess is to describe what steps are required when a change request accepted by a project team is outside of the authority level for that team and project manager. In general, this means the CR involves a scope change to the project, has a schedule impact greater than about two weeks, or will affect costs by more than 10% from the planning phase. It may be necessary for the project manager to request a special CRB or FB meeting, to reach a CR decision on a timely basis.

Figure 2.25 represents a flow chart of step 4.

STEP 5: MANAGE CHANGE ORDERS

The purpose of this step is to manage the implementation of the CRs by revising the project management plans and procedures to reflect the approved change and periodically checking the status of the associated CR.

The change management plan brings us to the end of the planning phase. By now, you and your team should be able to visualize all parts of the project and begin the execution phase.

FIGURE 2.24   Flow chart for making a decision

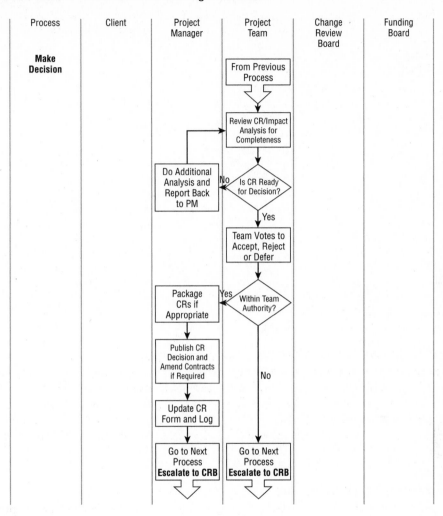

FIGURE 2.25 Flow chart for escalating to the CRB or funding board

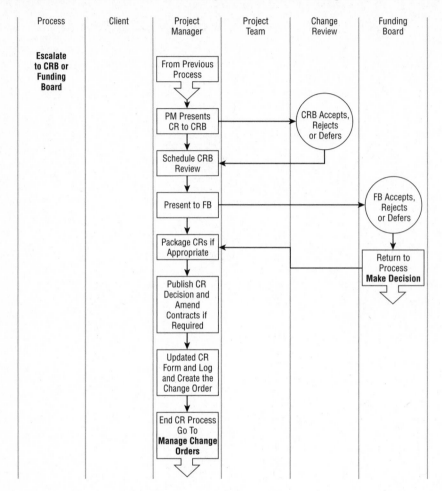

So How Do You Know If You Have a Good Plan?

You may think you have a good plan, but the proof is in the pudding! You will know the plan is done well if the following are true:

- Management is committed and supportive.
- Key personnel have reviewed and agreed to it.
- Team leaders have committed resources.
- Resources have reviewed and committed to tasks.
- The project manager has been fully acknowledged.
- Project funds are sufficient to do the job.
- The unknowns are discovered and documented.
- There are written contingency plans.
- There is a formal, approved, and published plan.

Phase 3

Executing Process

You now have a robust project plan. Your planning efforts should pay off here. The executing phase puts your plan in action. The project manager will now do the following:

- Direct and manage project execution
- Acquire a team
- Develop the team
- Manage the team
- Perform quality assurance
- Execute the communication plan
- Manage stakeholder expectations
- Conduct procurements

Task 3.1: Directing and Managing Project Execution

In this task you begin to implement your plan and collect performance information relative to the schedule, budget, status of deliverables, implementation status for approved change orders, as well as corrective action if needed and preventive activities associated with risk.

Directing and managing the project is the responsibility of the project manager. Efficient execution of the project relies on the direction and leadership of the project manager, the support of senior management, resource managers, and the commitment of team members, but mostly on the project manager.

Scenario

Olivia Ross has signed off on the plans and is excited to finally begin the implementation of this project. Ms. Ross took you (Carrie MacIntyre, project manager) to lunch and had a candid discussion about the Apples and Pears project. Ms. Ross wanted to be sure that you were aware of how important the due date was, and you wanted to be sure that she was aware of the real-world facts as you know them up to this point.

Even though the project management plan has been formally approved, you want to show Ms. Ross the items within your "project control book" to assure her that you have your arms wrapped around this project. She was impressed and assured you that she has an open-door policy, as do all members of her senior team, and that if you need anything at all, to go straight to the source for information. You are pleased by this but will always keep Jim Stevens, your sponsor, in the loop as well.

Scope of Task

Duration

This task will run the length of the project.

Setup

None.

Caveat

None.

Procedure

In this task you will use your expert judgment and the project management information system to execute the tasks on your project.

Details

According to the *PMBOK® Guide, 4th ed.,* p. 55, "The Executing Process Group consists of those processes performed to complete the work found in the project management plan to satisfy the project specifications." It is here where you will coordinate all of the activities of the project and manage the resources.

There are two tools and techniques associated with this task: *expert judgment* and your *project management information system.*

Expert Judgment

You were chosen to be a project manager because you have proven that you have the leadership and managerial expertise to bring the project to fruition. This, along with your team members and the technical expertise they provide, is a great start in managing project tasks. Other avenues of expertise are also available to you and your team, including your in-house experts, outside consultants, your stakeholders, as well as professional and technical associations. Use other experts when you need them, and your expertise will improve exponentially.

Hands-on 3.1: Testing Your Knowledge of Expertise

1.   As a project manager, what should you do when you are assigned to a project but feel you don't have the expertise to do the work?

2.   What should a team member do when it is clear the assigned project manager simply doesn't have the skills needed to manage the project (for example, the project is behind schedule, meetings have become finger-pointing sessions, or the project manager doesn't return calls and sits in the office all day with the door shut)?

Project Management Information System (PMIS)

As you may recall from Phase 1, your project management information system (PMIS) is part of your enterprise environmental factors. A PMIS provides you with an information collection and distribution process for all of your project management documents, access to intranet or Internet sites, scheduling software, configuration management databases, and so forth.

Not all people should have access to your project information, so you should establish passwords for those with a need for certain information. For example, your sponsor may want an executive summary, instead of all the details you typically provide to the project team. Or, you may provide contractors and suppliers with a portal and a password that bypasses your PMIS so confidential and proprietary information is not available to them.

In the absence of an active PMIS, you will have to create your own *project control book* to manage the project. This control book should include the project charter, the project management plan, forms and checklists, and so on. If possible, build a digital project control book. Your forms should have "write" abilities enabling you to simply tab through your document to fill in the answers.

Let's take a look at some tools that may be useful to you as you create your project control book and manage the project.

WORK AUTHORIZATION FORM

Most of your resources are internal, but for those who are external to the project, you must provide a notice to proceed. Table 3.1 represents a work authorization form.

EXTRA WORK AUTHORIZATION FORM

You want to be sure that suppliers and vendors understand that work not approved is work not paid. Table 3.2 represents a form for extra work authorization.

TABLE 3.1   Work Authorization Form

Work Authorization		
Project Name	Project Manager	Date
Contract Type		
☐ Firm Fixed Price		☐ Cost Plus Percentage of Cost
☐ Cost Sharing Ratio		☐ Cost Plus Fixed Fee
☐ Fixed Price Incentive Fee		☐ Cost Plus Incentive Fee
☐ The contractor's bid accepted by the customer is:		
Start Date:	Completion Date:	
Special Instructions:		
I have reviewed and accepted this project: Please keep me informed of progress and any changes in the scope as work proceeds.		
Signature:	Date:	
Position:		
Distribution List:		
☐ Scheduler	☐ Estimating staff with a copy of drawings	
☐ Contract General Supervisor	☐ Contract Inspector with three copies of drawings	
☐ Accounting	☐ Project file with a copy of drawings	

TABLE 3.2   Extra Work Authorization Form

Extra Work Authorization					
CONTRACT:		PROJECT:		DATE:	
WBS CODE:					
DESCRIPTION OF WORK PERFORMED:					
IS THIS THE FINAL DAILY REPORT AGAINST THIS WORK ORDER? YES NO					
PHYSICAL PERCENT COMPLETE:					

LABOR						
NAME	TRADE	HOURS WORKED			RATE	STANDARD AMOUNT	PREMIUM AMOUNT
		ST	OT	DT			
				SUBTOTAL LABOR		

EQUIPMENT					
DESCRIPTION		HOURS WORKED	TOTAL HOURS	RATE	AMOUNT
		SUBTOTAL EQUIPMENT			

MATERIAL			
DESCRIPTION	UNITS	UNIT PRICE	AMOUNT
	SUBTOTAL MATERIAL		

SUBMITTED BY:		DATE:	
ACCEPTED BY:		DATE:	

MEETINGS

Meetings are the order of the day for project managers. You want to make this time as productive as possible—not only for yourself, but also for your team members. You never want to hear that your meeting was a total waste of time, which it can be if you do not prepare for the meeting properly.

There are rules to harness the power of a meeting. These rules have been around for more than 30 years but are as valid today as they were then. Here is a suggested list of rules to help you harness the power of a meeting:

1. Do not call a meeting to decide something you could and should decide on your own.

2. Never get people together if a series of phone calls would serve you better.

3. Never invite anyone who is not vital to the discussion, but do make sure that everyone who would be of value is included.

4. Insist on punctuality. If you are 2 minutes late for a 20-person meeting, you have wasted 40 minutes.

5. Keep the purpose of your meeting firmly in mind and be sure it can be achieved.

6. Draft an agenda that breaks all subjects down into their simplest constituents.

7. Before sending out the agenda, read it through and examine points that can be misunderstood. In most meetings, disagreements occur because people are not talking about the same thing. If the issues are crystal clear, there is less chance for confusion.

8. See that the agenda is circulated in sufficient time for people to read it before they come—but not so far ahead that they will have forgotten it when the meeting time arrives.

9. Set time limits for each phase of the discussion and make sure everyone can see the clock. "Discussion, like work, expands to fill the time available."

10. See that whoever acts as chairperson states the issues, keeps to the agenda, lets everyone have a fair crack at the subject, cuts speakers short if they wander, and sums up succinctly as soon as all participants have their say.

11. Ask open questions to uncover necessary information.

12. If your budget allows, serve refreshments.

Your next item of business is to set up your meeting schedule. You will be meeting in person several times, but you will also have conference calls and video calls for those who are overseas. You will save a lot of time if you prepare the entire schedule in advance. Reserve your meeting locations and set up conference and video calls in advance as well. Table 3.3 represents a meeting schedule form that could be sent out to each team member and others as appropriate for the meetings.

But that's not the end of it. Be sure to send out reminders as well. Some people will forget they received this schedule. Or, prepare this for yourself and send out a notice to your participants at least two days in advance.

TABLE 3.3 Meeting Schedule

Project													
Project Manager													
Participants	Conference Calls				Video Conference				Face-to-Face Meetings			
	Date	Time	Location	Subject	Date	Time	Location	Subject	Date	Time	Location	Subject

Meeting Schedule

ESCALATIONS

Nobody likes to go over someone's head to escalate an issue, but at times this has to happen. Escalations are not comfortable for some project managers. The way to make this less uncomfortable is to establish an escalation process with your project team in advance.

Most escalations are not caused by people not doing their work. Work is not getting done because of other factors, such as (1) the boss has pulled those workers away to do other work, (2) you were assigned someone who does not have adequate skills, or (3) work is not getting approved in a timely manner.

We discussed earlier that if you set the right expectations ahead of time, you may reduce some of these challenges. For example, say that you, as project manager, had a discussion with a functional line manager about dealing with challenges, problems, or issues. You and the functional manager agreed that the functional manager would handle any challenges that came up in their area of expertise and that the only reason the functional manager would bring it to you is if they are not able to escalate the issue on their own and/or may not be able to meet the commitment made to you to complete the project work. This keeps the project manager from stepping into the functional manager's work.

Table 3.4 is a sample of an escalation matrix that may be useful to you while executing the project. Everyone has brainstormed in advance the types of situations that may need escalating.

MANAGE ISSUES AND ACTION ITEMS

The objective of issue and action item management is to quickly resolve critical issues that arise as the project team undertakes major business and technical initiatives. Critical issues are obstacles that warrant management attention because they

- Could prevent the project from achieving scheduled milestones
- Are out of a given project team's realm of control
- Present significant risk to the success of a project
- Require management escalation or intervention

The issue management process encompasses the identification of critical issues, tracking progress, facilitating closure, and recording resolution for future reference. The main things to remember when dealing with issues are as follows:

- Assign a responsible person to deal with the issue. (This could be you.)
- Make sure to follow up at regular intervals.

Many times project managers give a due date for resolution of the issue after they have assigned a person to get it resolved. This could be a problem if you don't follow up until it is supposed to be resolved. Sometimes if the issue is critical, you may want a daily or even an hourly meeting with the appropriate people until it is resolved.

Managing issues provides a means of monitoring and resolving those things that may jeopardize a project from meeting scheduled milestones. Sound procedures for managing issues are key to preventing, controlling, and resolving project risk—not only for a single project, but also for interdependent projects. Project team members report issues to the project manager either immediately or on status reports, depending on the issues' criticality. The project manager then logs the issues and action items (Table 3.5).

TABLE 3.4 Escalation Matrix

Escalation Matrix										
Type of Escalation	**1st Escalation**		**2nd Escalation**		**3rd Escalation**		**4th Escalation**		**5th Escalation**	
Operational	Functional Manager		Project Manager		Sponsor		Client		Senior Management	
	1/4 hour	2 hours	1/4 hour	2 hours	1/4 hour	2 hours	1/4 hour	2 hours	1/4 hour	2 hours
Scheduling										
Obtaining Instructions										
Customer Information										
Service Information										
Obtaining Materials										
Performance Issues										
Service Cancellations										
Logistical	Functional Manager		Project Manager		Sponsor		Client		Senior Management	
	1/4 hour	2 hours	1/4 hour	2 hours	1/4 hour	2 hours	1/4 hour	2 hours	1/4 hour	2 hours
Product Delivery										
Product Is Damaged										
Missing Product										
Order Cancellations										
Order Verification										
Technical	Functional Manager		Project Manager		Sponsor		Client		Senior Management	
	1/4 hour	2 hours	1/4 hour	2 hours	1/4 hour	2 hours	1/4 hour	2 hours	1/4 hour	2 hours
Error Messages										
Instructions Incorrect										
Technical Questions										

The left side of the columns reflects time spent waiting to get a hold of someone prior to attempting to get a hold of someone else.
The right side of the columns reflects time spent not getting a resolution before escalating to the next level.

TABLE 3.5 Issues and Actions Log

		Issues and Actions Log						
	Project					Project Manager		
ID	Stakeholder	Issues	Owner	Resolution Needed By	Status	Actions	Status Report Date	Source
1								
2								
3								
4								
5								
6								
7								
8								

CORRESPONDENCE LOG

You will want to keep track of any correspondence you receive or create that may be of value in defending the decisions you make. You will also want to keep memorandums from management or your team that may be crucial in the future. Table 3.6 is a sample correspondence log.

DECISIONS LOG

You will make many decisions when working on a project. Sometimes others will make decisions. These decisions may affect the entire project (for example, decisions on whether to cancel or move to next phase) or they may affect only one portion of the project. It is important that you keep a decisions log so you can refer to it when needed. Table 3.7 is a sample of a decisions log.

VENDOR/CONSULTANT PROFILE

Vendors and consultants will come and go during the course of the project. Sometimes there are many vendors, and it can be difficult to keep track of who is doing what. You may consider creating vendor profiles to keep track of them and the deliverables they are providing. In the Comments field you can keep track of your conversations, encounters, issues, and so on. If the project is complex, it would be difficult to sort through notes to find information. Table 3.8 is a sample of a vendor profile.

STATUS REPORTS

Some project managers spend the majority of their time chasing the status of their project. We spoke earlier about proactive vs. reactive project management. If you feel you spend the best part of your day trying to get status from people (being reactive), you may want to try something different (being proactive).

Communicate with your team about what status looks like to you. Do you want a high-level report such as "I'm good" or would you rather have something that tells you exactly where team members are on their tasks?

If there are 15 people at your status meeting and you are the last to give your report, a lot of your time is wasted. Some people like to air their dirty laundry at these meetings. Sometimes these sessions become finger-pointing events or problem-solving meetings—not good. You may want to have a problem-solving meeting, but not at a status meeting.

Consider using your status report meeting as something you present back to your team. Collect the information in advance. Let's say you have a weekly status meeting. Tell your individuals in advance what day they are to report status to you. For example, team members A and B report on Mondays, C and D report on Tuesdays, and so on. You have instructed them on how to provide this information to you. Perhaps you have set up a status phone line or a web page. You check the status lines or web pages daily and do not have to spend the whole day looking for status.

If challenges are reported, work it out with the team member(s) involved. If only three people are involved, you can settle this without involving everyone else. If a team member reports on Wednesday but the next day has an urgency of some kind, tell that person to contact you immediately and not to wait until the following Wednesday.

Let's say you have your status meetings on Monday. You report back to your team what has progressed during the previous week. You may want to create a presentation showing whether you are on track, behind, or ahead of schedule and budget. Table 3.9 is an internal status report form you may consider using to extract information from internal sources.

TABLE 3.6 Correspondence Log

Correspondence Log											
Project					Project Manager						
	TO						FROM				
Type*	From Whom	Subject	Date Received	To Whom	Location		Type*	To Whom	Subject	Date Sent	Location

*Email, letter, memorandum, fax.

TABLE 3.7 Decisions Log

				Decisions Log				
Project					Project Manager			
#	Business Area	Decision Date	Person(s) Involved	Project Impact			Decision Agreed Upon	
				High	Medium	Low		

TABLE 3.8   Vendor/Consultant Profile

Vendor Profile				
Project		Project Manager		
Vendor/Consultant Name				
Vendor/Consultant Project				
Work Description				
Manager		Tel:		
Vendor/Consultant Manager		Tel:		
Contract Start Date				
Contract End Date				
Summary of Major Deliverables				
Comments				

TABLE 3.9   Internal Status Report

Internal Status Report					
Project			Project Manager		
Team Member			Date		
Status Summary					
Project Health	RED	☐	YELLOW	☐	GREEN ☐
Milestone	Percent Complete		Planned Completion		Forecast Completion
Resources (week)					
Items	Budgeted		Actual/Forecast		Variation
To Date					
Remaining					
Total					
Comments					
Costs ($0.00)					
Items	Budgeted		Actual/Forecast		Variation
To Date					
Remaining					
Total					
Comments					
Accomplishments This Period					
Milestones achieved					
Milestones planned but not achieved					
Deliverables completed					
Work products planned but not completed					
Issues and Lessons Learned					
Issues					
Lessons Learned					

DAILY WORK REPORT FOR PRIME CONTRACTORS

You also need to collect information from your outside contractors and suppliers. You do not manage the subcontractors if you have hired a prime contractor. If you are managing subcontractors because you are the prime contractor, you need a different type of status report. Table 3.10 is an example of a daily work report you can use for contractors and suppliers.

TABLE 3.10   Contractor Daily Work Report

CONTRACTOR DAILY WORK REPORT							
Contract #:		Project:			Date:		
WBS		Percent Complete:					
Description of Work Performed							
Is this the final daily work report against this order?					Yes ☐ No ☐		
LABOR							
Name	Trade	Hours Worked			Rate	Standard Pay	Premium Pay
		ST	OT	DT			
					Subtotal Labor		
EQUIPMENT							
Description			Total Hours	Rate		Amount	
			Subtotal Equipment				
MATERIAL							
Supplier	Invoice #	# Units	Cost Per Unit	Cash	Charge	Amount	
				☐	☐		
				☐	☐		
				☐	☐		
				☐	☐		
			Sub Total Material				
Submitted By:					Date:		
Accepted By:					Date:		

It is important that you collect status information daily so you can use the data to evaluate performance. If you do not collect it daily, it will be difficult for you to keep track if it.

Hands-on 3.2: Testing Your Knowledge of PMIS

1. What are the elements of an electronic PMIS?

2. If you are lacking a PMIS, what should you do?

3. When setting up electronic permission to a PMIS, what items should you consider?

Task 3.2: Acquiring the Project Team

Project resources are the most valuable commodity on your project. Some will be those with whom you have worked previously; some will be preassigned to your team. You may have to negotiate for others and be mindful that part of your team may be a virtual team, that is, those who are either geographically dispersed or working away from your office. If you do not have the in-house expertise to do a certain portion of the project, you may have to acquire others—such as consultants, temporary employees, and so forth.

Scenario

You have had several discussions with internal resource managers. You worked with them during the planning phase, and they are in tune with the project. You now want the resource managers to release the individuals in their work units to work on your project.

You have already sent out your statements of work to the contractors, and they are ready to begin as soon as you give them the go-ahead.

Scope of Task

Duration

This duration may be hours or days, depending on the complexity of the project.

Setup

None.

Caveat

None.

Procedure

In this task you will do the following:

- Acquire resources
- Activate resources
- Orient and assimilate your team
- Discuss the challenges associated with obtaining resources

Details

The purpose of this process is to fill open positions on the project with qualified persons from the available pool of candidates. If staff selection is not the role of the project manager, then the project manager should provide the sourcing organization with the information needed to choose the candidate.

Acquire Resources

There are nine steps to this process:

1. Review corporate guidelines for recruiting and staffing procedures, particularly regarding Equal Employment Opportunities (EEO) guidelines.
2. Review candidate résumés and compare to the staffing plan to see whether an interview should be conducted.
3. Conduct the interview.
4. Complete an interview assessment.
5. Review assessments and determine whether the candidate meets your requirements.
6. Contact the sourcing organization and provide feedback.
7. Plan for new staff training, if needed.
8. Update the resource and staffing plan.
9. Update the organizational chart.

Activate Resources

As the project progresses, staffing continues in order to extend those previously committed or to acquire replacement staff, and is dependent on the recruiting and procedures of the delivery organization. This process has six steps:

1. Review the resources and staffing.
2. Review constraints such as budget, specific staff providers only, citizenship requirements, availability for travel, and so on.
3. If external resources are needed, check the current labor pool.

4. Develop a staff requisition document in compliance with corporate standards and include special skill requirements if needed.

5. Evaluate trade-offs between numbers of personnel available and needed skills.

6. Agree on a timetable for completion of recruitment processes.

Orient and Assimilate the Project Team

The purpose of this process is to provide all new members of the project team with a clear understanding of the project, their roles within the project, and the facilities they will need to perform their duties on the project. This process is done in five steps:

1. Review the goals and objectives of the project, including information about the client, the project management system, technical approach, deliverables, and so on with the new team member.

2. Review the project plans.

3. Ensure that appropriate facilities or office space and tools needed are supplied (either by the functional manager or the project office).

4. Assign and review the work package with the new member.

5. Confirm work assumptions and gain commitment from the new member.

Hands-on 3.3: Testing Your Knowledge of Acquiring Resources

1. In your experience, what are the challenges associated with acquiring resources?

2. What could happen if a new team member is not oriented to the project?

Task 3.3: Developing the Project Team

We discussed in Phase 1 the attributes of a leader as well as the tasks of a manager. It is important to understand the difference between the two and use leadership and management wisely. You want to improve team performance by improving individual competencies and team interactions that enhance the culture of the team.

Before you can develop your team, however, you must develop trust between yourself and your team. Some people believe that trust must be earned. Others believe that you should trust until there is a compelling reason not to. In any case, trust between team members and yourself will make your project successful. In this task you will learn management tools and leadership skills in order to develop your team.

Scenario

You already know several of the individuals on your team; however, there are a few new people and you are sure that some of them do not know each other. None of them has worked for you before, and you are anxious for the team to get to know each other as well as you.

Your team hasn't synched up as a team; in fact, the experienced people tend to mock the newer ones if they make a mistake. You go to James Stevens, the project sponsor, for funding of three team-building activities over the course of the next six months. However, he tells you that there is no money in the budget for that. You are on your own for developing your team.

Scope of Task

Duration

You will perform this task throughout the project.

Setup

None.

Caveat

None.

Procedure

In this task you will use a variety of tools that will assist you in developing your team, such as these:

- Ground rules
- Team building
- Training
- Coaching

Details

Working with a team that runs like a well-oiled machine is a wonderful thing. Working with a dysfunctional team is the complete opposite. Here are characteristics of a highly functional team:

- Meets stakeholder expectations
- Reduces barriers through open, honest communication

- Improves processes as they go by applying lessons learned throughout the project rather than just talking about them at the end of the project

- Embraces and controls change

- Makes and uses ground rules

- Has mutual accountability

- Uses collaborative creativity

- Makes joint decisions

- Takes appropriate initiatives

Knowing the characteristics of a dysfunctional team will help the project manager realize the areas of improvement needed in the team as well as yourself. These are some of the characteristics of a dysfunctional team:

- Low performance

- Confusion, conflict, and inefficiency

- Low commitment to project objectives

- Subtle sabotage, fear, disinterest, or foot dragging

- Unclear commitment from upper management

- Cliques, collusion, and isolation of members

- Unproductive gamesmanship and manipulation of others

- Hidden agendas

- Lethargy and unresponsiveness

So how do you begin? Start with ground rules, conduct team-building activities, follow with training where needed, and then mentor your team with an open-door, always-available policy.

Ground Rules

When the team gets together for the first time, ground rules should be established and set by the team. Ground rules determine how the team should function. The project manager should facilitate this activity but not take over the process. If the team helps to set the rules, they are most likely to follow them, Here is a sample of team rules that you may consider using:

- Plans set in concrete are not as useful as plans that reflect current reality.

- Credibility is indispensable—without it, quality is impossible. If credibility is lost, regaining it will be our top priority.

- Consider how we've handled problems before; it is not always necessary to reinvent the wheel.

- Do not be lured into giving preliminary results—we want the full picture, good or bad.

- We don't fix the blame if things go wrong—we fix the problem.

- We will take pleasure in doing a task well; in other words, we'll do it right the first time.

- Meetings are essential. Our individual and collective participation is required, so if you are unable to attend, send someone who can *make decisions* in your absence.

- Status reporting structures (schedule, costing information, and so forth) will be consistent across all projects.

- We will measure progress by monitoring the production of deliverables. This can be a tangible document or visual inspection of physical work to see that performance specifications are met.

- *Believe it or not, we are supposed to have fun!*

Team Building

It takes a while for a team to start working as a team—even if individually, team members are superior workers. A high level of conflict exists at the beginning of a project's life cycle. This is normal and all teams go through this, but team-building activities force the team to remove conflict early in the project to establish a team culture that uses conflict resolution techniques. Most project managers neglect to allocate time and budget for team-building activities. Considering how important it is for teams to achieve high performance, team building is one of those essential budget items.

In 1965, Bruce Tuckman theorized that teams have to go through five stages before they truly become a team: forming, storming, norming, performing, and adjourning.

Let's take a closer look at these stages:

Forming   People are usually guarded, polite, reserved, and impersonal.

Storming   People exhibit infighting, chaos, conflict, opting out, turf battles, cliques, and power plays.

Norming   People are organized, developing skills, solving problems, and resolving conflicts.

Performing   People are cooperative, productive, resourceful, and capable.

Adjourning   People exhibit a sense of loss and anxiety at having to break up.

As the project manager, you must allow time for these stages to occur. Forming and storming do not take as long as you might think, and soon you will see norming and performing. Also you may want to go to `http://wilderdom.com` for dozens of free team-building activities. Table 3.11 represents a team-building plan. On a stressful project, it is wise to schedule team-building activities and get funded for them before the project starts. Use as many team-building activities as your team needs and are appropriate for the duration of your project.

Team building is especially useful when everyone is at a high stress level. Perhaps you can plan to take a day or a half day off and do something fun. This really rejuvenates a team.

TABLE 3.11   Team-Building Plan

Team-Building Plan		
Team Building #1	Activity:	
	Planned Date:	
	Owner:	
	Cost Estimate:	
	Approved By:	
Team Building #2	Activity:	
	Planned Date:	
	Owner:	
	Cost Estimate:	
	Approved By:	
Team Building #3	Activity:	
	Planned Date:	
	Owner:	
	Cost Estimate:	
	Approved By:	

Training

Some individuals dive right in and can do their job well. Others may need some training. You may have established some links to an automated team room, or a file for status input, or even a data repository for retrieving or sending information. Do not assume that your team knows how to access these items. They may be password protected, and your team may need special access privileges. If training is necessary, be sure to allow time and budget for it.

Coaching

As a project leader you may need to "coach" an individual who may be having difficulty of one sort or another. With your open-door policy, this is something you may do often or not so often, depending on the maturity level of the individual. Most of us have a coaching style, and we tend to always coach in our own style. This is not always a good thing.

In their book *Management of Organizational Behavior* (Prentice Hall, 2007), Kenneth Blanchard, PhD., and Spencer Johnson, M.D. created a situational leadership model that is still widely used today. This model is found in Figure 3.1.

FIGURE 3.1   Blanchard and Johnson's situational leadership model

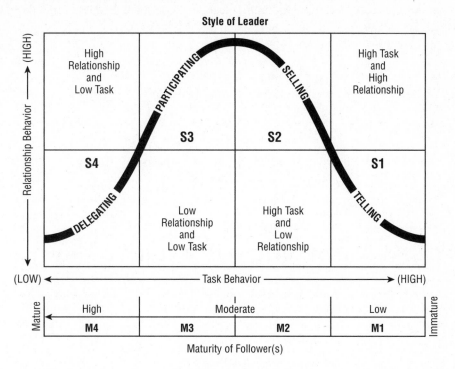

When you begin a new relationship as the boss, typically you participate in one-way conversations, that is, you are the one teaching and telling your new person what to do. The new person doesn't even know what to ask at this point. You are in the *telling mode*. The new person is "unwilling" to do the work because they are "unable" to perform the job yet. Trust between the manager and worker is low.

Soon, the relationship changes. The new person understands the work but still must come to you with questions. Two-way communications are established, and you are now in the *selling mode*. The new person is "willing" to do the job but is "unable" to go it alone. Trust is building.

Now the person knows the job and doesn't need you anymore. You are in the *participating mode* with your team. The person is willing and able to do the job without your guidance. However, this person may become "unwilling" to do the job if they become bored or demotivated. Trust is higher between everyone in this mode.

Finally, you trust everyone on your team completely and may delegate your own work to the now fully functional team. They are more than willing and able to perform their tasks, and trust is highest here. You are now in the *delegating mode*. By the way, you should delegate important tasks as well as small, insignificant tasks.

You can see that your personal style of managing needs to change according to the maturity levels of the people on your team. Let's say, for example, that you are more comfortable in the delegating mode. You must adjust your personal style if you have a new person. If you delegated work in this example, the new person would be frustrated and may think they are being set up to fail. They would feel more comfortable if you were in the telling mode. Likewise, if you are more comfortable in the telling mode, it would be disastrous to tell people what to do if they are fully functional.

Hands-On 3.4: Testing Your Knowledge of Developing Your Project Team

1.   Based on the scenario at the beginning of this task, describe three things you can do to develop your team that don't cost money but will take extra time.

2.   Describe five additional ground rules you believe would help your team perform better.

Task 3.4: Managing the Project Team

Now that you have acquired and developed your team, it becomes routine for you to manage them. You should make sure your team knows that even if you are managing on a horizontal plane, your job is not higher or better than theirs; you simply perform a different job than they do.

Scenario

You have successfully pulled together your team and have conducted a few team-building activities. They seemed to help the team get along, but now you find that certain members of your team seem hesitant to ask for help until it is way too late. You know you must handle this conflict, but managing conflict does not come easy for you. You have attended a class on conflict management and are eager to try some of the new concepts you have learned.

Scope of Task

Duration

This task is performed for the duration of the project.

Setup

None.

Caveat

None.

Procedure

In this task we will discuss the following:

- Abraham Maslow's hierarchy of needs
- Frederick Herzberg's hygiene theory
- Theory X and theory Y
- Expectancy theory
- Achievement theory
- Types of power
- Performance problems
- Rewards and recognition
- Conflict resolutions

Details

It really isn't about the money anymore—or is it? Motivational theories such as Maslow's hierarchy of needs, Herzberg's hygiene theory, and the concept of expectancy theory take different looks at motivation and the use of money.

The notion of power and its effect on you and others is important to understand, because the misuse of power can alienate you from your team.

Managing your team well is critical to the success of you and your team and as a result, your project. At times you may instantly try to correct a problem before you even know what the problem is. You may overstate the criticality of a problem or turn a blind eye because you are not comfortable with conflict. In any case, you must use your leadership as well as your management skills to resolve performance problems.

On the flip side of the coin are recognition and rewards. Everyone wants to be recognized for their efforts, and rewards need not be costly.

Maslow's Hierarchy of Needs

Psychologist Abraham Maslow wrote an article in 1943 that was published in the *Psychological Review*. It was the first time that a publication looked at a motivational study of humans rather than animals. In Figure 3.2 you can see in the pyramid the five strata of the human condition, as Maslow defines it.

Suppose you have an employee whose performance is superior. That person may be at the *self-actualization* stratum. Then you learn that your department is shutting down and all employees will be laid off. Suddenly, that person and the rest of the employees drop to the *basic physical needs* stratum. The employees may not be able to focus on anything but getting a new job in order to keep their homes. A person cannot get to a higher level unless their lower-level needs are met.

It is important for you to understand Maslow's theory, because it may explain changes in behavior, attitude, and performance.

FIGURE 3.2

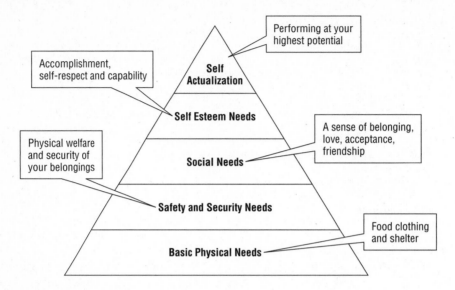

Herzberg's Hygiene Theory

Psychologist Frederick Herzberg published his findings about motivation in *The Motivation to Work* (John Wiley & Sons, 1959). He observed that man has two sets of needs: the first to avoid pain (hygiene needs) and the second to grow mentally (motivators). Hygiene theory is one way of determining satisfaction or dissatisfaction in the workplace.

Motivators, or satisfiers, consist of elements such as learning opportunities, gaining competency, achievement, and recognition.

Hygiene factors are more concerned with the items that may cause dissatisfaction in the workplace, such as working conditions, job security, relationships with peers and supervision, salary discrepancies, technical issues, policies and procedures, and so forth.

Considering hygiene theory, you may conclude that performance problems may not always be the employee's fault after all.

Theory X and Theory Y

Douglas McGregor, in his book *The Human Side of Enterprise* (McGraw-Hill Education, 1960), postulated that managers hold one of two sets of assumptions about human motivation. These assumptions will affect the manager's behavior and management style.

Theory X assumptions:

- People inherently dislike work and will avoid it if possible.

- The average person wants security, avoids responsibility, has little ambition, and prefers to be directed.

If these assumptions are true, the theory X project managers will do the following:

- Pressure or control people to achieve work objectives or organizational goals

- Closely supervise, punish poor performance, give workers little latitude and few rewards, and provide only negative feedback to "help them improve"

Theory Y assumptions:

- The average person likes work; it is as natural as play.
- If a person is committed to goals, that person will work toward them without external control.
- Goal commitment follows from the satisfaction of a person's desire to achieve.
- Creativity, ingenuity, imagination, and other widely dispersed human characteristics exist.

If these assumptions are true, theory Y project managers will do the following:

- Give workers more responsibility
- Rely on the self-motivation of employees

Other Motivational Theories

Several other motivational theories are worth exploring. One of them is *expectancy theory*, postulated by Victor Vroom, which states that if expectations are high, you will receive positive outcomes. Conversely, if there are low expectations, the outcome may not be so positive. You should not set expectations that are unachievable, as these will de-motivate people. People usually perform what is expected of them if they know their effort will be recognized or even rewarded. Do not offer insincere praise, though, as that may appear patronizing.

Another motivational theory is *achievement theory*, which is credited to David McClelland. People are motivated based on their ability to acquire achievement, power, and affiliation. People want to establish camaraderie with other team members and want to be affiliated with a team. If each individual on your team wants to achieve, chances are that team will be successful.

Types of Power

There are several types of power: legitimate power, referent power, expert power, reward power, penalty power, and personal power.

LEGITIMATE POWER

Project managers have *legitimate power* by being recognized in the project charter. Legitimate power is also established as a formal position within an organization. Organizational hierarchy defines the level of authority.

Project managers can use power in a variety of ways. The legitimacy that comes with their title, for some, may turn into "power trips." That is exactly the kind of power for which you don't want to be recognized. The need to understand the use of power is critical to project managers—both the power they have as well as the power of others. Let's take a look at other types of power.

REFERENT POWER

Referent power is based on the authority of an admired person. You may see prominent sports stars or movie stars doing advertising on TV. Somehow, because they are admired in the media, their support of a product or service may be meaningful to others.

As a project manager, referent power may be given to you by the people you influence in a positive way. They enjoy working with you and speak well of you to others. In this case, referent power is earned by your actions and the support you provide your team. Team members willingly accept what you have to say because they genuinely like you.

EXPERT POWER

Expert power occurs when another person believes you have knowledge or special skills that make you an expert. One of your project team members may have expert power, and it is expedient for you as the project manager to leverage that expertise. Feigning expertise will be found out in no time and will destroy any power perceived.

REWARD POWER

Reward power is based on positive reinforcement and the ability to award people something of value in exchange for their cooperation. The ability to use this power depends on the project manager's control over the project and relative position in the organization. For example, you may have money in the project budget for bonuses. The fact that you decide who gets them and when provides you with reward power.

COERCIVE OR PENALTY POWER

Penalty power (also known as punishment or coercive power) is predicated on fear. The employee fears reprisal if expectations are not met. The project manager may have the ability to render penalties, but the ability to use this power depends on the project manager's control over the project and relative position in the organization. Motivating by fear is never an option when working with teams.

PERSONAL POWER

Personal power works two ways: (1) Team members are attracted to the project manager and their management style and want to work for him or her, or (2) a person with personal power has a negative attitude and brings others down with them into negativity. They may not even know they have this power until someone points it out to them. At any rate, personal power can be the mark of a potential leader if they are able to influence others—down a good path or a bad path, with the result being based on the path they choose.

Performance Issues

This is where the rubber meets the road. Project managers must be willing to recognize and analyze performance problems before they act on them. You can use several steps to analyze performance problems:

1. Determine the problem.
   - Is this a training issue?
   - What makes me think there is a problem?
2. Determine its importance.
   - Is this problem going to cost the project?
   - Is correcting the problem worthwhile?

3. Determine whether there is a skill problem.
   - Has the person been allowed to get away with not doing the work?
   - Do they have the skills necessary to perform the work?
4. Determine the learning curve.
   - Is this person new to the task?
   - How long has the team member been doing the work?
5. Determine whether you can provide help.
   - Can you show how to do the work?
   - Are there checklists or other job aids that can help?
6. Determine what is keeping the person from doing the work.
   - Are their conflicting demands for this person between the project and the line manager?
   - Is the work environment conducive to achieving the task?
7. Determine the solution.
   - What is the cost of the solution?
   - Is the cost such that it is worth doing?
   - Ask whether there is anything you can do to help.
   - Ask the performer what she or he believes is the solution.

In reality, you will know the answers to most of these questions; others you will have to think about before you immediately act on the issue.

Hands-on 3.5: Testing Your Knowledge of Managing Your Project Team

You have a new person on your team, Lucy, who is an expert on procurement issues. You instruct her to find out the least expensive cost of a product you need for the project. Soon you get the invoice and see that she has purchased 1,000 units of the product at the cheapest price and has them stored in a warehouse. You see her signature on the invoice.

You immediately call her into your office. You do not want to stifle her initiative, but your main concern is that she signed the invoice. There are two ways to handle this, either positively or negatively.

1. Describe a negative way to handle this scenario.
2. Describe a positive way to handle the scenario.

Hands-on 3.6: Testing Your Knowledge of Motivational Theories

For the following, name the theory represented and the individual responsible for developing the theory:

1. Managers hold either of two sets of assumptions about human motivation. These assumptions will affect the manager's behavior and management style.

2. When a need is satisfied, it no longer motivates and the next-higher need takes its place.

3. Man has two sets of needs, one as an animal to avoid pain (hygiene needs) and a second as a human being to grow psychologically.

Hands-on 3.7: Testing Your Knowledge of Types of Power

Describe the type of power represented by the following statements:

1. A senior manager sends specific instructions to his employees and wants immediate action.

2. The project manager has arranged for the project team to attend a three-day retreat to celebrate success.

3. The project manager is asked to be a frequent speaker at industry symposiums.

4. A team member has asked to work on another project with the project manager who is leading the current project.

Leadership and Motivation

We discussed leadership and motivation earlier and determined that leadership is being able to influence people to do what they otherwise may not do. The following list shows typical leadership and motivational traits:

- Have vision, courage, and commitment.
- Encourage teamwork and participation.
- Adopt a positive attitude.
- Don't criticize the management.
- Keep your promises.
- Give each person the attention they desire.

- Provide constructive counsel.
- Provide a harmonious working environment.
- Provide honest appraisals.
- Provide clear performance expectations.
- Protect the team.
- Make sound and timely decisions.
- Communicate effectively.
- Empower team members.
- Know yourself and your team.
- Match skills with resources.
- Treat each person as an individual.
- Listen effectively.
- Emphasize long-term productivity.
- Give positive feedback.
- Establish direction.
- Seek responsibility and accept accountability.
- Motivate and inspire.
- Align individuals for success.

Rewards and Recognition

There may be differing schools of thought about rewards and recognition systems. Should the team be rewarded collectively? Teams succeed or fail, and the team members should share in the success and failure regardless of their individual contributions. If the team fails but individuals met their performance targets, should those individuals be singled out for rewards? Those are tough questions, and unfortunately there are no perfect answers. Here are a few suggestions for consideration:

- Rewards must be flexible enough to enable the teams to decide how their team members will be rewarded.
- It can be demoralizing to promote teamwork and continue to reward individuals.
- Define goals that can be achieved through collaboration as a team as opposed to a group of people acting as individuals in a cooperative manner.
- Team behaviors that are expected must be explicitly communicated to all those affected and an explanation given as to what defines success and how those behaviors will be recognized and rewarded.
- Be sure that team members perceive that the recognition and rewards are fair.
- Some of the most career-enhancing rewards are nonfinancial in nature.
- Whatever choice is made, recognize and reward good performance.

Conflict Resolution

Conflict is a natural occurrence in the project management experience. Resolving conflicts doesn't come naturally to most people. It is typically a learned trait, and if done well can be a great learning experience. You will perform conflict resolution many times in your project, and there are several approaches to conflict:

- *Forcing* or dictating a solution pushes one viewpoint at the expense of others and offers only win/lose solutions. Hard feelings may come back in other ways.

- When you avoid conflict, you *withdraw* or retreat from the actual or potential conflict situation. It does not solve the problem.

- When you accommodate conflict, you attempt to *smooth over* the situation. You emphasize areas of agreement rather than areas of difference, but this provides only short-term solutions.

- When you *compromise* your position, you are looking for bargains for solutions that bring a degree of satisfaction to all parties. This provides a definitive resolution.

- You can *collaborate* and reach consensus by incorporating multiple viewpoints and insights. This leads to consensus and commitment and provides long-term resolution.

- *Confronting* the situation treats conflict as a problem to be solved by examining alternatives and requires give-and-take and open dialogue. Confrontation provides the ultimate resolution.

Hands-on 3.8: Testing Your Knowledge of Managing Conflict

You are on site at the Portland Apples and Pears store. Todd Franks, the construction superintendent, is in Bellevue. You are anxious to see the final touches to the store, and when you arrive you are surprised to see the electrician high on a ladder putting up can lights and smoking a cigarette. The ladder is on newly installed carpet, and you can't believe he is smoking, particularly because during your last conversation with Todd, he specified to all the trades that after the carpet was installed, there would be no smoking in the store. You tell the contractor that he shouldn't be smoking in the store. He tells you to "deal with it."

1. Describe what the forcing method of dealing with conflict would be in this scenario. What would be the result of using this method?

2. Describe what the withdrawing method of dealing with conflict would be in this scenario. What would be the result of using this method?

3. Describe what the smoothing over method of dealing with conflict would be in this scenario. What would be the result of using this method?

4. Describe what the collaboration method of dealing with conflict would be in this scenario. What would be the result of using this method?

5. Describe what the confronting method of dealing with conflict would be in this scenario. What would be the result of using this method?

Task 3.5: Providing Quality Assurance

Quality assurance is a proactive process that helps control the project and delight the customer. In the absence of a quality manager, the project manager is responsible for the administration of the project quality plan. But that does not dismiss others from maintaining their own quality activities.

Quality assurance begins when you begin the work on the project. You want to be sure that your deliverables are "fit for use" and meet the quality characteristics that the client has specified. If your quality assurance processes do not allow you to meet quality objectives, it is time to change or improve your processes to achieve that goal.

The quality assurance plan should be multifunctional (so the plan can be repeated elsewhere in the organization) and prevention oriented. You will need to collect data and use that data to establish performance measures, and at times a quality audit will need to be performed.

During this phase, the project team is responsible for *executing the tasks* as described in the project management plan. The project manager is responsible for *performance measurements* achieved by comparing planned vs. actual results as well as for *providing status information* to all key stakeholders. The key stakeholders are responsible for *reviewing the metrics* that were put in place and any variances against those metrics. All team members are responsible for *taking whatever action is necessary to keep the variances within acceptable limits.*

Scenario

You have made visits to the store sites in Seattle and Portland. Progress at both sites is ahead of schedule, and the workmanship so far has been excellent. You breathe a sigh of relief, but inwardly you are not really surprised as you know that Todd Franks, the superintendent, always obtains superior results. Todd was surprised that you wanted to visit and you told him that you were anxious to see the stores. You were authorized to give Todd a bonus because he was ahead of schedule but wanted to give it to him in person. You arrange a lunch date and give him his bonus. He is surprised and pleased. You also give him gift certificates that he can give to his workers as he deems fit.

You have also visited the clothing manufacturing to see the quality of the clothes being made. You are shocked to discover that many shortcuts are being taken and that the quality of the clothes is not what you expected. There is single-seam construction where there should be two seams. The wedding dresses and formal wear have inferior fabrics lining the dresses. Fasteners fall off easily, and some of the fabrics used have flaws in them. You review your quality assurance plan and try to determine what went wrong and how much it will cost to either fix the clothing or throw it out and create new pieces.

Scope of Task

Duration
This will last the length of the project.

Setup
None.

Caveat
None.

Procedure

In this task you will learn about the following:
- Plan quality: tools and techniques
    - Cost/benefit analysis
    - Cost of quality
    - Control charts
    - Benchmarking
    - Design of experiments
    - Statistical sampling
    - Flowcharting
- Quality audits
- Process analysis
- Collecting metrics
- Variance management
- Managing deliverables
- Critical work products

Details

Quality to you may be different from quality to someone else. It is important that everyone be on the same page to avoid surprises in the quality of your deliverables. Earlier, we spoke about acceptance criteria for the deliverables on the project. Some may have been ignored or the workers might not have understood the instructions. In this task you will look for ways to make sure your quality process is being followed.

Using Quality Tools and Techniques
You have already created your quality plan; here is where you use some of the quality tools available to you.

COST/BENEFIT ANALYSIS

It is essential that you perform a cost/benefit analysis when deciding which processes you will use to measure or control quality. Although you certainly want to reduce rework and thereby improve productivity or production, the cost of that action should not outweigh the benefit you will receive. The items you should include in your cost/benefit analysis include strategic (why is this good for the business or project) as well as operational benefits, true costs using the time value of money, as well as a financial analysis.

COST OF QUALITY

Cost of quality refers to the total cost of all efforts to achieve product or service quality, such as reworking. *Prevention* refers to designing quality in, such as through appraisal activities. *Appraisal* refers to preproduction and production inspections, tests, or sampling that are done to ensure that the final product will be within the product specification levels. These are the costs associated with *conforming to quality.*

Design reviews, training, and quality planning are also associated with the costs of prevention activities. Inspections, lab tests, and in-process testing are costs associated with appraisal activities.

Joseph Juran, a noted quality expert, spoke often of the *cost of not conforming to quality,* referring to the impacts of internal and external failure. Internal failures are those that occur before leaving the organization and include scrapping, reworking, repairing, and evaluating defects. These cause costs to rise and employees to become disgruntled about having their efforts wasted. The goal is to design quality in, so there is little to catch at the inspection phase. External failures are those discovered by the customer and include returns, complaints, corrective action, and field maintenance. There is no way to know the true cost of external failures. Unhappy customers may complain to their friends and acquaintances about the failure, and you may never know the cost of that loss of business.

CONTROL CHARTS

A typical control chart is a graphical display of a quality characteristic that has been measured or computed from a sample or as results of a process *over time.* If you have repeatable processes, slight variation will still occur. The question is, will those variations still allow the process to meet the desired end result?

The quality control chart contains a line in the center that represents the average or mean when assessing processes or products. Management uses the upper control limit (UCL) and lower control limit (LCL) to set a control limit that should exceed customer expectations. Control limits are mathematically configured after collecting a sample size of data, so that if the process is in control, nearly all of the sample points will fall between the upper and lower control limits. As long as the points plot within the control limits, the process is assumed to be in control, and no action is necessary.

Customer expectations drive the upper and lower specifications on the control chart. The lower specification limit (LSL) is the lowest point in which a process or product is within the acceptable performance limits determined by the customer. Conversely, the upper specification limit (USL) is the highest point at which a process or product remains within the acceptable performance limits set by the customer. If your data stays within the control limits, you will meet customer expectations most of the time. However, a point that plots outside the control limits is interpreted as evidence that the process is out of control, and if the points get too close to the specification limits, you may not meet customer expectations. Investigation and corrective action are required to find and eliminate the assignable or special causes responsible for this result. The control points are connected with straight-line segments for easy visualization.

It is possible, however, that the USL and LSL may fall within the UCL and LCL, in which case, the process you are using is not capable of meeting customer expectations.

For example, say that as project manager, part of your job is to make sure your team knows that they will be given only 5 minutes of grace time to make it to your meeting. Although you start your meetings right on time, some people are usually a few minutes late. The meeting typically lasts 30 to 45 minutes. John, who is a key figure in the project, has been late getting to your meetings on time, so you decide to capture John's "on-time" status by using a control chart (Figure 3.3).

FIGURE 3.3 Control chart

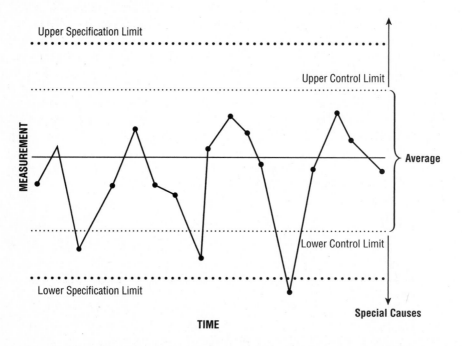

You have collected this data for 17 days, and John was late each Wednesday. In fact, in the third week he was so late that he missed the whole meeting. You call John into your office to discuss this with him. He tells you that he is not trying to be late but that on Wednesdays he has to take his daughter to day care and they don't allow parents to bring their children early. He simply can't make it on time.

You realize that on the other days he is within acceptable guidelines (upper and lower control limits). You discuss probable solutions. John agrees to let his trusted neighbor take his daughter to day care. (The neighbor has offered this many times, but he didn't want to take advantage of her.) He was able to change his process after you and he explored the special or assignable causes.

Customers will reject any item that is not within the specification limits they set. In the example, you have set control limits to be sure the specification limits will be met. Whenever you see more data points heading out of control, you will realize the process is out of control and needs to be fixed in order to stay within the specification limits. When fixing a process, you also need to realize that this is a cost of conforming to quality.

Even if all the points plot inside the control limits, if they behave in a systematic or non-random manner, then this is an indication that the process is out of control. For example, if the data points are "within limits" but appear below the average mark and are heading downward toward the lower control limit, you will want to look at your process because your process may soon be out of control.

BENCHMARKING

Benchmarking is simply comparing your results or planned project practices with other projects (internal or external) to determine standards with which to measure performance. It is useful to benchmark against other organizations within your own company and within the same industry, but much can be gained by benchmarking other industries as well.

There are typically five steps to the benchmarking process:

1. Define what you want to benchmark and define the content specifically.

2. Design a data structure to collect data.

3. Collect the data.

4. Verify and analyze the data to generate the results.

5. Present findings.

DESIGN OF EXPERIMENTS

Design of experiments (DOE) is a technique used in the quality planning process and is associated with engineer and statistician Genichi Taguchi. The basic premise of DOE is that quality should be measured by the deviation from a specification, rather than by conformance to predetermined tolerance limits, and that quality cannot be ensured through inspection and reworking, but must be built in through the appropriate design of the process and product.

In other words, DOE seeks to use the minimum number of trials required to achieve statistically sound results that allow valid conclusions to be drawn about the process. For example, as a manufacturer, you do not want to pay for a top-end suspension to go with mid-grade tires for the model of car being produced. That would be spending money on parts that would not improve the way the ride felt. Spending more than you need to, for functionality you will not be able to realize, is one form of "gold plating."

There are five steps associated with Taguchi's DOE:

1. Design the experiment.

2. Run a simulation and test.

3. Validate and evaluate the result.

4. Perform multi-objective optimizations.

5. Validate optimization results.

STATISTICAL SAMPLING

Remember the quote "Statistics are like swimsuits; what they reveal is interesting, what they conceal is vital"? Although the author is unknown, the quote is great at getting to the point. You need to be measuring what matters. Statistics are a tool that can help you make sense of available data. Although measuring the final product within a manufacturer's lot of products may meet the customer's specifications as a critical-to-quality (CTQ) characteristic, you may choose to select only a portion of the final lot to confirm that you met the mark. Testing some items, rather than all, can help substantially reduce the cost of conforming to quality, as long as you get a valid representation of the whole in the sample size you select.   There is a chance that when you choose to do sample testing, there is a chance for rejecting a good lot and obtaining a bad lot.

Let's take a look at some common statistical terms:

- An *attribute* is a characteristic of the product.

- *Attribute sampling* results in either conformance or nonconformance.

- *Attribute data* are sometimes referred to as discreet data.

- *Variable sampling* results are rated on a scale to measure the degree of conformity. The data are infinitely measurable, such as time or money.

- The *sample size* is the number of items in the sample, indicated by n.

- The *sampling plan* describes how sampling will occur.

Statistical terms describe numbers by using the following parameters:

- The *mean* is a sum of measurements divided by the number of measurements under consideration (also known as the *average*).

- The *median* is a value having as many observations above it as below it when the observations are arranged in increasing or decreasing sequence of value. (It is the middle number.) The median is the average of the two middle numbers when there is an even number of observations.

- The *mode* is the most frequently occurring observation.

- The *range* is the difference between the largest measurement and the smallest measurement.

FLOWCHARTING

Flowcharts are used to graphically display the steps within a process and the yes or no decisions that may be made along the way. Two types of flowcharts are generally used: a process flowchart and a system flowchart.

An example of a process flowchart is shown in Figure 3.4, which graphically displays how various elements of a process or system relate (in this case, how to manage an issue).

As a project progresses, understanding the tasks and decisions that occur in any given process can help the project team anticipate what quality problems might occur and where they may occur, which helps the team to develop approaches for dealing with them.

The following steps are used to create a flowchart:

1. Discuss the intended use of the flowchart.

2. Decide on the desired outcome of the charting session: a macro-level chart (high-level steps) or micro-level chart (very detailed steps).

3. Define the boundaries of the process—clearly establish first and last steps.

4. Document each step in sequence.

5. Determine inputs, outputs, and related steps.

6. Use appropriate charting symbols.

7. Draw the process accurately and consistently.

8. At each decision point, follow one branch through to completion.

9. If you encounter an unfamiliar segment, make a note of it and keep going.

10. Repeat steps 4, 5, and 6 until the process is completely charted, making sure to complete all decision branches.

11. Review the completed chart for possible gaps.

12. Determine how to fill in unfamiliar segments and verify the chart's accuracy.

13. After the chart is accurate and complete, analyze it for reasonableness.

Quality Audits

One of the quality assurance tools is a project audit. A project audit can be performed randomly or at specified times within each phase of the project. The intended outcome of the audit is to confirm the following:

- The planned project quality requirements are met.

- The products are safe and fit for the customers' use.

- All laws and regulations have been followed.

- Data systems to track, measure, and report quality attributes and quality characteristics are accurate and adequate.

- Any variances identified during quality checks are addressed by appropriate corrective action.

- Any opportunities for continuous improvement are noted for future action.

FIGURE 3.4   Flowchart example

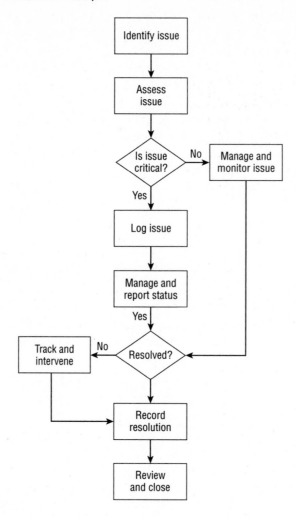

Process Analysis

Process analysis enables you to determine whether the processes you use meet your goals and objectives. You may have used a process for years, but it may not have fulfilled your expectations and you wouldn't know that until you collected some data on the process.

For example, say you own a pizza business and promise to deliver pizza within 30 minutes. Lately you find that customers are complaining because they are not receiving their pizzas in 30 minutes. So you check your internal process and find that the orders are not reaching the cook in a timely fashion. The person taking the orders also serves the drinks, and orders often sit on the counter for minutes at a time. You correct your process by using an ordering machine. The order now goes directly to the cook via a screen in the kitchen and prints out directions to the customer's home at the same time.

Collecting Metrics

One of the outputs of the plan quality process is quality metrics. You define what you want to measure to analyze performance. After you collect these measurements, you use the data within the quality control tools previously defined.

The size of the project should be proportional to the quantity of measurements and the effort it takes to collect them. For example:

- *Small projects* should concern themselves with basic information such as how the project is progressing in terms of cost, effort, and duration. There is usually no need to capture more-sophisticated metrics on the project deliverables or the internal project work processes, because there is not enough time to make improvements or take any actions based on the results of the metrics.

- *Medium projects* should collect the same information as small projects, but additional metric information may be of value. Expand the metric collection to quality of deliverables and how well processes worked. The differentiator would be the length of time available to respond to performance improvements.

- *Large projects* should collect the same metrics as for small and medium projects, but additionally it would be appropriate to look for metrics that provide information in the areas of cost, effort, duration, team performance, productivity, and business value, as well as the quality of deliverables and client satisfaction.

The following is a list of metrics that could be collected on your project. This list is not exhaustive by any means but may help provide additional ideas for your project:

- Cost
  - Actual cost vs. budget (variance) for project, for phase, for activity, and so on
  - Total support costs for x months after solution is completed
  - Total cost of employees vs. contract vs. consultant (vs. budget)
  - Actual labor costs vs. estimated labor costs
  - Actual equipment costs vs. estimated equipment costs
  - Actual material costs vs. estimated material costs
  - Amount of management reserve needed
  - Amount of contingency reserves actually used
  - Number of approved changes to the budget
  - Number of unapproved changes to the budget
  - Effective cost-reporting process
- Schedule
  - List of milestones with days early/late
  - List of impacted activities
  - Schedule performance index (SPI) (more about this in Phase 4)
  - SPI trend over time
  - Actual vs. estimated time spent on tasks

- How much slack was needed
- Whether the project end date was met
- The number of unknown constraints that hindered the project end date
- The number of tasks that should have been started but weren't
- The amount of free slack and slack that was used or not used
- Productivity
  - Work units produced per effort hour
  - Effort hours reduced from standard project processes
  - Effort hours saved through reuse of previous deliverables, models, and so forth
  - Number of process improvement ideas implemented
  - Number of hours/dollars saved from process improvements
- Quality of deliverables
  - Percentage of deliverables going through quality reviews
  - Percentage of deliverable reviews resulting in acceptance the first time
  - Number of defects discovered after initial acceptance
  - Number of client change requests to revise scope
  - Number of hours of reworking previously completed deliverables
- Quality of project
  - Number of best practices identified and applied on the project
  - Number of risks that were successfully mitigated
  - Project completed on time within approved schedule
  - Project completed within approved budget
  - Deliverable results traceable to requirements
  - Positive test results
  - Clear and unambiguous acceptance criteria

There are many other metrics; these are just a few. There is one important thing to remember, though: Don't measure something just because you can. Measure something that will provide meaningful information to help you meet the project objectives.

Variance Management

Project variance can be defined as the difference between a planned and actual time, cost, or performance measure. Project variance is a function of change requests or actual work results differing from those designed during the project-planning phase. After variation is identified, corrective action or reforecasting will follow. You will discover variances when you receive status reports. Another way to manage variances is to conduct informal reviews such as these:

- Managing by walking around
- Planning local peer reviews or walk-throughs

- Educating the team by exploring these questions:
  - What are the variance and deviation from the plan?
  - What is the standard variance?
  - Why are consistency and discipline important?
  - How can we accept criticism and avoid blaming?
  - Why is honesty (good and bad news) critical?

The important thing to remember is that identification of variance can not only help control project outcomes, but also help ensure customer satisfaction.

Quality Assurance Checkpoints

You can use the following checkpoints to ensure that quality work is being achieved:

- Identify the quality assurance activities that will be used across the project to validate the effectiveness of quality contributors (skills, standards, tools, methods, and procedures), and to ensure compliance with procedures.
- Identify key dates at which major reviews and other quality activities will occur.
- Review the project decision structure to validate and document that quality roles and responsibilities have been clearly identified, defined, and communicated throughout the project organization.
- Map quality contributors and procedures to quality standards that may be required on the project.

Managing Deliverables

The project manager has the responsibility to ensure the quality of all deliverables within a project. You have to view deliverables from the customer's perspective. If customers are unhappy with a deliverable, it isn't finished until the customer is happy. In other words, you want to remove any ambiguity from the acceptance criteria.

Acceptance criteria of a deliverable should include the following:

- Content properties (documents, software, and so on)
- Physical properties
- Ownership properties (trademarks, patents, and the like)

Critical Work Products

Critical work products are those work products that could cause the project to falter or fail if they do not meet quality expectations. In order to ensure that the deliverables will meet the acceptance criteria, the project team must make sure that these critical work products contain the requisite quality parameters. Complete one section of Table 3.12 for each critical work product. The first section of Table 3.12 explains what should be included for each item.

TABLE 3.12 Critical Work Products

Section No.	Section Items	Description
1	Work product	Provide the name of critical work product (or, possibly, a group of work products that are treated as one).
	Rationale	With reference to the acceptance criteria, explain why this work product is regarded as critical.
	Quality characteristics	Describe the attribute of the work product that will be used to assess its quality.
	Quality criteria	Define the target value of the quality characteristic.
	Quality contributors	Describe the factors such as skills, standards, and tools. This can also include the methods and procedures that will contribute toward the achievement of the set of quality criteria.
2	Work product	
	Rationale	
	Quality characteristics	
	Quality criteria	
	Quality contributors	
3	Work product	
	Rationale	
	Quality characteristics	
	Quality criteria	
	Quality contributors	

Hands-on 3.9: Testing Your Knowledge of Quality Assurance

1. Considering the scenario at the beginning of this task, what quality tools could you use to determine the problem? Why?

2. Describe items that are considered a cost of quality and items that are considered a cost of nonconformance.

3. Describe the Taguchi method (design of experiments). Is this a good tool to use in a society where change is constant? Why or why not?

4. What is the purpose of a quality audit?

5. List two metrics that can be taken during a project in each of the following categories:

    a. Cost

    b. Schedule

    c. Productivity

    d. Quality of deliverables

    e. Quality of the project

Task 3.6: Executing the Communications Plan

You have created a communications plan and have already used it to get this far in the project, but now more than ever communications are the key to success. You know what tools you will be using, have done your stakeholder interviews, and know when and how to send information and where information can be found. But there's more! You will want to know the correct way to communicate with your sponsor and your team as well as with those who are technical.

Scenario

The team is well in place now, and you have established guidelines on how project information is shared. You have created toll-free telephone numbers for your virtual team members, set up emails and voicemail, and provided a fax number dedicated to the project. You have sent everyone a meeting schedule and considered the different time zones. Considering the different time zones, you have also established your video conference schedule. You have set up manual and electronic filing structures and provided your team with a team directory, including emergency numbers.

Scope of Task

Duration

This task exists for the duration of the project.

Setup

None.

Caveat

None.

Procedure

In this task you will learn about these topics:

- A communication model
- Distributing information
- Reporting on performance
- Communicating with your sponsor and your team
- What executives really want to know
- Managing stakeholder expectations
- Listening skills

Details

Communicating is everything to a project. Project communications is often considered the most important job that a project has. You will spend upward of 90% of your time communicating, especially in this phase.

Communication Model

Figure 3.5 is from *Project Management: A Systems Approach to Planning, Scheduling, and Controlling* by Harold Kerzner (9th ed., p. 231; John Wiley & Sons, 2006). It is a communication model showing that when you are speaking (are the source or encoder), the message flows through your personality screen and to the receiver (decoder) through the receiver's perception screen. When the receiver provides feedback, the message flows through the receiver's personality screen and back through the sender's perception screen.

Information Distribution

A considerable amount of information must be distributed during a project. You will create project reports that describe the *status of the project, the status of issues, approved changes,* and *lessons learned* during the time cycle for the reports. When you provide lessons learned, you should document the causes of issues and the rationale behind the corrective action taken.

You may have to conduct project presentations, either to your team or executive management. It is helpful to use presentation software when doing this, but if you are adequately prepared, you can present your project information by using video conferencing or face-to-face meetings. When feasible, be sure to provide your audience a copy of what you will be presenting in advance so they have time to digest the information and prepare any questions they may have.

FIGURE 3.5   Communication model

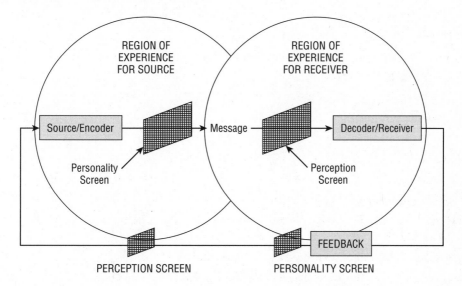

You will need to create *project records* that include meeting minutes, formal or informal correspondence or memos, emails, decisions made, and so forth. Remember that the distributed items need to be appropriate to the recipient based on their expectations. For example, your sponsor may ask you for an executive summary instead of the details that your team needs. By the way, an executive summary should always include cost information. Remember, at the top of the food chain it's all about the money!

All of this information should be placed with electronic project historical records, if possible, so that others can review your records and learn from them.

Performance Reporting

Performance reporting includes the processes of collecting and disseminating performance information. This includes status reporting, progress measurement, and forecasting.

STATUS REPORTING

Status reporting describes where the project now stands since the last status report. The elements of a comprehensive status report should include these elements:

- Status summary of the health of the project (red, the project is off track; yellow, the project is on track but will soon be off track; green, the project is on track).
- Accomplishments for the report period, including the following:
    - Milestones achieved
    - Milestones planned but not achieved
    - Deliverables completed
    - Work packages planned but not completed
- Accomplishments planned for the next period
    - Milestones to be achieved
    - Deliverables to be completed
    - Summary of issues
- Risks
- Changes
- Action items

PROGRESS REPORTING

Progress reporting describes what the project team has accomplished since the project began. These are elements of a progress report:

- Progress of deliverables identified in the work statement
- Comparisons of expenses to the expected budget to date
- Effectiveness of the project to date
- Current challenges in completing the project
- Quality assessment
    - Product assessment provides an assessment of the quality of deliverables to be produced by the project team based on criteria articulated in the quality plan. These may be supported by metrics such as the number of defects and nonconformities.
    - Project assessment provides an assessment of the quality contributors being used in the project. These may be supported by metrics such as number of compliance reviews, test results, and procedural changes.
- Risks

FORECASTING

Forecasting predicts future project performance. A forecast report can be presented as an S-curve—a graphical depiction of the project budget and schedule over time. The variances in cost and schedule can readily be seen, and by analyzing the results relative to the baseline plan S-curve, estimates can be made of anticipated (forecasted) variations at completion.

Figure 3.6 represents a sample of an S-curve diagram. You will learn more about S-curves in Phase 4.

FIGURE 3.6   S-curve

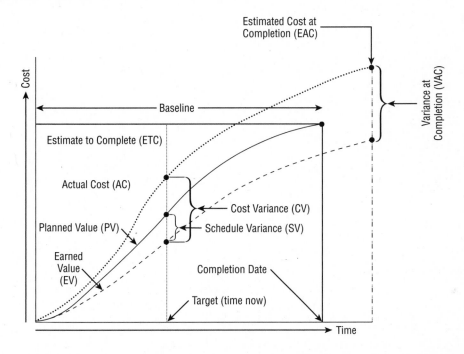

Now that you have your status, it is time to report on the results. If you have an online electronic PMIS, the form found in Table 3.13 should be completed by the task manager as well as the project manager. This form reports earned value calculations from the data received by the line manager. (You will learn about the earned value concept during Phase 4. We show the tool here because you will need a tool similar to this one in your arsenal of project tools.)

TABLE 3.13 Project Performance Report

			Project Performance Report									
				Project Manager								
Project						Project Manager Completes						
	Responsible Task Manager Completes				Earned Value			Cost Performance			Schedule Performance	
Date	Activity (WBS #)	Percent Complete	Weeks to Complete	Expenses per Week	Budgeted Cost for Work Scheduled	Budgeted Cost for Work Performed	Actual Cost for Work Performed	Cost Variance	Cost Performance Index	Schedule Variance $	Schedule Performance Index	
					PV	EV	AC	CV	CPI	SV	SVP	

Communicating with Your Sponsor, Team, and Executives

The success or failure of a project is directly proportional to the amount of time spent communicating to your sponsor and team as well as the quality of those communications. Communications is 80%–90% of a PM's job. The right people have to be kept informed in the right way at the right time as per their communication needs.

COMMUNICATING WITH YOUR SPONSOR

Other than friendly chatter, there are typically three other types of communications you will have with your sponsor:

- Incident communications
- Informal communications
- Formal communications

The first type, *incident communications*, occurs if there is a complaint from a client or a problem that needs solving with the sponsor's assistance. Base your need to communicate with your sponsor on the urgency of the incident or unfavorable visibility of your organization.

Never just hand over a problem to the sponsor. The sponsor will lose confidence in your ability to handle these situations. It is essential, then, to communicate an objective assessment of the situation, *including* a recommended approach for dealing with the problem. The sponsor *may* decide to handle the situation, perhaps because of politics or rank issues, but you will not be viewed in a negative way. Do your homework and obtain all the facts on both sides of the issue! Then, before you communicate with the sponsor, follow these steps:

1. Describe the full impact and how it will be addressed.
2. Consult with your management, if necessary.
3. Determine who should receive the information after the sponsor has been notified.
4. Determine who should deliver the communication, if not you.
5. Determine who should be in attendance when the communication is given. (Political protocol regarding rank, status, or title may be an issue, so be mindful of the corporate culture.)
6. Determine the method of communication.
7. Deliver the communication to the sponsor.
8. Document the communication to the sponsor—this may take the form of a note that it took place or may be more elaborate.
9. Determine actions and issues that need to be raised.
10. Enter a notation into your correspondence and decision log.

If you receive a written complaint, it is also important to do the following:

- Respond in writing to each element in the complaint.
- Acknowledge the incident and determine whether it is legitimate.
- Initiate actions to analyze the situation.

If the incident needs sponsor support, share the written document with your sponsor before sending it out. Otherwise, just copy the sponsor as an FYI or heads-up.

The second type is *informal communications*. You will want to meet with the sponsor on a regular basis to informally discuss the project (such items as overall state of the project, progress, and performance, as well as successes). Seek regular feedback to determine whether your sponsor is happy. If the sponsor is not happy, react quickly and discuss expectations once again.

Keep the sponsor in the loop. Communicate regularly via whatever media were chosen by the sponsor. You will avoid the "meddling sponsor" syndrome if you communicate regularly. The main rule is this: Never let the sponsor find out from someone else something that you should have communicated earlier!

The third type is *formal communications*. This is typically done in report form and includes the following:

- Summary of accomplishments for the current period and planned accomplishments at the next reporting period at the milestone and deliverable level

- Summary of cost and schedule information

- Review of change orders, issues, and risks

- Issues or risks that impact the sponsor and require the sponsor's involvement or support

- Discussion of sponsor concerns

- Identification of opportunities and threats related to actions requested by the sponsor

Remove technical issues too detailed for a sponsor. Sponsors do not want to be mired in the minutiae.

COMMUNICATING WITH YOUR PROJECT TEAM

The three types of communications you have with your sponsor will be the same for your project team. During incident communications, again you will assess the degree of urgency associated with the incident. Plan your communications accordingly:

1. Provide an objective appraisal of the situation.

2. Don't minimize but don't overstate either.

3. Be prepared to engage the team in looking for alternatives.

4. Make sure the full impact of the event is understood or determine the impact with the team.

5. Deliver the communication to the team.

6. Work with the team to determine the best course of action.

7. Discuss concerns and address them immediately or determine a date for responding.

8. Document the communication and the team response.

The second type is informal communications. You will meet with the project team (face to face or electronically) on a regular basis (daily, weekly, monthly, as appropriate) to informally discuss the project:

- Topics include overall state of the project, progress, performance, as well as successes, personnel changes, overview of new technology, and so forth.

- Meetings should be considered no-rank sessions in which the team members feel that everyone has a contribution to make.

- Learn to know what items are of special interest to the team.

- Sometimes the best information is received one-on-one over a cup of coffee or during a private telephone call.

Formal communications are the third type of communication. You should create pre-agreed-upon status reports that include the following:

- Summary of accomplishments for the current period and planned accomplishments at the next reporting period at the milestone and deliverable level

- Summary of cost, effort, and schedule information

- Review of changes, issues, and risks

- Opportunities and threats related to actions requested by the team

WHAT EXECUTIVES REALLY WANT TO KNOW

Remember, executives are looking out for the needs of the business, so your communications with them should include those items important for the business. When seeking help from an executive with a problem that you want them to do something about, make sure you have the answers to the following questions:

- Why was this undertaken?

- What is being done? By whom? Why?

- What exactly is the problem?

- What is the magnitude and importance of the problem?

- What approaches have been used so far to handle it?

- Was the approach thorough and complete?

- Do you have any suggested solution?

- Have you considered others?

- What's next?

- Who does it?

- What are the time factors?

- What do you expect me to do?

Hands-on 3.10: Testing your Knowledge of Communicating with Your Sponsor and Team

1. If a sponsor did not receive timely or accurate information, what might you as the project manager expect the sponsor to do?

2. You are in a meeting with your sponsor. You give the sponsor timely and accurate information about status, but the news is not good. There are unresolved issues. Before you can deliver your plan to deal with the problem, the sponsor says to you, "That is not what I want to hear, so let me ask again, what is the status of the project?" You tell the sponsor the same thing. He asks you the same question again. What should you do?

3. What items can you informally communicate with your project team?

4. What items *must* have a written response?

Managing Stakeholder Expectations

You have created a communications matrix and performed a stakeholder analysis regarding their concerns and interests. Those tools gave you the big picture about the expectations of stakeholders. But expectations are only half of the equation. You should use an expectations/commitment process to assist in the area of managing stakeholder expectations. The following represents sample expectations and commitments between the project manager and the project team. After these are shared with your project team, ask the team members what their expectations are of you and their commitments to you. You may have to add or change your original thoughts.

Project manager expectations of the project team are as follows:

-   Punctual attendance will be the order of the day at face-to-face or video meetings and conference calls. If you are unable to attend, please send someone who can *make decisions* in your absence.

-   Quantitative and qualitative commitments will be met.

-   Status and jeopardy conditions will be reported in a proactive and timely manner (good or bad news).

-   The team will participate with high energy and a good attitude.

-   Everyone will be supportive and respectful of other team members.

-   Everyone will be willing to accept responsibility for their tasks.

-   Solve conflicts without alienation and accept challenges cheerfully.

The following are project manager commitments to the project team:

-   I will involve you in appropriate planning efforts.

-   I will value and utilize your input.

-   I will provide timely notification of meetings, conference calls, and so on.

-   I will keep you informed of changes as soon as they occur.

- I will return your phone calls and other inquiries within 24 hours unless you designate otherwise.

- I will be as flexible as possible with changes that may occur within our plan.

- I will not get involved in your work effort unless you ask me.

- Standards of performance will be provided and communicated to everyone.

- My meetings will always be no-rank sessions.

- I will deal with conflicts quickly with the attitude of fixing the problem, not assigning blame.

What to Do When the Communications Plan Is Not Being Followed

If your project team is not following the communications plan, you should gather your team, sponsor, and others as necessary to have a meeting and discuss the problem. There are seven steps you can follow that do not assign blame but provide an open forum for discussion:

1. Apologize to everyone and tell them what this meeting is about: "I am sorry; I must not have communicated with you the expectations I have regarding our communications plan. As a result, several items have come to my attention that require revisiting the plan and hopefully gaining agreement from everyone today regarding those expectations."

2. Explain to them specific actions that did not comply with the communications plan, such as failure to report status on time, hearing from someone else something that should have been communicated to you, and so on.

3. Describe the impact of not following the plan, such as, "Because I did not receive timely status, I reported incorrect information to our sponsor that made it look as if we weren't on track with the schedule or the budget. Because status was late, our sponsor did not have the correct information when meeting with senior management. This made it impossible for our sponsor to respond to their questions. I should have contacted you, so I will take responsibility for that, but it was our agreement that you would proactively report status to me so that I would not have to ask everyone for status."

4. Ask for feedback: "Is there anything else *I* can do that will bring us into compliance with the plan?

5. Ask your meeting participants, "Is there anything *you* would like to do differently to bring us into compliance? What questions do you have about everything we have discussed today?"

6. Ask for commitment: "Are we now in agreement that we will follow the plan with the changes we have discussed today?"

7. Thank them for their participation.

Hands-on 3.11: Testing Your Knowledge of Expectations and Commitments

List at least five expectations a project sponsor may have of you (the project manager) and five commitments a sponsor will make to you (the project manager).

Listening Skills

It seems that one of the most difficult communication skills we as humans have is listening. Television journalist Diane Sawyer says it best: "I think one lesson I have learned is that there is no substitute for paying attention."

Attentive listening is a learned skill. It is not automatic but requires conscious effort and intent. So how can we improve how we listen? By first becoming aware of the skills involved in listening and then practicing these skills.

What specific skills are involved in attentive listening? The following are critical:

- Pay attention to verbal and nonverbal signals.
  - Look at the speaker.
  - Lean forward.
  - Use "listening noises" (oh? yes, uh-huh).
- Verify using feedback and clarification.
  - This shows the other person (or *decoder*) you are listening and that you understand what is being said.
  - This helps you to determine whether you are interpreting the message correctly.
  - This helps the receiver, or decoder, to look at the issue from another perspective.
- Think about what the sender has to say.
  - Listen for facts as well as ideas, and be sure you ask the speaker questions if necessary to ensure that you understand what was said. Ask yourself questions such as, "Is this meaningful to me?" and "What can I do with this information?"
  - Listen for what is not being communicated. Is the speaker preparing me for good or bad news?
  - Listen to the passion and the attitude of the speaker.
  - Use your thought processes to internalize what you're hearing so you can question and evaluate what is being said.
- Respond to what the speaker has said.
  - Be sincere, not patronizing.
  - Reply to the speaker's concerns or points.

Hands-on 3.12: Testing Your Knowledge of Listening Habits

The following listening assessment tool has been around for many years. Unfortunately, the author of this self-assessment listening IQ is unknown, but this is an effective tool.

1. Read each statement in Table 3.14. Reflect on whether you have experienced or felt the thought expressed in the statements in the past year. To the left of each numbered statement, circle one response.

TABLE 3.14 Listening Questions

Y N ■ 1. It is difficult for me to listen because I have so many other demands on my time and energy.

Y N ■ 2. I can listen effectively while doing other things, like signing my correspondence or logging onto my computer.

Y N ● 3. After someone has explained a concept, I ask several probing questions to help clarify or understand the concept.

Y N ▲ 4. I have frequently left meetings with no idea what decisions we made or who was accountable for action.

Y N ▲ 5. During meetings, people rarely ask questions exploring issues that are raised and points that are made.

Y N ● 6. When someone is speaking, I let my mind find ways to remember key facts.

Y N ■ 7. If I am tired or distracted, I try to give the illusion I am listening, but really I mentally "check out."

Y N ● 8. I write down the most important ideas in a message when someone speaks.

Y N ▲ 9. In meetings, subgroups have formed that don't appear to listen (or even be willing to listen) to one another.

Y N ■ 10. When people come to talk to me about personal matters, I try to think of ways to help them solve the problem.

Y N ▲ 11. After presentations, discussions, or major parts of meetings, rarely does anyone summarize or extract clear and specific points to then feed back to the group.

Y N ■ 12. I interrupt people to save them the time of explaining something I already understand.

Y N ▲ 13. In meetings, I see myself as the "devil's advocate," and am always trying to help the group see "the other side."

Y N ● 14. I restate or read key details to the speaker before our conversation ends so I am sure our understanding is clear.

Y N ● 15. I am in the habit of listening for key points when people talk, and then reflecting those key points back to the speaker.

Y N ■ 16. I tend not to listen when I am distracted by the outfit someone is wearing or something they do that "puts me off."

Y N ● 17. I filter out distractions when I am trying to listen, or I suggest we move to a quieter place.

Y N ▲ 18. During meetings, questions are asked that have already been covered in the meeting.

Y N ● 19. I use phrases like "Let me be sure I understand..." quite regularly when I have listened to someone else.

Y N ▲ 20. In meetings, while someone makes a point, I am already thinking about how I will give my "yes, but..." response.

Y N ● 21. When someone is talking with me, I stop whatever I am doing and give them my full, absolute, sincere attention.

Y N ■ 22. When people begin to talk to me about personal matters (like their divorce), I get very uncomfortable and don't want to listen.

Y N ▲ 23. I feel that if I listen to someone else, I will lose something important (such as my job, our uniqueness, our power, etc.)

Y N ■ 24. Emotional words or ideas that don't fit my view of the world make me not want to listen to the speaker.

2. Now you will compute your score for this assessment. Your score is based only on yes responses in each of the three key categories.

On the survey form, you may have noticed a symbol to the left of each question number. Compute the score for each symbol category, scoring 5 points for each *yes* response *in that category only.* (Score 0 points for each *no* response in a category.) Place the total number of points for each category in Table 3.15.

TABLE 3.15   Listening Scores

Listening Survey Scores		
Group 1	●	Points
Group 2	■	Points
Group 3	▲	Points

These values will be interpreted in the "Phase 3 Solutions" section in the Appendix.

Task 3.7: Conducting Procurements

In this task you will perform procurement procedures that provide guidance on the strategies that will be used to request bids from the marketplace, select sellers, and award contracts. Sellers may be obtained through advertising and bidder conferences. Independent estimates and proposal evaluation criteria are used to select sellers, and procurement negotiations bring you to awarding the contract.

Scenario

This project is your first chance to be a part of the procurement process. You have aligned yourself with Bud Bergstrom, the director of procurement, and he has allowed you to be present during bidder conferences as well as contract negotiations. You are learning more about contracts than you previously imagined and can see how important the project manager's role is in procurement processes. Your master project plan and statements of work drive much of what goes into a contract, and you have conveyed this information to your team.

Scope of Task

Duration

The duration begins in the executing phase and lasts until project closeout.

Setup

None.

Caveat

None.

Procedure

In this task you will learn about the following:

- Obtaining sellers
- Selecting sellers
- Awarding contracts
- Scope-related contract components
- Cost-related contract components
- Schedule-related contract components
- Contract approvals

Details

Procurement procedures should provide guidance on the strategies that will be used to solicit the marketplace. Procurement procedures will impact *how many* suppliers will be approached in a given procurement event, *in what manner* the agency will go to the market, and the *type of contract* that is intended to be established. These factors must be considered before you can actually choose a vendor or contractor. Additionally, a system of selecting sellers without prejudice needs to be in place so that contracts can be awarded fairly.

Obtain Seller Responses

The process of requesting seller responses involves announcing the opportunity to respond to a buyer's request (advertising), and holding bidder conferences where questions are asked and responded to by an audience of all potential bidders.

BIDDER CONFERENCES

Bidder conferences are held before potential sellers submit their proposals. The procurement office typically conducts the conference and invites all potential sellers. Project managers are not usually trained in the legalities of selecting sellers but attend the bidder conference to provide support as needed to the procurement officer.

The purpose of a bidder conference is to ensure that all parties hear the same things at the same time and that all questions and corresponding answers are heard by all. This also gives the sellers an opportunity to see who they are bidding against—they may even opt out of the bidding if they know they cannot compete with certain parties.

When planning for the bidder's conference, an agenda with the following items may be used:

- The *introduction* should introduce key players and include the purpose of this meeting, information about your company, and any pertinent background information.

- *Requirements* should be listed within the RFP or other solicitation document.

- *Business items* should include why the project is important to your business and performance expectations, among other things.

- The *process* should include the negotiation procedure, timetable, and an outline for the award criteria.

- The *questions-and-answers session* should be handled with great care and precise administration. The facilitator of the bidder conference should record questions that are received and include who submitted them, their reference to the solicitation section, and the specific paragraph and line of the contract in question.

All answers must be provided to all active bidders so that everyone has the same information. In addition, these answers must become part of the solicitation from which bidders will submit the final offer and, subsequently, part of the awarded contract.

ADVERTISING

Advertising or publishing a request for information (RFI) in trade journals, newspapers, or other industry publications expands exposure to potential bidders. Include in your advertising a project brief and an abbreviated statement of work to solicit information from potential sellers to meet your needs. In most government agencies, a buyer is required to publicly advertise pending government contracts.

INTERNET SEARCH

Many commodities can be obtained over the Internet for a firm fixed price. However, if the commodities are highly complex or are associated with high risk, you should not use the Internet because of the costs involved. What if the item wasn't what you thought you would get? You lose all of the time you spent obtaining the product and now have to do it again. As long as ordering the product does not involve any risk to the project, the Internet is a great place to order items.

Select the Seller

The process of selecting the seller involves determining the best-value contractors by considering price, schedule, technical issues, and other factors. The project manager works closely with the procurement officer (buyer) to evaluate proposals, review independent estimates, and score proposals against evaluation criteria.

INDEPENDENT ESTIMATES

In order to validate the reasonableness of proposals, your organization may choose to bring either in-house or external expertise to create their own independent estimate of the project. If there are major differences between the independent estimate and contractors' proposals, it may indicate that the statements of work were ambiguous or otherwise failed to consider all items necessary to complete a proposal.

PROPOSAL EVALUATION TECHNIQUES

There are several ways to evaluate a proposal. A *weighting system* is one method for quantifying qualitative data to minimize the effect of personal prejudice on source selection. Earlier you used a weighted scoring process when you were choosing one project over another. You can do the same thing to evaluate a proposal. There are four steps to this process:

1. Assign a numerical weight to each of the evaluation criteria.

2. Rate the prospective sellers in each criterion with a raw score.

3. Multiply the rate score by the weight given that proposal element.

4. Total the resultant products to compare an overall score.

Table 3.16 looks at weighted scores of vendors based on predetermined selection criteria.

TABLE 3.16 Choosing Vendors via a Scoring Model

Evaluation Criteria	Vendors						
	Raw Score				Weighted Score		
	A	B	C	Weight	A	B	C
Ability to Deliver Technology				5			
Financial Capacity				5			
Understanding Our Need				4			
Management Approach				3			
Life Cycle Costs				4			
Totals							

A *screening system* establishes minimum performance requirements for one or more of the evaluation criteria; for example, the buyer may want individuals to have specific credentials or companies to have specialized certifications, such as ISO 9000.

Another evaluation technique is the use of a *compliance matrix*, through which bidders indicate their ability to fulfill specific performance criteria or functionality.

Award Contract

Buyers and sellers usually start out with different goals. The buyer wants maximum value for minimal cost. The seller wants to provide the minimal value for the maximum amount possible. Procurement negotiations, if done well, enable both buyer and seller to reach a meeting of the minds so that both sides are pleased with the outcome. It starts with procurement negotiations.

PROCUREMENT NEGOTIATIONS

Henry Ford said it best, "If there is any secret to success, it lies in the ability to get the other person's point of view and see things from his angle as well as from your own."

Procurement negotiations are used to clarify and gain mutual agreement on the elements and requirements of the contract prior to signing the contract. Final contract language should include all terms and agreements that were negotiated. Planning for negotiations requires several steps:

Develop objectives.   If you are the buyer, what is the maximum you are willing to pay? If you are the seller, what is the minimum you are willing to accept?

Assess your opponent to see what motivates them.   Is your opponent interested in profitability, keeping people employed, developing a new technology, or wanting to use your name for future reference?

Describe your strategy and tactics.   Know before you begin what techniques you will use to swing your opponent to your point of view.

Assemble your facts.   Do your financial and other homework! Your opponents are doing their homework about you and your business, and will use these facts to their favor.

Conduct a complete price/cost analysis.   That way, you know what the contract items should cost before committing to a fee or type of contract.

Arrange the details of the negotiations.   Specify where the negotiations will occur, the type of table to be used (round or square), who will face the windows, and so on.

Project negotiation objectives are to obtain a fair and reasonable price while still getting the contract performed within certain time and performance limitations and developing a good relationship with the seller.

According to the *PMBOK® Guide, 4th ed.*, p. 332, negotiations are used to "clarify the structure, requirements, and other terms of the purchase so that mutual agreement can be reached prior to signing the contract." Final contract language reflects all agreements reached including, as per the *PMBOK® Guide, 4th ed.*, pp. 332–333:

- Responsibilities
- Authority to make changes
- Applicable terms and governing law
- Technical and business management approaches
- Proprietary rights

- Contract financing
- Technical solutions
- Overall schedule
- Payments
- Price

There are typically five stages of negotiation for project management:

Orientation   Introductions are made.

Exploring   Issues are searched and identified.

Bargaining and decision making   This is where bargaining occurs and concessions are made.

Resolution   The two positions are summed up, and final concessions are made and documented.

Closing   The ultimate goal; this ensures that both parties have identical agreement and marks the end of negotiations.

Planning ahead of time for the negotiations can minimize the negative aspects of negotiation. Remember, you are the buyer. The seller wants your business. You are in control.

Hands-on 3.13: Testing Your Knowledge of Conduct Procurements

1. What is the importance of a bidder's conference when obtaining seller responses?

2. When selecting a seller, what are the differences among a weighting system, a screening system, and a compliance matrix?

3. What research and preparations need to be made before contract negotiations begin? Why?

Scope-related contract components include the following:

Statements of work   The statement of work is a written document that includes the labor, materials, equipment, and services that are to be supplied by an outside contractor. The statement of work can be written internally or during a bid process; for example, the supplier can provide a contractual statement of work (CSOW).

Drawings   Drawings or pictorial portions of a contract show graphical depictions of a design(s) or dimensions of the work.

The following are cost-related contract components:

Contract sum   The contract sum is stated in the contract and is the total amount payable by the owner to the contractor for performance of the work defined under the contract.

Retention amount   This is a contractually stipulated amount, withheld by the owner from each progress payment, which gives the owner protection from incomplete or insufficient work. Issues related to the retention amount include the amount, duration, and release of funds.

Final payment   This is the owner's last payment to the contractor, upon the contractor's completion of the work, and includes any accrued retention amounts. Issues relative to the final payment are timing of the final payment, final inspections, and handling disputes over the final payment.

Liquidated damages   The owner reduces a contractor's fee if the project is not completed. This is usually a per diem amount and must be established in the contract before it can be enforced. Liquidated damages cannot be a penalty. Penalties will be enforced typically when balanced by a reward or incentive.

Schedule-related contract components include these:

Date of commencement   The date the work is established in the contract; this may require a work authorization to proceed.

Notice to proceed   Determines when the contractor may begin work and when the "clock starts" for billing.

Substantial completion   The stage in the progress of the work that is sufficiently complete in accordance with the contract documents so that the owner can occupy or utilize the work for its intended use.

Acceleration   The hastening of the work pace by the owner. Causes of acceleration may include increased scope without extension of time, owner-caused delays without extension of time, or decreased schedule.

Delays can be excusable, nonexcusable, or compensable:

- *Excusable delays* occur because of factors beyond the control of any party involved in the project (for example, inclement weather). The contractor may be afforded extra time without penalty but no additional money.

- *Nonexcusable delays* occur when the contractor fails to live up to contractual obligations. For example, if materials are not obtained in time or if there is insufficient labor, the contractor is due neither additional time nor money.

- *Compensable delays* are caused by the owner's failure to live up to contractual obligations—for example, the owner fails to provide access to a building. The contractor is due additional time and money.

Kerzner (8th ed., p. 817) explains that the two most common contract forms are completion contracts and term contracts:

Completion contracts   The contractor is required to deliver a definitive end product. Upon delivery and formal acceptance by the customer, the contract is considered complete and final payment can be made.

Term contracts   The contractor is required to deliver a "specific level of effort," not an end product. The effort is expressed in woman/man-days (months or years) over a specific period of time using specified personnel skill levels and facilities. When the contract effort is performed, the contractor is under no further obligation. Final payment is made, irrespective of what is actually accomplished technically.

CONTRACT APPROVALS

Most businesses and organizations have written policies and procedures that state who has the authority to sign a contract. Contracts still should be reviewed for contract language that fulfills the identified need for an end product or service.

The U.S. government typically uses compliance matrices to review their contracts. (These matrices are also used to choose vendors.) Table 3.17 is a modified version of the government's contract compliance matrix.

TABLE 3.17   Sample Contract Compliance Matrix

Clause	Item	Descriptions	Met or Not Met
Section A: Standard			
None	Solicitation, offer and award	Standard form used to award a contract.	**Met** ❑ **Not Met** ❑
Section B: Supplies or Services and Costs/Prices			
B.1	Service being acquired	States the nature of the work to be performed.	**Met** ❑ **Not Met** ❑
B.2	Estimated cost and fees	States that the estimated cost of the contract is \$_____ and the potential fee is \$_____.	**Met** ❑ **Not Met** ❑
B.3	Availability of funds	States that there are no funds available until the buyer states that funds are available and any action by the contractor before funds are available will not be reimbursed.	**Met** ❑ **Not Met** ❑
Section C: Description/Specification/Statement of Work			
C.1	General information	Sets forth the basic requirements under the contract.	**Met** ❑ **Not Met** ❑

TABLE 3.17 Sample Contract Compliance Matrix *(continued)*

Clause	Item	Descriptions	Met or Not Met
C.2	Statement of work	Sets forth specific requirements. See program/project plans for details available from the program/project manager.	**Met** ❑ **Not Met** ❑
C.3	Deliverables	Specifies deliverables the customer is expecting to see and due dates for each. Refer to the project plan.	**Met** ❑ **Not Met** ❑

Section D: Packaging and Marking

Clause	Item	Descriptions	Met or Not Met
D.1	General information	Requires use of standard commercial practices in packing and marking shipments.	**Met** ❑ **Not Met** ❑

Section E: Inspection of Services

Clause	Item	Descriptions	Met or Not Met
E.1	Inspection and cost reimbursement	Establishes the right of the buyer to inspect all services called for by the contract at all places and times.	**Met** ❑ **Not Met** ❑
E.2	Acceptance	Acceptance of all work is by the contracting officer or duly authorized representative.	**Met** ❑ **Not Met** ❑

Section F: Deliveries or Performance

Clause	Item	Descriptions	Met or Not Met
F.1	Term of contract	Establishes the contract term.	**Met** ❑ **Not Met** ❑
F.2	Option to extend the term of the contract	Allows the buyer to extend the term of the contract with 30 days notice as long as intent was communicated at least three months before expiration.	**Met** ❑ **Not Met** ❑
F.3	Stop work order	Establishes the buyer's right to issue a written order for the contractor to stop all or any part of the work under the contract. The contracting officer shall make an equitable adjustment (e.g., delivery schedule, estimated cost, fee, etc.) as appropriate.	

In summary, executing the project is like launching a rocket—you may have a few tough moments while it is being launched, but once it's in orbit, you can breathe a sigh of relief that you have put in place all that you need to set it on its planned course.

Now that the execution phase has started, monitoring and controlling (which you have been doing since early in the project) play the critical role of keeping the project on course.

Hands-on 3.14: Testing Your Knowledge of Contract Negotiation

Cimarron is participating in a contract negotiation with a clothing manufacturer that is certified by ISO 9000. They have agreed to reproduce the line of clothing for the Apples and Pears project that Cimarron's former outside manufacturer couldn't complete without making too many errors. Introductions have been created, but the potential manufacturer has already begun offering solutions in your meeting before the problem details have been discussed. They are so excited to get the business that they fail to realize they won't have the business until the contract is signed.

1. If you were a project manager, what would you do?

2. What should Cimarron's procurement officer do?

3. What are the next steps after introductions and issues are identified?

Phase 4

Monitoring and Controlling Process

The project is well underway now, and it is time to monitor the performance of the project against the master project management plan and to control changes that may occur by ensuring that those changes go through the change management process. It is here that you will monitor previously identified risk events and work closely with a contract administrator.

Controlling the project simply means keeping it on track. This may well be the most important work of the project; if the deviations are significant and not managed carefully, the objectives of the project may not be met.

Task 4.1: Monitoring and Controlling Project Work

As you can see by now, you have been interacting with the other project processes we discussed in the previous phases. The controlling phase has been going on since slightly after the project began. Although we cover this in a separate phase, all phases are iterative and thus need monitoring and control.

It is during the work of monitoring and controlling that you can see the progress of a project, which is determined by comparing the actual work results against the project plan. Visibility of project results provides a window of opportunity for you to provide corrective and preventive action as needed.

Scenario

The Apples and Pears project is well into the execution phase, and Carrie, the project manager, has actually been monitoring and controlling the work for a while. Now James Stevens, her sponsor, is asking for performance information relative to money. Carrie knows that the best way to prepare the report is to use the earned value technique because it shows the costs used as well as the costs associated with scheduled tasks that have not been performed according to the original schedule.

Carrie has decided to explain the process to her team members so they understand the implications to the project if they are late or over budget.

There haven't been any changes so far, but Carrie is prepared to use integrated change control when any changes occur.

Scope of Task

Duration

This task will last for the duration of the project.

Setup

None.

Caveat

None.

Procedure

In this task you will monitor and control changes, verify that deliverables have been completed and accepted, and monitor and control scope, schedule, cost, and quality.

Details

In order to verify that the project stays within the approved scope, cost, schedule, resources, and quality (we will discuss monitoring and controlling *risk* later in this task), you will collect data and report on the performance of the project. The reports should be in a consistent format; the data needs to be measured in regular intervals and include the status of the project, the progress of the project, and a forecast of future project events. If the project is "out of plan," you will have to establish preventive or corrective action to bring the project back on track.

The validity of the project status, progress, and forecasting is accomplished through integrated change control.

Additionally, this phase will cover verification of scope; scope, cost, and schedule control; earned value concepts; and quality control.

Integrated Change Control

Integrated change control is the process of managing changes to the project plan, project documents, and organizational process assets, as well as monitoring changes and seeing that the approval process is followed. Unmanaged changes will disrupt the flow of the project; the right hand will not know what the left hand is doing, and the project will be considered out of control.

Changes are inevitable. You know more now than you did when planning the project. To minimize the number of changes, make sure the questions in Table 4.1 are asked and answered by a responsible party before asking for a formal change request.

TABLE 4.1   Change Control Responsibilities

Questions	Answered By
Why is the change necessary?	Initiator
What is the cost of the change?	Initiator
Does the change improve quality?	Initiator
Is the additional cost for this quality justifiable?	Initiator
What risks are associated with this change?	Initiator and project manager
Are additional resources needed?	Project manager
What is the impact on the delivery date?	Project manager
What is the impact on the budget?	Project manager

Inevitably, some of the changes will be "nice to have" or "nice to do" but fall out of the original scope. If the initiator of the change is passionate about it, that person will provide the necessary details to justify the change. Remember, an approved change necessitates that you change the project plan, the schedule, the budget, and all other documents impacted by the change.

Hands-on 4.1: Testing Your Knowledge of Integrated Change Control

You have just received approval that a change is going to be made to the Apples and Pears project. It seems that when the furniture arrived for the two stores in Bellevue and Portland, the chairs were the wrong color and the love seats were actually full-size sofas. The procurement officer investigates and finds that if he reorders the furniture, delivery will take eight weeks but the stores are due to open in five weeks. He tries to expedite a new order, but it can't be done. The original order will be refunded. He decides to purchase the new furniture locally for an increased price of $5,000, which will come out of the management reserve fund.

1.   What project documents need to be changed to accommodate this change?

2.   Who needs to be notified of the change?

3. Answer the following questions based on this scenario:

    a. Why is the change necessary?

    b. What is the cost of the change?

    c. Does the change improve quality?

    d. Is the additional cost for this quality justifiable?

    e. What risks are associated with this change?

    f. Are additional resources needed?

    g. What is the impact on the delivery date?

    h. What is the impact on the budget?

Verification of Scope

When you verify scope, you are formalizing acceptance of project deliverables. Verification of scope provides an audit trail for changes made to the project. For example, if the deliverable isn't the same as was planned, there should be a change request that caused the deliverable to be different. Verification measures also help to make future decisions based on the outcomes of the deliverables associated with the scope of the project.

When deliverables are not accepted before the customer sees them, they are considered internal failures and require reworking, perhaps scrapping, and most important, a change in the project plan. The rework could cause schedule delays, cost overruns, and the like.

Hands-on 4.2: Testing Your Knowledge of Scope Verification

So far, the deliverables on the Apples and Pears project have been accepted because they were produced following the plan. A problem surfaced, however, in the switch room for telecom equipment at the home office. A new cooling system was put in place to control temperature and humidity. It was supposed to be installed without ducts to allow for free flow of air. When you arrived to inspect the new system, the noise was so high you couldn't hear yourself speak. You then noticed that the cooling system had been ducted. When asking the vendor why it was ducted, he said that he thought a mistake had been made when the plan called for open cooling and had taken it upon himself to "correct" the problem. He thought Cimarron would be pleased. This task is on the critical path.

1. What action would you take to fix this problem?

2. How should payment of the service be handled?

Scope Control

Scope control requires adjustments to cost, schedule, or other project objectives. Scope changes are iterative and require constant comparison to the original plan. They may require corrective action, must be documented, and may be severe enough to cause a baseline change. Any changes to scope must be integrated into the change control system put in place by your change control plan. A baseline change usually requires approval from the change control board. Work that affects the scope and is *not approved* falls under the term *scope creep*. Scope creep is deadly to the project. Failure to manage scope creep will cause unauthorized schedule delays and budget overruns.

Hands-on 4.3: Testing Your Knowledge of Controlling Project Scope

The Apples and Pears project has been moving along quite well, but in the third month of the project, Todd Franks called Carrie, the project manager, to hire a different construction superintendent in Bellevue. Todd Franks is unable to be at both sites at the same time and spends a lot of time and money traveling to both sites. The requested budget is $50,000 for this new hire, and Todd has agreed to interview the candidates.

Name the five steps needed for this change request to be processed.

Schedule Control

Schedule control is all about managing the schedule baseline. In Phase 2 you learned about fast-tracking and crashing a project to stay within the schedule baseline, but if schedule changes are approved, the schedule baseline changes. At every status meeting you should emphasize that the project needs to stay on schedule. For example, if someone tells you that they are one week behind on their task, you should be able to equate that week to money and say, "You are now $2,000 worth of work behind schedule. How will you be making that up?" (We will show you how to do this a little later in this task under the topic of "Earned Value.")

Hands-on 4.4: Testing Your Knowledge of Controlling the Project Schedule

You have been given the assignment to "work in" a new task. The task has been approved for cost, but the schedule date is cast in stone per upper management. The name of the new task is *review article*. You have been told the duration will be three days because many senior managers will want to review it. You have the network diagram shown in Figure 4.1.

FIGURE 4.1   Network diagram

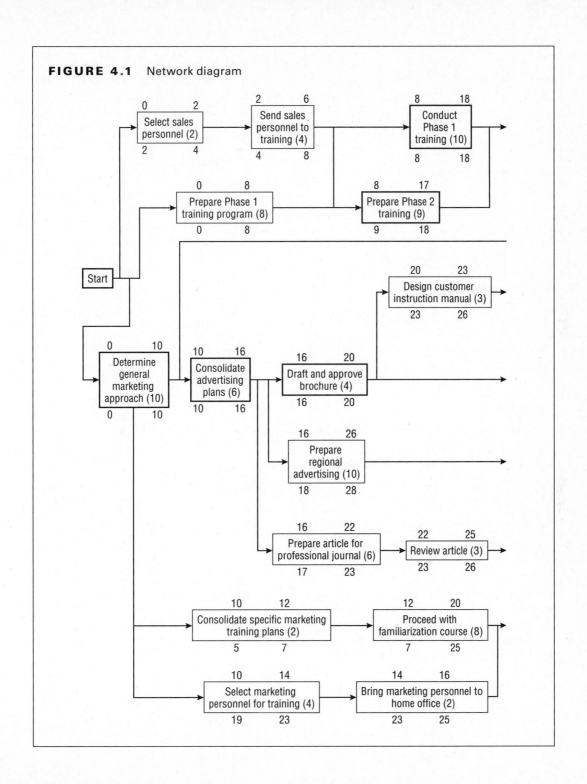

FIGURE 4.1   *(continued)*

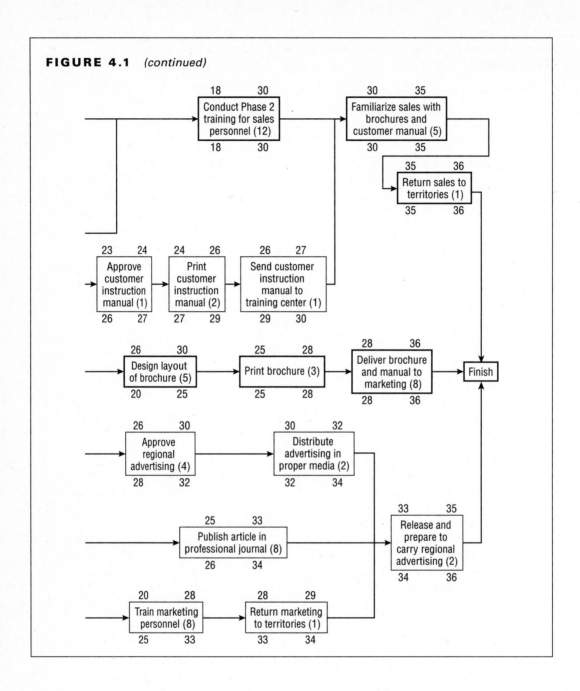

You decide that the review article task needs to come after "prepare article for professional journal" and before "publish article in professional journal."

1. What is the impact to the project?

2. What is the impact to the project if the task duration is 5 days?

3. What can you do to reduce the schedule risk?

4. Your client comes back to you and wants the project finished 5 days earlier than the 36 days previously planned. You decide to crash the project. How would you do this?

Cost Control

Keeping the budget under control can happen only if you know exactly where you stand on the budget. Elements affected by cost include the following:

- Controlling changes to the project budget
- Cost estimating
- Project cash flow
- Company cash flow
- Direct labor costing
- Overhead rate costing
- Others, such as incentives, penalties, profit-sharing, and the like

EARNED VALUE

Earned value is a technique that is very effective for looking at cost and scheduling elements. When you are collecting status from your team, someone might say to you, "I'm on track." What does that actually mean? Does that mean that you are scheduled to be working on week 5 and you are in week 5? If so, that is a good thing.

You may ask another person whether she completed her task this week as planned. She replies, "No, I didn't get to it this week but I will be able to finish it next week." Many new project managers would simply say, "OK" and slip the date out one week. It may be more helpful if your team members understood the impacts of allowing the schedule to slip and that it is not appropriate to just say, "I didn't get to it." For example, the schedule has two parameters:

- The actual scheduled time to perform the work
- The cost of the work that has been done or the cost of the work that has not been completed

Table 4.2 takes a closer look at earned value concepts.

TABLE 4.2   Earned Value Concepts

What Is It?	What Does It Mean?	Acronym	How to Calculate
Weeks to complete	How long will it take to complete at the rate we are going?	None	Determine percentage of tasks completed thus far to determine where you want to be.
Expense per week	What does this task cost this week?	None	Use whatever tool you are using to collect cost information.
Planned value (budgeted cost of work scheduled)	How much work should be done?	PV (BCWS)	Use planned figures.
Budgeted cost of work performed	How much work is done? (Task A, which was supposed to be completed last week was scheduled to cost $2,000. I am only 75% complete. Therefore, I have done $1,500 worth of work, which is my earned value.)	EV (BCWP)	Determine cost per week and compare where you want to be to where you are.
Actual cost of work performed	How much did the completed work cost?	AC (ACWP)	Use whatever tool you are using to collect actual cost information.
Cost variance	The difference between what the cost should be and what it actually is. ("I have completed $1,000 worth of work [EV], but it cost me $1,200 to do the task [AC]. It has cost me $200 more to do what I have done than was originally planned.)	CV	$EV - AC = CV$
Cost variance percentage	Cost variances that are converted to percentages.	CVP	$CV/EV \times 100 = CVP$
Cost performance index	How efficiently has the work been performed? CPI is often used to predict possible cost overruns. (I have performed $1,000 worth of work [EV]. It has cost me $1,100 to do so [AC]. Each dollar of scheduled work generated 90.9 cents worth of work, which is the cost performance index.)	CPI	$EV/AC = CPI$

TABLE 4.2   Earned Value Concepts *(continued)*

What Is It?	What Does It Mean?	Acronym	How to Calculate
Schedule variance	The difference between what the schedule should be and what it actually is. (As of today, I was supposed to have completed $1,000 worth of work [PV]. I have only done $900 worth of work [EV]. Therefore, I am behind schedule by $100 worth of work [SV].)	SV	EV – PV = SV
Schedule variance percentage	Schedule variances that are converted to percentages.	SVP	SV/PV × 100 = SVP
Schedule performance index	Used to measure the performance of the schedule. It is often used to predict possible schedule overruns. (I have done $1,000 worth of work [EV]. The value of the work scheduled [PV] is $750. Therefore, each dollar of scheduled work generated $1.33 worth of work, which is my schedule performance index.) This measures how efficiently the work is being performed.	SPI	EV/PV = SPI
Budget at completion	What was the total job supposed to cost? The sum of all budgets allocated to the project.	BAC	Total budget
Estimate at completion	What do we now expect the total job to cost? The sum of all direct and indirect costs to date plus the estimate of all work remaining.	EAC	AC + ETC = EAC
Estimate to complete	What is the expected remaining cost of an activity or group of activities in the project?	ETC	EAC – AC = ETC
Variance at completion	The difference between what the job was supposed to cost and what we now expect it to cost.	VAC	BAC – EAC = VAC

If you are planning to take the Project Manager Professional (PMP®) exam, you will need to know the earned value formulas. *Hint:* As soon as you sit for the exam, write your memorized formulas on a piece of scratch paper. That way, you won't get confused.

OVERHEAD

When planning the project in Phase 2, you learned about the cost of overhead or "burdened" labor rates. This is a reminder that your company will specify a percentage that includes an average of all labor plus benefits, pensions, and so on. In the absence of this information, it is appropriate to use 100% as overhead. For example, if the total labor budget is $250,000, you can add a line item on your budget equal to that amount and call it overhead.

Quality Control

In Phase 3 we discussed quality assurance tools such as flow charts, control charts, cost/benefit analysis, benchmarking, and so on. All of the quality control tools used in Phase 3 can be used in this phase as well. We are going to focus on cause-and-effect diagrams, histograms, Pareto charts, run charts, and scatter diagrams. Of course, it goes without saying that you will also use inspection techniques.

CAUSE-AND-EFFECT DIAGRAMS

Kaoru Ishikawa worked in the Kawasaki shipyards and pioneered the use of a performance measurement tool that could plot the cause and effect of a stated problem that results in a single output. Causes are arranged by level of importance or detail that result in a representation of relationships and hierarchy of events. Many call this tool the *Ishikawa diagram*, or the *fishbone diagram* or because it looks like a fish skeleton. Figure 4.2 represents a sample of a fishbone diagram.

Hands-on 4.5: Testing Your Knowledge of Earned Value

1. Consider the scenario shown in Table 4.3. As you can see, the work is linear with time but not linear with cost. One of your team member's tasks is planned to take five weeks. When you collect status, your team member advises you that he is only 60% complete and has spent $10,000 on that portion that has been completed. You were expecting a report that this particular task was 80% complete and that $8,000 had been spent (weeks 1–4). What is the earned value for this task?

TABLE 4.3 Earned Value Scenario

SCHEDULE COST	WEEK 1 (20%)	WEEK 2 (20%)	WEEK 3 (20%)	WEEK 4 (20%)	WEEK 5 (20%)
	$2,000	$1,000	$3,000	$2,000	$1,000

2. What is the status of this task?

3. Using your knowledge of earned value, record the formula you will use to calculate the earned value elements found in Table 4.4 and the rationale for your choice.

TABLE 4.4 Earned Value Worksheet

Earned Value Elements	What Does the Acronym Stand For?	Formula	Answer	Rationale
PV		None		
AC		None		
EV		None		
CV				
SV				
CPI				
SPI				
BAC				
ETC				
EAC				
VAC				

FIGURE 4.2 Fishbone diagram

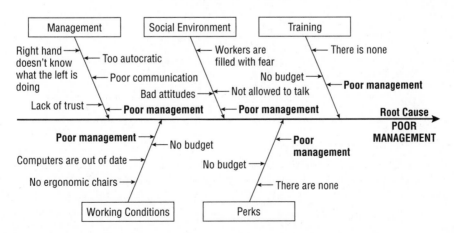

There are four steps to this process:

1. Identify the problem and identify the factors involved with the problem.
2. Draw the factors off a middle line so that each factor has its own "bone."
3. Identify possible causes by using the factors you described in step 2.
4. Analyze your diagram and use the "why" question until you get to the root cause of the problem.

HISTOGRAMS

Histograms are used to determine process capability at a snapshot in time. A *histogram* is a type of bar graph that shows how frequently something occurred. It looks like a bar graph, but there are no spaces between the bars. Without any space between the bars, you can see how the values relate to each other.

Suppose a pizza company wants to deliver pizzas in less than 30 minutes, 100% of the time. The first thing you must do is collect data on the subparts of the process, such as taking the order, making the pizza, and delivering it. Figure 4.3 is a histogram that shows that the current process is unable to deliver pizzas within 30 minutes (the average is 37.06 minutes).

FIGURE 4.3   Histogram sample

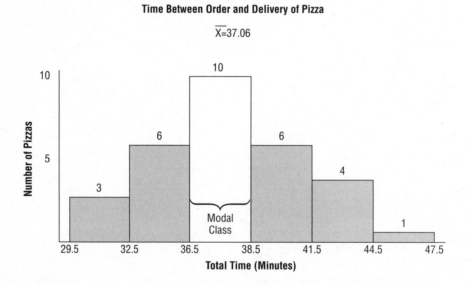

Time Between Order and Delivery of Pizza

$\overline{X}=37.06$

PARETO CHARTS

The Pareto diagram is named after Vilfredo Pareto, a 19th-century Italian economist who postulated that a large share of wealth was owned by a small percentage of the population. This basic principle translates well into quality problems — most quality problems result from a small number of causes. Joseph Juran, a noted quality expert, created a corollary to

Pareto's rule that says 80% of problems are caused by 20% of the potential sources. Quality experts today often refer to the principle as the 80/20 rule.

A *Pareto chart* (Figure 4.4) is a histogram, ordered by frequency of occurrence, that shows how many results were generated by type or category of identified cause. It places data in a hierarchical order from most occurrences to least occurrences, suggesting that the highest number of occurrences, if resolved, would produce the greatest improvement.

When seeking operational or process improvement project opportunities within an organization, this can be a helpful tool in deciding what to fix first. While the Pareto diagram will point to the biggest culprit of failed throughput, the other factor to consider is the cost of correcting that error. Although it can summarize all types of data, the Pareto analysis technique is used primarily to identify and evaluate nonconformities.

FIGURE 4.4   Pareto chart

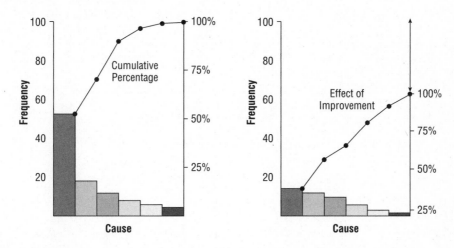

RUN CHARTS

A *run chart* looks very much like a control chart but without control limits; instead it has a target to compare the data with (the dashed line in Figure 4.5).

SCATTER DIAGRAMS

Scatter diagrams are another way that you can observe process control data. *Scatter diagrams* organize data by plotting independent vs. dependent data. The independent variables are plotted on the x-axis (horizontal), and the dependent variables on the y-axis (vertical). If a relationship or correlation can be found between the variables, it can be a predictor that if one variable changes, the other will also. It does not necessarily mean that a cause and effect is in place. Both parameters may be the effect of another independent or variable data set not included in your scatter diagram. Figure 4.6 shows a relationship between the independent variables and dependent variables.

FIGURE 4.5   Run chart

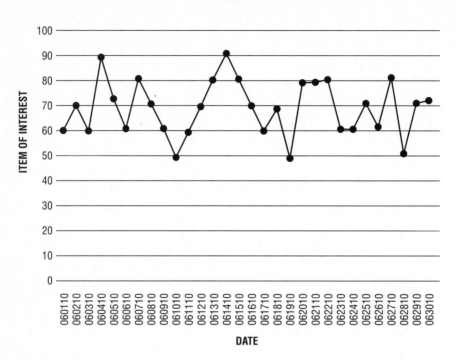

INSPECTIONS

Inspections include reviews, audits, and walk-throughs, among other things. You will want to be sure that you, team leaders, or technical specialists are measuring, examining, and testing results to see whether they conform to requirements. These inspections should be conducted at regular intervals and also at unscheduled times.

Hands-on 4.6   Testing Your Knowledge of Quality Tools

1.   What information can a fishbone diagram give you?

2.   A histogram is used for what purpose?

3.   What is a Pareto chart?

4.   What quality control tool is used when data are displayed on a graph that shows observed data in a time sequence in order to see the output or performance of a manufacturing or other business process?

5.   When should a scatter diagram be used?

FIGURE 4.6   Scatter diagram

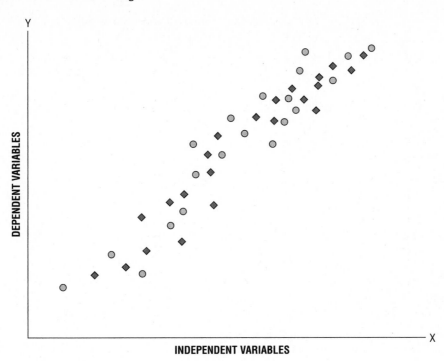

Performance Reporting

Performance reporting begins after the project has started and data can be collected. It is not useful to use earned value as a performance tool until the project has been on its way for a number of weeks or even months, depending on the planned duration of the project. You simply don't know as much at the beginning of a project, and variances can be quite large. When the variances are within 5% to 10% of the plan, earned value can be used to manage variances.

VARIANCE ANALYSIS AND FORECASTING

The variances in cost and schedule can readily be seen in Figure 4.7, which is called an *S-curve*. By analyzing the results relative to the baseline plan, estimates can be made of anticipated (forecasted) variations at completion. The CPI, SPI, ETC, EAC, and VAC are part of the earned value concepts we discussed earlier in this task and are valuable tools for monitoring, analyzing, and forecasting work performance.

FIGURE 4.7   S-curve

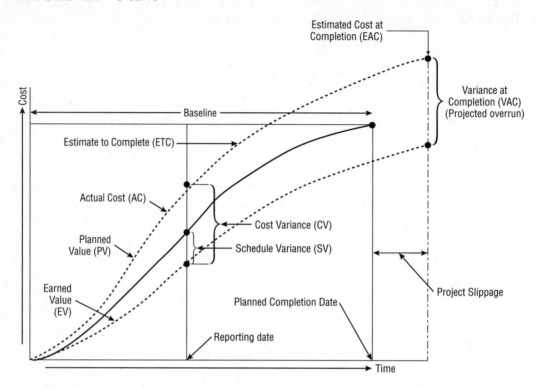

After you are fully comfortable with the earned value concept, you can begin to make useful interpretations of the data. Having said that, it is important *not* to rest on the numbers alone. You cannot make assumptions. For example, if the actual cost of a particular task was $5,000 and the planned value for that task was $3,000, you might assume that the task manager was out of control — but you might get a different response.

"I told you that I didn't have enough people, and you arbitrarily placed the date and budget on me. I had to pay overtime — we are lucky we accomplished what we did." Maybe, in response, you should be looking at more-realistic expectations.

The net is this: Do your homework. Ask the right questions, get the appropriate data, and you will be able to defend both the budget and the schedule brilliantly.

COMMUNICATING METHODS

You will be receiving information from many people, and it is your job to create performance reports that are sent to sponsors and senior management. These reports typically have cost data related to variances in the project due to budget, schedule, quality, and so on. Now is the time to use your communication plan.

Hands-on 4.7: Testing Your Knowledge of Performance Reporting

The Cimarron Construction Project

The Top Notch Construction Company has received a contractual order from Cimarron to build the new store located in Portland. The project started several months ago. Table 4.5 shows the monthly cost summary for May. Some of the entries in the table have been purposely omitted, but the following additional information is provided to help you answer the following questions:

- Assume that the overhead of 100% is fixed over the period of performance.

- The report you are given is at a month's end (May).

- The 80/20 sharing ratio says that the customer (that is, Cimarron) will pay 80% of the dollars above the target cost up to the ceiling cost, and Top Notch will be responsible for 20% of the overrun. If the cost is below the target, Cimarron will retain 80% of the underrun and Top Notch will receive 20% of the underrun.

- The ceiling price is based on cost (that is, without profit).

Answer the following questions by extracting data from Top Notch's monthly summary report shown in Table 4.5:

1. What is the total negotiated value of the contract?

2. What is the budgeted value for all work authorized under this contract?

3. What is the total budgetary amount that Cimarron had originally allocated/released to Top Notch?

4. What is the new/revised total budgetary amount that Cimarron has released to Top Notch?

5. How much money, if any, has Cimarron set aside as a management reserve based on the original released budget (burdened)?

6. Has the management reserve been revised, and if so, by how much (burdened)?

7. Which level-2 WBS elements make up the revised management reserve?

8. Based on the revised PV completion costs, how much profit can Top Notch expect to make on the Cimarron project? (Hint: Don't forget sharing ratio.)

9. How much of the distributed budget that has been identified for accomplishment of work is only indirectly attributed to this contract (that is, overhead)?

Answer the following questions for direct labor only:

10. Of the total direct effort budgeted on this contract, how much work did Top Notch *schedule* to be performed this month?

11. How much of the work scheduled for accomplishment this month was actually earned (that is, earned value)?

12. Did Top Notch do more or less work than planned for this month? How much was the schedule variance percentage (SVP)?

13. What did it actually cost Top Notch for the work performed this month?

14. What is the difference between the amount that Top Notch budgeted for the work performed this month and the actual cost (that is, CV)?

15. Which WBS level-2 elements are the primary causes for this month's cost and schedule variances?

16. How much cost variance has Top Notch experienced to date?

17. How much schedule variance has Top Notch experienced to date?

18. Is the cost variance improving or getting worse?

19. Is the schedule variance improving or getting worse?

20. Does it appear that the scheduled end date will be met?

21. What is the new estimated burdened cost at completion?

22. How much profitability/loss (variance at completion) can Top Notch expect from the new estimated cost at completion?

23. If Top Notch's final burdened cost for the program was $3,150,000, how much profit/ loss would they experience?

TABLE 4.5 Performance Reporting Data

Monthly Cost Summary: May

Contract:	Top Notch Construction	Negotiated Cost:	$2,500,000	Sharing Ratio:	80/20	Reporting Period:	May 1–May 31
Project Manager:	Eldred Moore	Target Fee:	12%	Ceiling Price:	$3,000,000	Contract Period:	Jan 1–Oct 31

Level 2 WBS Items	Current Month $$					Cumulative to Date $$					At Completion $$			
	PV	EV	AC	SV	CV	PV	EV	AC	SV	CV	Contracted PV	Original Released PV	Revised PV	Variance
Project Management	19,300	19,300	19,300	0	0	108,000	108,000	108,000	0	0	200,000	200,000	200,000	
Construction A	23,000	16,600	24,200	<6,400>	<7,600>	158,000	181,700	234,700	23,700	<53,000>	250,000	200,000	225,000	<25000>
Construction B	14,000	15,200	16,800	1,200	<1,600>	96,000	94,200	93,000	<1,800>	1,200	200,000	200,000	200,000	
Construction C	0	0	0	0	0	0	0	0	0	0	300,000	275,000	275,000	
Construction Support	11,600	10,400	12,000	<1,200>	<1,600>	73,000	74,300	75,600	1,300	<1,300>	200,000	190,000	190,000	
Quality Control	5,900	6,000	6,000	100	0	5,900	6,000	6,000	100	0	100,000	100,000	100,000	
Notes:														
Total Direct Overhead	73,800	67,500	78,300								1,250,000	1,165,000	1,190,000	
x100%	73,800	67,500	78,300								1,250,000	1,165,000	1,190,000	
TOTAL	147,600	135,000	156,600								2,500,000	2,330,000	2,380,000	

Task 4.2: Managing Risks

You identified risks in Phase 2. In this task risks that were previously identified may surface and new risks could occur. Fortunately, you have a risk management plan and know what you have to do when other risks occur.

Scenario

You have several balls in the air by this time, and one of the concerns you have is whether a project that is external to the A&P project could impact the grand opening on November 1. You have been brought into the picture along with Diana Featherston, the telecommunications manager, as well as Bud Bergstrom, the contracts manager, to discuss the situation.

Diana explained that Data Mentors Phone Company (DMPC) has just won the business of installing a new communication system for Cimarron Industries. Cimarron has decided to provide a new communications system for all of its organizations and link them together.

Currently, Cimarron is served by a 10-year-old system that has served its users well but it is not capable of providing the new services required for a progressive institution. The new system must have category 5 data lines, voice, LAN connectivity, and wireless telephones, to name a few features.

The new communications system for Cimarron is scheduled for conversion by October 15 according to the contract. The contract is very clear about missed dates, specifically the cutover. Cimarron wants the new system in and ready for use by October 31, two weeks after the cutover, so the users can get used to the new system in time for the completion of the A&P project.

Failure to meet the cutover date would result in liquidated damages of $1,000 per day for DMPC. Brendon Edwards, the experienced project manager for DMPC, just came from a meeting with Olivia Ross and Jim Stevens. Brendon explained that there was an extremely tight time frame for the implementation of the new system (that is, very little slack time in the schedule to offset unexpected delays). Brendon was advised to set up a meeting with Carrie MacIntyre, the project manager for the A&P project, and the telecommunications manager, Diana Featherston, as well as contract manager Bud Bergstrom to discuss some of the finer points of interest.

The meeting was typical for a first-time meeting. Brendon wanted to make sure that if there was a possibility of missing the October 15 cutover date, a two-week window would be available between the cutover and the "go live" date. Diana replied, "So that there is no misunderstanding, Brendon, the contract spells out a cutover date of October 15. We expect the system to be working flawlessly well before that time. We need you to provide us with an implementation plan and an analysis of the risks for this system conversion within the next few weeks. I must insist that this cutover to the new system is not, I repeat, not to jeopardize the October 15 date." With that said, Bud left the meeting to allow Diana, Carrie, and Brendon to continue their discussions.

Brendon knew the limitations all too well as a $1,000 per day penalty was included in the project. "Well, Carrie, the way I see it, to make the conversion date, there are some items that Cimarron must provide us. The date in our contract states that you will have an equipment room for us by June 1, so that we can begin installing the system. The date is very critical to us; if you do not meet it, the cutover date may be in jeopardy."

Diana thought about that and said, "You're right, Brendon, but remember, we don't have much leeway on that October 15 date. Everyone is geared to the October 15 date."

The contract had its bad points. It seemed that the only date that Cimarron had to meet was the equipment room to be ready by June 1. Anything else that they missed was not part of the bargain, but made it acceptable. However, if DMPC missed their dates, the penalties were high.

On May 23, Brendon was becoming frustrated about the promises of Cimarron's contractor to finish the equipment room. A special meeting was scheduled to discuss the problem.

"Diana, your contractor has not even started the job for you. I have been sending you messages regarding the criticality of completing the equipment room per your promise and our contract. I have put the project in jeopardy because of this situation. I need your help in making your contractor comply with the contract," stated Brendon.

"I passed that information along to Carrie, and she advised that the contractor was having difficulties obtaining a permit to remove the steam pipes overhead. Apparently there are some overhead water pipes that must be routed around the new room. He is being delayed by the city. The city must provide a permit before those pipes can be moved. It is some special city ordinance — no one knew about this, not even the contractor. We should have it in a few days, but you know how slow the city can be in these matters. I'm sure you understand," said Diana.

"Perhaps you could start placing your equipment, terminating the cable on the new frame, and so on. The contractor said he would have temporary electrical power, lighting, and the floors sealed, but he would have to work in the equipment room overhead and around you while your people are installing the equipment. The other items, such as air conditioning and proper power for your system, will not be available when you start. Can you work around this problem and still make the October 15 cut date?" Brendon was now becoming concerned about meeting that October cutover date.

Scope of Task

Duration

The duration is the length of the project.

Setup

None.

Caveat

None.

Procedure

In this task you will learn how to manage a risk event.

Details

Managing risks is something you will do throughout the life of the project. It should be a topic covered in every status meeting. Risks pop up unexpectedly, and you can't possibly predict what risks will surface at the beginning of the project. You need to manage them as soon as they occur — with help from your team, of course.

The first thing you have to do is document the risk event. Table 4.6 shows a sample of a risk event worksheet that can be used to manage the risk event. This table is using a qualitative approach to determine probability and impact.

After documenting the risk event, you will post it into your risk register and monitor it as appropriate for the type of risk it is (that is, risks that could jeopardize the objectives of the project should be monitored very closely).

Preventive and Corrective Action

You can't possibly identify all of the risk events that may occur at the planning stage of your project. Risks do occur during the execution phase and have to be controlled. When you are managing a risk event that was not previously identified, you may think of ways the risk could have been avoided. Preventive action should be documented as part of your lessons learned.

Corrective action is simply correcting the situation after it has been identified and updating your risk register to include the risk and what you did, to prevent it from happening again.

TABLE 4.6 Risk Event Worksheet

Risk Event Worksheet				
1. Risk				
Probability	Impact	Category	Risk Response	Comments
Very Low ☐ Low ☐ Medium ☐ High ☐ Very High ☐	Very Low ☐ Low ☐ Medium ☐ High ☐ Very High ☐	Technical ☐ Project Management ☐ Organizational ☐ External ☐	Avoid ☐ Transfer ☐ Mitigate ☐ Accept ☐	
2. Risk				
Probability	Impact	Category	Risk Response	Comments
Very Low ☐ Low ☐ Medium ☐ High ☐ Very High ☐	Very Low ☐ Low ☐ Medium ☐ High ☐ Very High ☐	Technical ☐ Project Management ☐ Organizational ☐ External ☐	Avoid ☐ Transfer ☐ Mitigate ☐ Accept ☐	
3. Risk				
Probability	Impact	Category	Risk Response	Comments
Very Low ☐ Low ☐ Medium ☐ High ☐ Very High ☐	Very Low ☐ Low ☐ Medium ☐ High ☐ Very High ☐	Technical ☐ Project Management ☐ Organizational ☐ External ☐	Avoid ☐ Transfer ☐ Mitigate ☐ Accept ☐	
4. Risk				
Probability	Impact	Category	Risk Response	Comments
Very Low ☐ Low ☐ Medium ☐ High ☐ Very High ☐	Very Low ☐ Low ☐ Medium ☐ High ☐ Very High ☐	Technical ☐ Project Management ☐ Organizational ☐ External ☐	Avoid ☐ Transfer ☐ Mitigate ☐ Accept ☐	

Hands-on 4.8: Testing Your Knowledge of Managing Risk

Using the scenario at the beginning of this task, answer the following questions:

1. Describe the risk events.

2. What corrective action would you suggest for Brendon to consider?

3. How does DMPC maintain equilibrium between Cimarron and the recommended mitigation strategy(s)?

4. What were the factors that produced the circumstances described in this task?

5. Which of these risk events could have been identified ahead of time?

6. What type of preventive action could Brendon have used to overcome these risk events if they had been identified?

Task 4.3: Administering Procurements

Contract administration is the process of ensuring that the company and project obtain the products and services from suppliers as specified in the contract as well as the seller ensuring they are paid as per terms negotiated. In other words, both parties will be responsible for monitoring the results of contract work for compliance with contract terms.

On the buyer side, this means the project manager, working with the contract manager, monitors contractor performance and ensures that all changes are processed as required by the change control process specified in the project plan, elements of which have been added to the contract.

Contract performance that deviates from contract requirements is addressed, and appropriate remedies, both administrative and legal, for nonperformance are applied as necessary.

Scenario

Carrie, the project manager from Cimarron, has been assigned a contract administrator, Riley Avalon. Riley, who also has training as a legal assistant, will assist Carrie on the Apples and Pears project. Riley has worked on many contracts and will be Carrie's team member representing procurements.

Scope of Task

Duration

The duration of this task begins at Phase 3 and finishes at the end of Phase 4.

Setup

None.

Caveat

None.

Procedure

In this task you will learn about the following:

- Duties of a contract administrator
- Claims administration
- Procurement performance reviews
- Inspections and audits
- Contractor performance report
- Records management system

Details

Knowledge and management of contracts usually reside with a contract administrator. Most organizations have contract administrators in either the legal department or procurement department. If this is the case for you, then you are in luck. Contract administrators will take away the stress of having to manage the contract yourself. Typically, they are trained in all aspects of managing contracts and are essential to your project team.

Duties of a Contractor Administrator

As you will soon see, your contract administrator will become your best friend. The contract administrator has many duties and partners with the project manager as needed to perform their functions. They have to have an understanding of legal perspectives associated with the contract as well. Let's explore the many duties of a contract administrator.

CONTRACT CHANGE CONTROL

Change is inevitable in a project, whether that change is related to contracted items or not. This process defines the types of items that could be affected by a contract change and utilizes the change control procedures identified in Phase 2. Table 4.7 describes the types of changes that could occur within a contract.

TABLE 4.7 Types of Contract Changes

Type of Change	Description
Administrative change	Change that does not affect project work, such as changing mailing addresses or telephone numbers
Change order	A written order, following change management processes and signed by the contracting officer, so that a seller can make a change
Incomplete contractual action	Work that has started before a final contract is complete
Supplemental agreement	A contract modification that has been agreed to between the buyer and seller
Constructive change (also known as directive change)	Changes to the contract that may include the following: • Incorrect direction of the buyer that results in an unacceptable product or service • Specifications that are impossible to achieve • Incorrect understanding of the contract • Overinspection • Failure by the buyer to disclose knowledge that changes the seller's work • Acceleration of performance • Late or unsuitable owner- or customer-furnished property • Misusing proprietary data

INTERPRETATION OF SPECIFICATIONS

The specifications for a project are included in contract documents and consist of written requirements for these elements:

- Materials
- Equipment
- Systems
- Standards
- Workmanship
- Performance of related services

The project manager, technical advisor, and/or contract administrator with knowledge of the defined specifications should monitor the project to be sure that specifications are achieved.

SUBCONTRACTOR MANAGEMENT

It is important to understand the relationships between the owner, a prime contractor, and subcontractors. The prime contractor has a two-way relationship with suppliers, a vertical two-way relationship with the project owner, and a downward two-way relationship with subcontractors.

It would be inappropriate, for example, for the project *owner* to engage in a work request with the *prime* contractor's *subcontractor*. The subcontractor's contract is with the prime contractor and not the owner.

Formal, written subcontract agreements are usually signed only after the prime contractor has been awarded the prime contract.

PRODUCTION SURVEILLANCE

Production surveillance is usually accomplished through performance reporting and typically includes the results of tests and inspections, as required in the contract or by laws, rules, regulations, and so on.

PAYMENT SYSTEM

There are two types of payments to which a contractor and buyer agree. One of them is *progress payments*, whereby payment is completed upon reaching certain progress parameters. The second is *completion payments*, which apply when a specified amount is withheld from a contractor until all contract items have been satisfied, including last-minute punchlist items. Progress schedules should be defined in the contract; whatever is agreed upon becomes part of the contract language.

You are charged with signing off on completion items so that your accounts payable department is confident that the work was completed as per the contract.

Claims Administration

There may be claims against the contract if the buyer and seller disagree on payments or other issues. Let's take a look at items that could be included in the contract that would minimize claim from a legal perspective.

BONDS

To avoid these legal claims, bonds and warranties may have been included in the contract. The parties involved in bonds include the following:

- Project owner, known as the *oblige*
- Contractor, known as the *principal*
- Bonding company, known as the *surety*

The owner must pay the premium on the bond. There are three types of bonds that might be used, for example, in a construction contract:

Bid bonds   These compensate the owner for the additional costs incurred because of the low bidder's failure to honor its bid. It is customary for public project owners to require bidders to submit a bid bond with their bid. Options to a bid bond include cash, a certified check, or an irrevocable letter of credit.

Performance bonds   These are legal instruments whereby a third party, usually a corporate surety, guarantees the project contractor's performance to the project owner.

Payment bonds   These offer security for unpaid subcontractors and suppliers. The purpose is to avoid liens against the owner's property.

WARRANTIES AND PRODUCT LIABILITY

Warranties apply to owners and sellers as follows:

Owner's implied warranty   Exists when the project owner extends an implied warranty to the general contractor that all documents relating to the project are accurate, complete, and legal. If they are not, the contractor is entitled to recovery of damages.

Contractor's warranty   There are three contractor warrantees:

- Materials/equipment will be of good quality and new unless otherwise permitted.
- Work will be free of defects not inherent in the quality permitted.
- Work will conform to requirements of the contract document.

WAIVERS

A *waiver* is the refusal to accept a legal right. In practice, everyone takes advantage of their rights at appropriate times; neglecting to do so is considered a waiver. In contracts, if, after knowledge of a supposed fraud, surprise, or mistake, a party performs the agreement in part, he or she will be considered as having waived any objections to fraud, surprise, or the like.

RESOLUTIONS OF DISPUTES

Several remedies are available to resolve disputes:

Dispute review board   A board of three experts is convened shortly after the contract award. Regular meetings are held, and the board's compensation is split between the owner and the contractor. The board makes recommendations, which may be accepted or rejected.

Mediation   Normally created by contract and uses an objective third party to facilitate an amicable resolution.

Binding arbitration   Is normally created by contract, and there may be one or three arbitrators. Courts will enforce their decisions; therefore it is *binding*.

Litigation   Uses a judge and jury in a court of law and/or administrative boards (state and federal agencies).

CONTRACT BREACH

A *contract breach* is a violation of an obligation, engagement, or duty to fulfill a contract. There are two types of contract breaches:

Material breach   A material breach involves one of the vital aspects of the agreement, such as the contractor failing to appear on the job site for an extended period of time.

Immaterial breach   Involves a less important aspect of the agreement, such as a contractor failing to clean up the job site at the end the day.

The following types of legal action can be taken for a breach of contract:

- Excuse the breach.

- Rescind the contract — the nonbreaching party elects to rescind the contract (that is, the contract no longer has any legal force or effect).

- Terminate the contract for default and sue for damages (materials and goods, but not labor).

CONTRACT TERMINATION

There are legal ways to terminate a contract.

A buyer can *terminate for convenience* anytime. Possible reasons for termination for convenience include:

- Requirement is eliminated.

- Technical obsolescence.

- Budget can no longer support the project.

If a contract is terminated for convenience, the seller is paid for all work completed and accepted by the buyer including preparation time and money.

When a contract is *terminated for default*, that is, the seller did not perform the work of the contract as stated in the contract, the contractor may not be entitled to payment for work in progress but not yet accepted by the customer. The buyer, depending on the situation, may be entitled to repayment of any payments made to date on the unaccepted work.

Hands-on 4.9: Testing Your Knowledge of Contract Changes

Name the type of change associated with the following descriptions:

1. Changes to the contract that may include these elements:

- Incorrect direction of the buyer that results in an unacceptable product or service

- Specifications that are impossible to achieve

- Incorrect understanding of the contract

- Overinspection

- Failure by the buyer to disclose knowledge that changes the seller's work

- Acceleration of performance

- Late or unsuitable owner- or customer-furnished property

- Misusing proprietary data

2. A written order, following change management processes and signed by the contracting officer, so that a seller can make a change

3. Work that has started before a final contract is complete

4. Change that does not affect project work, such as changing mailing addresses or telephone numbers

5. A contract modification agreed to by the buyer and seller

Hands-on 4.10: Testing Your Knowledge of Legal Contract Issues

1. What is the difference between a material and an immaterial breach of contract?

2. Describe termination of a contract for convenience.

3. What is the difference between mediation and binding arbitration?

4. Under what conditions can you terminate a contract for default?

5. Name the three warranties that a seller should provide.

6. What is a surety bond?

Procurement Performance Reviews

The essence of procurement performance reviews is to make sure that all procurement items are following the procurement plan. The objective of the reviews is to determine whether the contractor is following the contracted statement of work (CSOW) and if not, according to the *PMBOK® Guide*, 4th ed., p. 339, "allows the buyer to quantify the seller's demonstrated ability or inability to perform work."

Items may be identified that do not comply and become part of a *punch list*, which is a list of all corrections that need to be completed before final payment is made.

To assist with the review relative to the contractor's progress (as stated in the contract), the contract administrator or you (if you don't have one) should ask these questions:

- Who will review the seller's documentation?

- Is the work completed within scope?

- Does the work completed comply with stated quality parameters?

- Will a quality audit be necessary?
- Is the project within budget and on schedule?
- Will a buyer inspection be needed?

You may use status meetings with your contractors to collect some of this information.

 It is not always wise to have contractors in the same status meetings as your internal team members. Many things are discussed in these meetings that contractors do not need to know.

Inspections and Audits

Inspections and audits can be required by the buyer and supported by the seller if they were included in the contract. If they were not included in the contract, they could be misconstrued as overinspection of work. These inspections can be conducted by buyer procurement personnel and others named in the contract.

Contractor Performance Report

During this phase you report on the performance of the contractor to determine whether the contractor is meeting the needs of the project according to the contract. You want to identify strengths and weaknesses of the entire owner-contractor relationship. Table 4.8 is a mid-project performance review of your contractor, vendor, or supplier. If the vendor fails any question with an "Almost Met" or "Not Met" answer, corrections are in order.

Records Management System

All records are the responsibility of the project manager, who must use corporate policies, standards, and guidelines to manage procurements records. A records management system should be a part of your project management information system (PMIS) that allows for retrieval of all contracts and associated correspondence and documentation.

TABLE 4.8 Contractor Performance Report

	Please respond with a grade from A to F or N/A to the following statements.	A	B	C	D	F	N/A
1	Does the vendor/contractor keep you informed of project status in a timely manner?						
2	Does the vendor/contractor offer alternative recommendations for any requests that could not be granted?						
3	Does the vendor/contractor provide an impact analysis of time, cost, or performance for client-initiated scope changes?						
4	Does the vendor/contractor maintain strong leadership and control of the project?						
5	Does the vendor/contractor maintain a positive and supportive attitude and set an example of flexibility?						
6	Does the vendor/contractor ensure timely monitoring and follow-up of project objectives and milestones?						
7	Does the vendor/contractor use effective escalation procedures?						
8	Did the vendor/contractor provide timely and appropriate documentation to you?						
9	Did the vendor/contractor protect proprietary information?						
10	Did the vendor/contractor present a competent and professional image?						
11	Did the vendor/contractor reflect strong interpersonal skills?						
12	Did the vendor/contractor display acceptable technical knowledge of the products and services that were managed in this project?						

Phase

5

Closing Process

There are many reasons why projects close. They can close because they become an ongoing operation or lack funds and resources. The need for the project may have gone away because of technological advances, or the project may simply become extinct because it is completed and accepted by all stakeholders. The Apples and Pears project is coming to a close because it is almost finished. There are a few things left to do, however.

You want to be sure that all work has been completed and accepted by the customer. The closing phase consists of the following:

Project closure   Finalize all activities across all of the project process groups to formally close the project or a project phase.

Contract closure   Complete and settle each contract, including the resolution of any open items.

Task 5.1: Formalizing Project Acceptance

It has been said that no project is 100% complete. That may be true on IT projects to some degree and also for research and development (R&D) projects. R&D projects continue as long as they are funded or finally obtain the intended result; but most projects have a formal project acceptance and closure process. This task also applies to end-of-phase reviews as well. Why wait until the end of the project to verify deliverables or to provide feedback to your team and client?

Scenario

The project is just about over. All issues have been resolved, and the Apples and Pears stores will be ready to open by November 1 as planned. Carrie, the project manager, knows that even if the work is done, some things still have to happen before she can formally close out the project, such as formal acceptance by the customer, closing out the contract, and record keeping.

Scope of Task

Duration

This task occurs throughout the project, but most of the activities will be performed after the monitoring and controlling phase, through the end of the closure phase.

Setup

None.

Caveat

None.

Procedure

In this task you will learn how to obtain acceptance from the customer.

Details

It is time to obtain signed acceptance from the customer. A formal acceptance document (see Table 5.1) officially records the results of reviews, inspections, and tests conducted throughout the project to validate that deliverables meet acceptance criteria. The product as a whole receives final acceptance upon project completion. This final acceptance comes from the customer and the organizations that will use and support the product.

Acknowledgement That Objectives Are Met

When the objectives have been met, you need to get acknowledgement from the customer and others to officially end the project. This acknowledgement may be formal acceptance, usually the signing of an acceptance document (sign-off), or it may come in a more informal way, such as when the customer pays for the product and uses it over a period of time.

Product Acceptance

Acceptance should be based on an evaluation of the product using acceptance criteria set during the early phases of the project. You set requirements when the project began, and those have to be met for the product to be accepted. Testing the product against the acceptance criteria validates it.

Nonacceptance of the Product

At this stage of the project, you shouldn't have any deliverables that are not acceptable. You have been monitoring and controlling the progress of deliverables since the execution phase started. You cannot expect the client to accept anything that is not complete or correct.

If you find that the deliverables are incomplete or not correct, penalties may be assessed for noncompletion (if spelled out in the contract) and final payment to the contractor may be withheld.

Operations Turnover

Those products that have a long life may require manufacturing, ongoing maintenance, ongoing support, and/or ongoing operational use. Turning the product over requires that training, documentation, and initial support activities be part of the project deliverables.

It is important to plan for the turnover. A meeting should be held to discuss knowledge transfer and documentation transfer as well as the physical product or service. Be sure that the people with the right skills are available and that those who will take responsibility for the product are in attendance.

A formal document should be signed by the operations manager and the project manager acknowledging transfer and control. Table 5.2 is a sample of a formal transfer document.

TABLE 5.1   Deliverable Acceptance Document

Deliverable Acceptance					
Date		Project #		Project Name	
Sponsor				Telephone #	
Project Manager				Telephone #	
Description of Deliverable					
Acceptance Criteria					
Reviews, Inspections, and Test Results (Attach supporting documents.)					
Business, Operations, and/or Support Areas Involved					
☐ Support Desk			☐ Operations		
☐ Sales			☐ Management		
☐ Users			☐ Others		
Accepted By					
Sponsor			Date		
External Customer			Date		
Internal Customer			Date		
For Project Office Use Only					

TABLE 5.2   Formal Product Transfer to Operations

Formal Product Transfer to Operations			
Project Name		Project Completion Date	
Project Manager			
Name of Product or Service	<Describe the service being turned over.>		
Operations Owner Signature		Turnover Date	
Project Manager Signature		Turnover Date	
Name of Product or Service	<Describe the service being turned over.>		
Operations Owner Signature		Turnover Date	
Project Manager Signature		Turnover Date	
Name of Product or Service	<Describe the service being turned over.>		
Operations Owner Signature		Turnover Date	
Project Manager Signature		Turnover Date	
Name of Product or Service	<Describe the service being turned over.>		
Operations Owner Signature		Turnover Date	
Project Manager Signature		Turnover Date	
Name of Product or Service	<Describe the service being turned over.>		
Operations Owner Signature		Turnover Date	
Project Manager Signature		Turnover Date	

Hands-on 5.1: Testing Your Knowledge of Project Acceptance

1. What happens when a deliverable is not accepted?

2. Can the contract be closed out if a deliverable is not accepted? Why or why not?

3. A service representative works the help desk in her IT department. She receives a call concerning a new product that was just released. She has never heard of the product. What has happened?

4. What can happen to the product or service if it cannot be maintained?

Task 5.2: Performing Personnel Performance Reviews

Performance reviews are a critical part of personal development, yours as well as the team's. Most of the project personnel have come and gone, and vendors may have come and gone, but you have been managing the project from beginning to end. You want to be sure that you provide performance feedback for your team members and are willing to receive feedback from them.

Scenario

Most of the team members have left the project, and you are ready to provide feedback to their managers about their performance on your project. This will be easy because the hard work is already done. At the beginning of the project, you shared with your team what items they would be measured on and spent time at regular intervals with each of them to share their strengths and weaknesses.

Scope of Task

Duration

This task starts soon after the project starts, and ends soon after the project is complete.

Setup

None.

Caveat

None.

Procedure

In this task you will learn about the following:

- Providing team performance reviews
- Your team's performance review of you, the project manager
- Buyers' evaluations of sellers

Details

Providing feedback on team and project manager performance is essential. Even though your team members may not directly report to you, you must provide their managers with feedback on their performance on your project so the managers will have the information necessary to write an appraisal on their direct report.

If you are in a projectized organization, you would, of course, write an appraisal rather than just provide feedback because the team members would be your direct reports.

You should also provide feedback throughout the life of the project or anytime a team member has completed a task and left the project. Many times lessons learned are conducted only at the end of the project, and the team members who have left the project are forgotten.

Project managers also need feedback on their performance. A project manager's boss needs the input from those who interacted with the project manager so that an accurate assessment of their performance can be documented on their appraisal.

Provide Feedback on the Team's Performance

Table 5.3 represents a sample of feedback from the project manager to a team member. Because many of the questions are subjective, you must be specific with the feedback if the score was below or above a C.

Some project managers take the easy way out and only provide a C, or average, rating to their team. However, you have been working with your team for weeks or months, and it is vital that you spend the extra time documenting above-average or superior performance with specific examples. The same is true for below-average performance, though if performance was poor, the project manager should have handled the performance issue during the project.

Provide Feedback on the Project Manager's Performance

One of the most useful tools you will use is feedback on yourself as the project manager. Ask your team, sponsor, and customer to be candid and truthful with the feedback they provide because it is important for your personal development as a project manager. Take the feedback graciously and be honest with yourself about the improvements you need to make. Table 5.4 is a sample of a project manager's performance review.

Your manager will also want to write an appraisal of you. Although you have received feedback from your team, your manager may be appraising other things, such as feedback from vendors, other internal personnel, and those external to the project.

Provide Feedback on the Seller's Performance

Most organizations have a *preferred vendor list*, consisting of vendors who have proved themselves to you in the past. But as everything else changes, so do your vendor organizations. There may be new ownership or new leadership or a myriad of other changes that could affect the quality of their previous performance. A vendor evaluation should be provided to your procurement department so they can see whether this vendor should continue to be on the preferred list. Table 5.5 is a sample vendor evaluation questionnaire you may consider using.

TABLE 5.3   Team Member Performance Report

Team Member Performance Report						
Name of Project						
Project End Date						
Project Manager						
Please respond with a grade from A to F or N/A to the following statements. My team member:	A	B	C	D	F	N/A
Was punctual at meetings and conference calls.						
Met quantitative and qualitative commitments.						
Participated with high energy and a good attitude.						
Reported status in a timely manner as agreed.						
Was supportive and respectful of team members and others.						
Was willing to accept responsibility and accountability.						
Solved conflicts without alienating others.						
Accepted challenges cheerfully.						
Displayed a total commitment to the project.						
Applied technical judgment when necessary.						
Communicated effectively with other team members, the project manager, and others associated with the project.						
Set an example of flexibility.						
Used timely, effective escalation procedures.						
Met individual project objectives and milestones.						
Was an honest steward of time and expenses.						
Added value to the project.						

TABLE 5.4 Project Manager Performance Review

Project Manager Performance Review						
Name of Project						
Project End Date						
Name (Optional)						
Please respond with a grade from A to F or N/A to the following statements. My team member:	A	B	C	D	F	N/A
Displayed a total commitment to the project.						
Clearly defined team member roles and responsibilities and held them accountable.						
Met due date commitments or provided the best possible alternative if the original due date could not be met.						
Communicated customer/project goals to all team members and kept them involved.						
Maintained strong leadership and support of the project team; set an example of flexibility.						
Effectively utilized project management tools when applicable (e.g., network diagrams and Gantt charts).						
Ensured timely monitoring and follow-up of project objectives and milestones.						
Used timely, effective escalation to ensure customer satisfaction.						
Conducted timely project meetings and conference calls with team members; had control of meetings.						
Negotiated and published project plans.						
Provided on-site support or was otherwise available.						
Added value to the project.						
Had good knowledge of products and services involved in the project.						
Conducted a post-project evaluation and provided feedback on successes or suggestions for improvement.						
Was courteous and professional.						
Comments:						

TABLE 5.5 Sample Vendor Evaluation

	SELLER EVALUATION		
Project Name		**Project End Date**	
Project Manager		**Date**	
#	**Questions**	**Yes or No**	**Why or Why Not?**
1	Did the vendor/contractor display a total understanding and commitment to the project?	☐ Yes ☐ No	
2	Did the vendor/contractor keep you informed of project status in a timely manner?	☐ Yes ☐ No	
3	Did the vendor/contractor offer alternative recommendations for any requests that could not be granted?	☐ Yes ☐ No	
4	Did the vendor/contractor provide an impact analysis of time, cost, or performance for client-initiated scope changes?	☐ Yes ☐ No	
5	If the vendor/contractor was also the project manager, did the vendor/contractor maintain strong leadership and control of the project?	☐ Yes ☐ No	
6	Did the vendor/contractor ensure timely monitoring and follow-up of project objectives and milestones?	☐ Yes ☐ No	
7	Did the vendor/contractor use effective escalation procedures?	☐ Yes ☐ No	
8	Did the vendor/contractor provide timely and appropriate documentation for you?	☐ Yes ☐ No	
9	Was a post-project assessment meeting conducted with the client?	☐ Yes ☐ No	
10	Did the vendor/contractor protect proprietary information?	☐ Yes ☐ No	

TABLE 5.5 Sample Vendor Evaluation *(continued)*

11	Did the vendor/contractor present a competent and professional image?	☐ Yes ☐ No	
12	Did the vendor/contractor reflect strong interpersonal skills?	☐ Yes ☐ No	
13	Did the vendor/contractor display acceptable technical knowledge of the products and services that were managed in this project?	☐ Yes ☐ No	
14	Were appropriate vendors/contractors identified?	☐ Yes ☐ No	
15	Did the vendor/contractor provide an adequate description of products and services they were to provide?	☐ Yes ☐ No	
16	Were roles and responsibilities understood among vendors/contractors?	☐ Yes ☐ No	
17	Was the vendor/contractor aware of the criteria for evaluation? (product acceptance criteria)?	☐ Yes ☐ No	
18	Was the vendor/contractor made aware of actual costs vs. expected costs?	☐ Yes ☐ No	
19	Did the vendor/contractor adhere to the schedule?	☐ Yes ☐ No	
20	Was the vendor/contractor cooperative?	☐ Yes ☐ No	
21	Did the vendor/contractor maintain a positive and supportive attitude and set an example of flexibility?	☐ Yes ☐ No	
22	Were any specific problems or issues attributable to the vendor/contractor?	☐ Yes ☐ No	
23	Would you recommend the vendor/contractor used on this project for future projects?	☐ Yes ☐ No	

Hands-on 5.2: Testing Your Knowledge of Performance Reviews

1. Why should the project manager write a performance review of team members when feedback has been provided to the team members since the project began?

2. What should you do if you are uncomfortable providing less-than-satisfactory feedback?

3. Is it appropriate to ask your team members to write their own performance reports?

Task 5.3: Obtaining Contract Closure

Closing a contract includes the formal acceptance of the product, service, or result purchased and agreement that the contract has met all line items.

Scenario

Carrie, the project manager for Cimarron, has just completed a walk-through with Todd, the superintendent of construction at the Apples and Pears store in Portland. The vision has for the most part become a reality, but several items are not totally completed. Todd has prepared a *punch list* (a list of all items not completed) and has reviewed this list with the contractor. The contractor advises he will have it done in a few days.

Scope of Task

Duration

This task starts as soon as contract items are completed and could last for the duration of the project.

Setup

None.

Caveat

None.

Procedure

In this task you will learn how to close out a contract.

Details

Most of the time a procurement officer and someone in the legal department actually close out the project, but they need information from you as the project manager. Procurement personnel want to know that all contract line items are fulfilled so that final payments can be made, and that a contractor closeout letter has been sent to the contractor.

Contract Closeout Template

It's difficult to remember everything that has to be done during this phase, so using a template will guide you through the process of closing out a contract. Table 5.6 is a sample of a contract closeout template you may wish to use. This table contains some elements of the government process for closing out a contract.

Contract Closeout Letter to Contractor

Figure 5.1 represents a memorandum that can be used to formally acknowledge that the contract has been closed. This memo should be sent to each vendor, contractor, or seller that has a negotiated contract. Your procurement department typically has a letter such as this and will send it out, but if you don't, this will suffice.

Hands-on 5.3: Testing Your Knowledge of Contract Closure

1. In the scenario at the beginning of this task, the contractor has still not returned to finish up the punch list. The store will open on November 1, whether the items are fixed or not. Should Carrie close out the contract? After all, the items are just little things. Why or why not?

2. If the contractor never returns, what should you do?

TABLE 5.6　Contract Closeout Template

Contract Closeout Template					
Contract #		**Last Modification # and Date**		**Contract Amount**	
Task			**Completed: Yes or No**	**If Not, Why Not?**	
1. Does the contract file contain an executed copy of the contract, negotiation background data, appropriate determinations, and all required documentation?			☐ Yes ☐ No		
2. Have all contract changes been formalized, and does the file contain executed copies of the related modifications with appropriate backup information?			☐ Yes ☐ No		
3. Does the contract file contain copies of all applicable delegations of authority to administer the contract?			☐ Yes ☐ No		
4. Have all financial matters been resolved (disputes, liabilities, credits, or refunds, etc.)?			☐ Yes ☐ No		
5. Does the file include adequate documentation to evidence receipt, inspection, and acceptance of all deliverables?			☐ Yes ☐ No		
6. Have all reports required under clauses been received? 　a. Reporting of royalties 　b. Notice and assistance regarding patent and copyright infringement 　c. Patent rights			☐ Yes ☐ No		
7. Have security items been retrieved, such as badges and building access entry?			☐ Yes ☐ No		
8. Has equipment been returned, such as laptops and printers?			☐ Yes ☐ No		
9. Has there been a closeout meeting with the supplier?			☐ Yes ☐ No		
10. Has the supplier performance evaluation been sent to the contract administrator?			☐ Yes ☐ No		
11. Has a final invoice for this supplier been sent to accounting?			☐ Yes ☐ No		
12. Have lessons learned been documented for this supplier?			☐ Yes ☐ No		
13. Have all unused funds been closed from financial systems?			☐ Yes ☐ No		
14. Have all other outstanding actions been taken and adequately documented in the file?			☐ Yes ☐ No		

FIGURE 5.1   Sample project closeout letter

MEMORANDUM TO: <Name of contractor>

FROM: Procurement officer

DATE: <Insert date>

SUBJECT: Formal contract closeout letter

Section I

    1. The contractor has completed the required deliveries and/or performed all services, and the client has inspected and accepted the deliverables and/or services.

    2. Below is <your company> information:

       Contractor Administration Office Name   _____

       Contractor administration address   _____

                                                _____

    3. Below is <contractor> information:

       Contractor name   _____

       Contractor address   _____

                                      _____

Section II

    1. Dollar amount of excess funds, if any.

    2. Voucher number and date, if final payment has been made, or invoice number and date, if the final approved invoice has been forwarded to contract administration.

    3. All required contract administration actions have been fully and satisfactorily accomplished (see Section III).

    Name of contracting officer _____

    Signature _____ Date _____

Section III

    The following requirements have been met for closure of the subject contract:

    1. Disposition of confidential or proprietary material is completed.

    2. Final patent report is cleared.

    3. Final royalty report is cleared.

    4. There is no outstanding value engineering proposal.

    5. All interim or disallowed costs are settled.

    6. Price revision is completed.

    7. Subcontracts are settled by the prime contractor.

    8. Prior year indirect cost rates are settled.

    9. Contract audit is completed.

    10. Contractor's closing statement is completed.

    11. Contractor's final invoice has been submitted.

    12. Contractor's closing statement is completed.

    13. Contractor's final invoice has been submitted.

Task 5.4: Understanding the Lessons Learned

On a project of any size, there will be lessons learned. There is no value to these lessons, however, if they are not heeded or if they are simply documented and filed away.

Scenario

Carrie, the project manager at Cimarron, has been capturing lessons learned throughout the project and is preparing the lessons learned thus far. She has prepared a document that she will send to team members ahead of her lessons-learned meeting so the team can ponder the questions prior to the meeting. She has monitored corrective and preventive actions, and her team is well versed on lessons learned because Carrie and her team have held lessons-learned meetings after each phase as well as after challenges have been overcome. Carrie is now about to conduct the lessons-learned meeting for the project and is going to use a template so she does not forget anything.

Scope of Task

Duration

This task is performed throughout the life of the project.

Setup

None.

Caveat

None.

Procedure

In this task you will learn how to determine and document lessons learned.

Details

Lessons learned are also referred to as a *post-project assessment* and are meant to be a learning tool. The lessons learned are simply that—a means for learning from issues, challenges, and successes. This learning should not be limited to the current project team members but should include anyone who will work on projects in the future, provided the lessons are archived appropriately.

The purpose of a post-project assessment is to assess product, project, and contract acceptance. The assessment can be conducted by independent evaluators or by the project team.

Independent Evaluators

When a very large project is complete, it is recommended that a third party or parties not connected with the project conduct the evaluation. The evaluators should have access to people with the technical and business expertise needed to evaluate the various aspects of the project and the product.

Project Team Reviews

If an external review is not conducted, the project team itself can perform the review because they most likely have all project records available to them and have been intimately involved throughout the project. It is important to remember to invite team members who have left the project, not just those who remain at the end.

Planning for the Review

A post-project review requires some planning; unless the project is quite small, you may not be able to be conduct it in one meeting. The following represents what needs to be done to prepare for the final evaluation:

- Review the project files.
- Conduct interviews.
- Gather and analyze data.
- Review client/user acceptance.
- Evaluate realized costs, benefits, operational efficiency, and product performance—this may not be known until a product has been in the marketplace for a while and can produce measurable results.
- Measure operating efficiency and product performance.
- Evaluate the technical approach.
- Evaluate training and documentation provided to external customers and internal clients.
- Evaluate relationships and communications.
- Evaluate vendors and vendor-provided products.
- Verify attainment of project goals.
- Measure the success of quality improvement.
- Evaluate work efforts.
- Recommend changes to standards and procedures.

Evaluation Review Questions

Table 5.7 represents project evaluation review questions to assist you in preparing your lessons learned.

TABLE 5.7 Project Evaluation Review Questions

	PROJECT EVALUATION REVIEW QUESTIONS		
Name of Project		**Project End Date**	
Name of Evaluator		**Date**	
#	**Questions**	**Yes or No**	**Why or Why Not?**
1	Were project expectations well managed, defined, and met?	☐ Yes ☐ No	
2	Were products thoroughly analyzed and acceptance criteria clearly stated?	☐ Yes ☐ No	
3	Were meetings and reviews well organized?	☐ Yes ☐ No	
4	Were project phases well planned?	☐ Yes ☐ No	
5	Were checkpoints adequate for control?	☐ Yes ☐ No	
6	Were the roles and responsibilities of all project participants clearly defined?	☐ Yes ☐ No	
7	Was the project schedule well coordinated?	☐ Yes ☐ No	
8	Was the schedule followed?	☐ Yes ☐ No	
9	Was project documentation prepared so that it met professional project standards?	☐ Yes ☐ No	
10	Was project status provided in a timely fashion?	☐ Yes ☐ No	
11	Did internal customers fulfill their responsibilities to provide resources?	☐ Yes ☐ No	

TABLE 5.7 Project Evaluation Review Questions *(continued)*

12	Were approvals provided in a timely fashion?	☐ Yes ☐ No	
13	Did internal and external customers take part in work sessions, reviews, and testing of the product, and did they provide accurate information?	☐ Yes ☐ No	
14	Were issues adequately researched and appropriate decisions made?	☐ Yes ☐ No	
15	Was the change control procedure agreed upon in advance?	☐ Yes ☐ No	
16	Was the change control procedure followed?	☐ Yes ☐ No	
17	Did the product satisfy the expectations of its sponsors, clients, and users?	☐ Yes ☐ No	
18	Did the product conform to its specifications, including performance constraints?	☐ Yes ☐ No	
19	Were training programs effective?	☐ Yes ☐ No	
20	Were business objectives (including quality improvements) achieved?	☐ Yes ☐ No	

After these questions have been answered, you will want to document the answers in a post-project assessment form, such as the one in Table 5.8. Notice that this template doesn't include a box for what went wrong. When people start thinking about what went wrong, negatives come to mind, and finger-pointing and blame enter the picture. As a project manager, you may wish to facilitate what can be done differently next time to be sure no blame is cast. You are here to fix a problem, not to fix the blame.

TABLE 5.8   Lessons Learned Template

Lessons Learned		
Items that went well		
1.		
2.		
3.		
4.		
What are the challenges the project had?		
1.		
2.		
3.		
4.		
What can be done differently next time?		
1.		
2.		
3.		
4.		
What did we do to celebrate our success?		
1.		
2.		
3.		
4.		
Action Items		
	Responsible Party	**Date to Be Completed**
1.		
2.		
3.		
4.		
5.		

Hands-on 5.4: Testing Your Knowledge of Lessons Learned

1. If an action item that is not completed exists on your lessons-learned document, can you close out the project? Why or why not?

2. How do you handle a problem identified in your lessons-learned meeting that is clearly attributable to a team member who left the project in an earlier phase because their work was completed?

Task 5.5: Creating and Distributing Final Reports

In this task you will make sure you have captured all relevant data about the project and will create and distribute the final project report. Then all of this data will be archived according to your company procedures and retained according to statutory guidelines.

Scenario

You have gathered all pertinent information and are well on your way to finalizing all of the documents.

Scope of Task

Duration

The duration of this task should be two to three hours or more, depending on the complexity and duration of the project.

Setup

None.

Caveat

None.

Procedure

In this task you will learn to do the following:

- Apply appropriate updates to organizational process assets
- Retain organizational knowledge
- Comply with statutory requirements
- Release project participants
- Create a final report

Details

You can see by now just how many documents you have prepared for the project. Some of those documents caused changes to your organizational process assets. You will need to update them. Also, you must retain the organizational knowledge you have learned from the project as well as comply with statutory requirements.

Update Organizational Process Assets

Many times during a project, particularly if the project has significant duration or high complexity, normal processes will be bypassed by using work-arounds. In fact, some work-arounds may improve the bypassed process, so it is important to keep process records up-to-date.

For example, on telephone company projects, a variety of equipment is used. Most of the equipment is assigned from existing inventories. If the assigned piece of equipment fails, another will be used. But unless the completed records show the actual piece of equipment used, it would be a maintenance and an inventory nightmare if the records were not updated.

The updating is needed on construction projects or any other type of project for which the final records must reflect the approved and accepted deliverable. You always want the records to match all of the change orders. These records are sometimes called *as built*. You sure wouldn't want to look at a set of working plans showing that a wall was missing or that the electrical plan had changed but was not reflected on the as-built document, or on an IT project that used hardware that was different from the planned hardware.

Table 5.9 is a checklist that mirrors the organizational process assets in the *PMBOK® Guide, 4th edition*, p. 32. You can use it as a reminder of what items need to be updated.

Retain Organizational Knowledge

The overall project management process should include procedures for transferring knowledge to people throughout the organization.

A *knowledge database* creates the foundation for both coaching and peer group activities. The database takes the lessons learned from individuals and projects and records them so that they are easily accessible to anyone with a need to learn. A knowledge database is particularly useful for project managers who want to learn from previous projects.

Knowledge databases can be placed wherever appropriate for your organization but are typically maintained by the project management office (PMO), if there is one. If a knowledge database doesn't already exist, you will have to create your own and see that it is maintained. They are certainly useful, but it should be required that whoever posted a particular piece of knowledge should consistently keep the information current. If this doesn't happen, the information may be erroneous or out-of-date.

Project documents to be included in the knowledge database could include, but are not limited to, the following:

- Project control book
- Phase 1 initiation documents including project charter
- Phase 2 project plans
- Phase 3 execution documents
- Phase 4 project management monitoring and control documents
- Phase 5 project and contract closure documents
- All phases' correspondence, meeting notes, technical files, and so on

Comply with Statutory Requirements

Your organization has a record retention policy for all types of records. Most project management documents are kept indefinitely. Why? Some project results, such as building a bridge, have a very long life span, and if the bridge should fail, going back to the original project documents might help uncover the cause of the failure.

Release Project Participants

Some employees have been on your project temporarily, others part-time, and a few for the entire duration. In any case, you must make sure that their working hours on your project are accounted for and are included in your final report. Team members who work in a matrix organization should return to their regular position with appropriate feedback to their manager. If team members are in a projectized organization and are no longer needed, the project manager may have to lay them off or find them another position within the organization.

Create Final Project Report

Table 5.10 is a template you may consider using in order to create a final project report. This report is a key document summarizing the project and its results, and should be sent to your sponsor and others in senior management with a need to know.

TABLE 5.9   Organizational Process Assets

Organizational Process Assets		
Process and Procedures		
Organizational standard processes	Standards	Y☐ N☐
	Policies	Y☐ N☐
	Standard product and life cycles	Y☐ N☐
	Quality policies and procedures	Y☐ N☐
Guidelines	Standardized guidelines	Y☐ N☐
	Work instructions	Y☐ N☐
	Evaluation criteria	Y☐ N☐
	Performance measurement criteria	Y☐ N☐
Templates	Risk	Y☐ N☐
	WBS	Y☐ N☐
	Network diagram	Y☐ N☐
	Contract templates	Y☐ N☐
Organizational communication requirements	Specific technology available	Y☐ N☐
	Allowed communication technology	Y☐ N☐
	Record retention policies	Y☐ N☐
	Security requirements	Y☐ N☐
Organization's set of standard processes tailored to fit the project		Y☐ N☐
Project closure guideline or requirements	Final project audit	Y☐ N☐
	Project evaluations	Y☐ N☐
	Product validations	Y☐ N☐
	Acceptance criteria	Y☐ N☐
Financial controls procedures	Time reporting	Y☐ N☐
	Required expenditure and disbursement reviews	Y☐ N☐
	Accounting codes	Y☐ N☐
	Standard contract provisions	Y☐ N☐
Issue and defect management procedures defining issue and defect controls	Issue/defect identification and resolution	Y☐ N☐
	Action item tracking	Y☐ N☐
Change control procedures that determine:	How documents will be modified	Y☐ N☐
	How changes will be approved	Y☐ N☐
	How changes will be validated	Y☐ N☐
Risk control procedures	Risk categories	Y☐ N☐
	Probability definition and impact	Y☐ N☐
	Probability and impact matrix	Y☐ N☐
Procedures for prioritizing, approving, and issuing work authorizations		Y☐ N☐

TABLE 5.9   Organizational Process Assets *(continued)*

Corporate Knowledge Base (Process measurement databases used to store and retrieve information.) Again, use this reminder checklist to determine what if anything needs to be updated based on your project.		
Process measurement databases		Y☐ N☐
Project files	Scope baseline	Y☐ N☐
	Cost baseline	Y☐ N☐
	Schedule baseline	Y☐ N☐
	Quality baseline	Y☐ N☐
	Performance measurement baselines	Y☐ N☐
	Project calendars	Y☐ N☐
	Network diagrams	Y☐ N☐
	Risk registers	Y☐ N☐
	Planned risk-response actions	Y☐ N☐
	Defined risk impacts	Y☐ N☐
Historical information and lessons learned knowledge bases	Project documents	Y☐ N☐
	Project closure information	Y☐ N☐
	Project closure documentation	Y☐ N☐
	Results of previous project selection decisions	Y☐ N☐
	Previous performance information	Y☐ N☐
	Information from the risk management effort	Y☐ N☐
Issue and defect management database		Y☐ N☐
Configuration management knowledge bases	Baselines of all company standards	Y☐ N☐
	Policies and procedures	Y☐ N☐
Financial databases	Labor hours	Y☐ N☐
	Incurred costs	Y☐ N☐
	Budgets	Y☐ N☐
	Project cost overruns	Y☐ N☐

TABLE 5.10   Ten-Step Final Report Template

Ten-Step Final Project Report			
Project Name		Completion Date	
Project Manager		Telephone Number	

#	Item
1.	**Executive Summary** <Include the main results of the project in general (not technical terms) by summarizing the rest of the items below.>
2.	**Project introduction** <Include why the project was initiated and how it aligns with corporate goals.>
3.	**Major Project Activities** <Include description of major work packages that were undertaken to fulfill the objectives of the project.>
4.	**Project Results** <Describe the results of scope changes, schedule cost, quality, and risk results as compared to the baseline plan; if the results are +/– 10%, explain why.>
5.	**Communications** <Describe your communication efforts with the tools you used and whether they were effective.>
6.	**Key Project Changes** <Describe the approved key changes made to the project and how they affected the original project plan.>
7.	**How Defects Were Managed** <Describe product inspection or test results; if there were defects, describe what was done to bring them up to specifications.>
8.	**Vendor Performance** <Describe how well or poorly vendors, contractors, sellers, and suppliers performed relative to contract items and/or commitments.>
9.	**Project Challenges** <Describe your key project challenges, why they were challenges, and what you did to overcome them.>
10.	**Transition to Operations** <Describe how project products were turned over to operations and discuss any problems there may have been and how they were resolved.>

Perform Final Project Closure

Finally, you are done with the project. Or are you? Use the checklist found in Table 5.11. If any of your answers are no, you must revisit the item to be sure it is complete before final project closure occurs.

TABLE 5.11   Closure Phase Checklist

	CLOSURE PHASE CHECKOUT LIST		
1.	Are any deliverables outstanding?	☐ Yes	☐ No
2.	Are there any internal outstanding commitments?	☐ Yes	☐ No
3.	Have all costs, internal and external, been appropriately charged to the project?	☐ Yes	☐ No
4.	Have all work packages and work orders been completed?	☐ Yes	☐ No
5.	Have any incomplete work packages been documented and rationalized?	☐ Yes	☐ No
6.	Has management been notified regarding the availability of project personnel?	☐ Yes	☐ No
7.	Has management been notified regarding the availability of project facilities?	☐ Yes	☐ No
8.	Has the project plan been archived with all support data?	☐ Yes	☐ No
9.	Has agreement been reached with the project sponsor on disposition of remaining deliverables?	☐ Yes	☐ No
10.	Have suppliers been notified regarding any outstanding commitments?	☐ Yes	☐ No
11.	Have operations and maintenance procedures been put into place and activated?	☐ Yes	☐ No
12.	Has the final project report been written and sent back to the sponsor?	☐ Yes	☐ No
	PERSONNEL		
13.	Have project team concerns regarding future assignments been addressed if this project took place in a projectized organization?	☐ Yes	☐ No
14.	Is the project team dedicated to the remaining project commitments?	☐ Yes	☐ No
15.	Have personnel been reassigned or notified of reassignment methodology?	☐ Yes	☐ No

Hands-on 5.5: Testing Your Knowledge of Creating and Documenting the Project's Final Report

1. What would happen if a knowledge database or similar instrument did not exist in your organization?

2. If a knowledge database is in place, what could happen if it wasn't regularly maintained?

3. If a process was improved during the execution and completion of a project, what should the project manager do?

4. Should the final project report be given to team members?

The project is now complete. As with most projects, you and your team have learned many new things that you may be able to use in future project assignments. As you have seen, project management is never boring. And it is now considered a key management business strategy. Hopefully, you will eagerly continue your project management voyage. Our best wishes to you on your journey.

Appendix A

Solutions

Phase 1 Solutions

The following are the solutions for the Hands-on sections for Phase 1.

Hands-on 1.1: Testing Your Knowledge of Finance Principals

Here are the correct answers and how we arrived at them.

1. $98.00 now is equivalent to $105.60 one year from now.

    False: Total amount accrued = $98.00 (1.05) = $102.90

2. $200.00 one year past is equivalent to $205.00 now.

    False: Required investment = $205.00/1.05 = $195.24

3. $3,000.00 now is equivalent to $3,150.00 one year from now.

    True: Total amount accrued = $3,000.00 (1.05) = $3,150.00

4. $3,000.00 now is equivalent to $2,887.14 one year ago.

    False: Total amount accrued = $2,887.14 (1.05) = $3,031.50

5. Interest accumulated in one year on an investment of $2,000.00 is $100.00.

    True: Interest = $2,000.00 (1.05) = $100.00

Hands-on 1.2: Testing Your Knowledge of NPV

1. The following table shows the answers to the net present value (NPV) questions and how the answers were derived.

Period	Cash Flow	Present Value Factor	Present Value
0	−$12,337	1.000	−$12,337.00
1	$10,000	0.9091	$9,091.00
2	−$5,000	0.8264	−$4,132.00
		NPV =	−$7,378.00

2. The following table shows how present value (PV) is used to calculate the NPV of a project. Always remember to show your initial investment as a negative number.

Period	Cash Flow	Present Value Factor	Present Value
0	−$5,000,000	1.000	−$5,000,000
1	$1,000,000	0.9174	$917,400
2	$900,000	0.8417	$757,530
3	$900,000	0.7722	$694,980
4	$750,000	0.7084	$531,300
5	$750,000	0.6499	$487,425
6	$750,000	0.5963	$447,225
		NPV=	−$1,164,140

3. The NPV for the remodel project is -$1,164,140.00.

4. The present value for each year of the Apples and Pears project is shown below.

Period	Cash Flow	Present Value Factor	Present Value
0	−$7,000,000	1.000	−$7,000,000
1	$3,000,000	0.9174	$2,752,200
2	$2,000,000	0.8417	$1,683,400
3	$2,000,000	0.7722	$1,544,400
4	$1,500,000	0.7084	$1,062,600
5	$1,500,000	0.6499	$974,850
6	$1,500,000	0.5963	$894,450
		NPV=	$1,911,900

5. The NPV of the Apples and Pears project is $1,911,900. Because this is a positive number, it is a good project to pursue.

6. The new NPV would be $161,900. The number is positive so it is still a good project to pursue.

7. The Apples and Pears project.

8. Other ways to select a project include cost benefit analysis, IRR, and comparative analysis as well as a weighted scoring model.

Hands-on 1.3: Testing Your Knowledge of Benefit Measurement Methods—Scoring Models

1. Additional information that can be provided for the eight criteria is as follows:

   - Provide a synopsis of the project that shows how it aligns with corporate strategy. For example, use a presentation that shows how the business goals map to the project objectives.

   - Provide the results of an NPV comparison.

   - Provide a document that maps how the projects are related and the impacts of each.

   - Provide results of alternative analysis (for example, IRR or payback period).

   - Describe how the project meets standards; but if it does not, explain what the impacts might be.

   - Provide a skills and availability matrix.

   - Describe how the other projects relate and the advantage of continuing with this one.

2. The scores for projects 1 and 2 were 108 and 104, respectively. Adding these scores changes the choice from accepting Project 1 to accepting Project 2 instead.

Questions	Project 1			Project 2		
	Weight	Rating	Score	Weight	Rating	Score
1. Project enhances corporate image	4	2	8	4	4	16
2. Project creates competitive advantage	5	5	25	5	5	25
3. Project increases public awareness	3	3	9	3	3	9
4. Process improvement is enhanced	3	1	3	3	3	6
5. Company infrastructure is improved	2	2	4	2	1	2
	Total Score		49	Total Score		58

3. Scoring models are simple and provide consistency in the approach.

4. For small projects (and your company would have to decide what is considered *small*), a comparative approach may be enough. But most companies use an economic model as well.

5. There could be challenges with scoring models. Projects may be ranked and scored subjectively (without data and facts) instead of objectively. There may be inconsistencies in the selection committee based on politics, personal agenda, and so on. Senior management may override the decision. If these challenges do exist, consider revamping the criteria so that all are in agreement.

Hands-on 1.4: Testing Your Knowledge of Business Cases

1. A business case is usually created by a team—which may or may not include the project manager. A project manager is *not* expected to be on the selection committee or the scoring committee. He or she acts more as a consultant, providing data and facts as needed to complete the case.

2. Project managers are closer to the real-world implications of high-level decision making and can help avoid major pitfalls if brought into the process early enough.

3. There may be disadvantages if the project manager does not understand financial, corporate, and internal issues at a high level. Project managers are typically a lower rank than those who create and approve business cases. Other team members may not understand the internal workings of the business and override a project manager of lesser rank. Trust issues may develop between the PM and the business case team if they do not see added value in the PM's participation.

4. It can be; but if it is not thorough enough, wrong decisions can be made, and the implications of those decisions may not be known until too many costs have been expended. Then a cycle of "Well, we've spent this much money on it—let's make it work" exists. If it is perceived that the business case is not complete, it may be tabled in favor of a less-demanding comparative or financial-only approach.

Hands-on 1.5: Testing Your Knowledge of Leadership Analysis

If you circled most of your answers in the 1, 2, and 3 columns, project management may not be the best fit for you. If you had several 4s or 5s, leverage those so that project management can be in your future.

If you circled most of your answers in the 3, 4, and 5 columns, project management may be a good fit for you.

Most individuals are not gifted in all of these characteristics. If you circled mostly 3s, 4s, and 5s but had one or two or three 1s and 2s, then those are the ones you need to work on.

You may also ask your supervisor or mentor to do the test based on their opinions of you. Then compare your answers with theirs to get a truer picture of your skills.

You can also use the 360-degree feedback process with your peers. The feedback you receive can assist in making changes if needed, or provide reinforcement that you are doing well.

Hands-on 1.6: Testing Your Knowledge of Stakeholder Analysis

1. See the following table for concern/interests/support, impact, and strategies. You can see that you do not have enough information on Darcy Moore, Louise Rose, Todd Franks, and Harry Edwards. Now is the time to get that information!

Identify and Interview Stakeholders	Determine Concern or Interest	Impact Assessment	Strategies to Reduce Challenges and Gain Support
Megan Holly	Megan has high support for the project but she has low influence.	May be overzealous in the beginning.	Megan needs to be reined in so she doesn't begin work prematurely. Keep Megan informed and include her opinions and ideas as appropriate.
James Stevens	James has high power but low support for the project.	James can block the project.	James should be one of the recipients of a progressive business case, participate in risk management tasks, and receive budget and cost information as often as he wants.
Jacob Patrick	Jacob has low power and high support.	None.	Keep Jacob informed and let him head up the construction piece of the project because it will be a subproject all by itself.

Identify and Interview Stakeholders	Determine Concern or Interest	Impact Assessment	Strategies to Reduce Challenges and Gain Support
Jordyn Kelly	Jordyn has high support and high power.	Keep Jordyn satisfied about project issues and concerns that affect HR.	Leverage Jordyn to assist in obtaining resources.
Skylar Janes	Skylar has high support but low power.	Keep Skylar in the loop.	Make sure Skylar uses other stakeholders' opinions about the brand for A&P.
Carolyn Lee	Carolyn has high support but low power.	Keep Carolyn informed.	Whenever a union is involved, it is important that the project manager have a reasonable understanding of the union contract.
Madison Adams	Madison has low power but high concern.	Keep Madison satisfied every step of the way.	IT issues can make or break a project. Involve Madison early and often.
Allison Jones	Allison has low power but high concern.	Keep Allison satisfied every step of the way.	IT issues can make or break a project. Involve Allison early and often.
Darcy Moore	Not enough info.	Not enough info.	Not enough info.
Louise Rose	Not enough info.	Not enough info.	Not enough info.
Todd Franks	Not enough info.	Not enough info.	Not enough info.
Harry Edwards	Not enough info.	Not enough info.	Not enough info.

2. The benefits of interviewing stakeholders and conducting a stakeholder analysis are as follows:

    - High-level individuals that are engaged early in the process can help build personal support and trust.

    - The stakeholders' input and opinions may increase the quality of your project.

    - You may be able to obtain the right people at the right time, and this could improve the outcome of the project.

    - Keeping stakeholders informed builds their confidence in your ability to manage the project.

    - Using stakeholders' opinions and other input will also lend additional trust and support when you need it.

3. Other stakeholders may include shareholders, suppliers, customers, your team, government agencies, local agencies, and lenders.

4. The information you may want to know to help understand stakeholders includes the following:

    - What information they want

    - How and how often they wish to receive information

    - Emotional interests

    - If they are positive about the project

    - If they are negative about the project

    - Financial interests

    - Who else might be influenced by their opinions

5. Some project managers feel they can plan the project on their own and assign people to tasks. But a team of one is not a team. By including as many people as you can, you develop support with those who are positive about the project. You may even earn trust with those who are not positive about the project, because you have heard their concerns and mapped a strategy to help overcome their fears and concerns.

Hands-on 1.7: Testing Your Knowledge of Stakeholder Mapping

The following diagram represents a completed stakeholder map, given the information you have so far on the Apples and Pears project.

High

Low Concern/Interest/Support High Power	High Concern/Interest/Support High Power
	James Stevens
Keep Satisfied	**Manage Closely**
	Jordyn Kelly

Power

Low Concern/Interest/Support Low Power	High Concern/Interest/Support Low Power Allison Jones
	Megan Holly
Normal Monitoring	**Keep Informed**
	Jacob Patrick
Carolyn Lee	Skylar Janes
	Madison Adams

Low

Low   **Concern**   High

Hands-on 1.8: Testing Your Knowledge of Corporate Strategy

1. Project managers want to be able to answer the question, "Why are we doing this?" and focus only on the elements of the project that support the corporate strategy. If a project manager does not understand the corporate strategy, the project could easily fall into *scope creep* mode.

2. The following are three elements of corporate strategy:

   - What kind of image do we want?
   - Where do we want to be five years from now?
   - What do we want to be known for?

3. Portfolio management is important because project selection is determined by what is good for the business based on all of the corporate strategy elements for a given time period instead of what is good for a particular business unit. If a business unit ties their project requests to corporate strategy, the project is more likely to be approved. There are several other advantages to portfolio management, such as more-efficient use of resources, a greater understanding of funding, and that it exposes redundant projects.

4. The business needs for Apples and Pears include the following:

   - Increases revenue

   - Promotes competitive advantage

   - Creates new products and services

   - Improves customer satisfaction

Hands-on 1.9: Testing Your Knowledge of Goals and Objectives

The following table shows the SMART goals and objectives of the Apples and Pears project.

SMART	Business Goals (What)	Project Objectives (How)
Specific	To increase revenue, promote competitive advantage, create new products and services, and improve customer satisfaction.	Cimarron will create two new stores—one in Bellevue, Washington, and the other in Portland, Oregon—that will showcase a new line of clothing for women who are shaped either as an "apple" or a "pear."
Measurable	The measure of financial success will not be known until two years of revenues have occurred. Marketing will determine whether we have increased our market share and competitive advantage.	Surveys will be conducted to determine customer satisfaction. The project manager will stay within the approved project budget of $8,750,000.
Accurate	In order to determine measurements of success, Cimarron will follow corporate guidelines and financial practices already in place. Accuracy of the data is paramount.	All reports to management will follow the corporate project management system for quality and accuracy.

SMART	Business Goals (What)	Project Objectives (How)
Realistic	Cimarron's other line of business is children's clothing. Those stores typically launch within the same time and budget constraints.	The project team has sufficient background and skills to determine that the order-of-magnitude budget and the approved schedule are adequate. Approved change orders may alter the budget and schedule.
Time-bound	Because the project will be complete by October 25, we will have the two-month holiday shopping window, from November 1 through December 31, to launch the new line of clothing.	The project is to be completed by October 25 so that the store can open by November 1.

Hands-on 1.10: Testing Your Knowledge of the Product Scope Description

The following list shows the initial scope of the Apples and Pears project. The A&P project has two major products that will be produced:

1. The stores in Bellevue and Portland are to be elegant and will include the following:
   - Plush carpeting
   - Nonobtrusive overhead music
   - Designer showcasing
   - Private dressing rooms with complete doors
   - Ambient lighting
   - Displays for jewelry, accessories, and perfume items
   - Second-floor bridal gallery

2. Clothing will have style and quality for bridal wear, evening wear, daywear, sportswear, outerwear, and lingerie:
   - They will fit properly.
   - They will be manufactured with no defects.
   - 90% of the clothing will be machine washable.
   - They will be available in all sizes.
   - They will be affordable (including the bridal wear).

Hands-on 1.11: Testing Your Knowledge of Deliverables

These are the deliverables expected from the Apples and Pears project:

1. Brand established for stores that includes logo for the stores, stationery, envelopes, receipts, invoices, business cards, and catalogs

2. Advertising plan to include newspapers and television promos

3. Designs for clothing to include bridal, evening wear, daywear, sportswear, lingerie, and outerwear

4. Clothing for Apples and Pears manufactured in the United States

5. Hired and trained personnel for counter, sales, and management

6. Retail stores open in Belleview, Washington, and Portland, Oregon, according to construction documents, space planning, lease requirements, and furnishings layout

Hands-on 1.12: Testing Your Knowledge of Requirements

This table shows the requirements of the Apples and Pears project.

Requirements	R	U	M	B	A
1. Clothing manufactured in the United States	Y	Y	Y	Y	Y
2. Both stores opened by November 1	Y	Y	Y	Y	Y
3. Clothing line meets Cimarron's standards of affordability, quality, and style	Y	Y	Y	Y	Y
4. Order-of-magnitude budget to be $8,750,000	Y	Y	Y	Y	Y
5. Advertising plan to be completed by June 30	Y	Y	Y	Y	Y

Hands-on 1.13: Testing Your Knowledge of Project Boundaries

The boundaries of the Apples and Pears project are as follows:

1. There are only two stores—one in Bellevue, Washington, and the other in Portland, Oregon.

2. IT will follow the project plan and not make any changes unless directed and approved to do so.

3. We will use designers from the United States and Europe if necessary.

4. Clothing will be manufactured in the United States only.

5. We will hire only personnel within the local communities around Bellevue, Washington, and Portland, Oregon. Nobody from Cimarron will be transferred.

6. Advertising for the stores will include the Seattle and Portland metro areas only.

7. Advertising will use local publications and television only.

Hands-on 1.14: Testing Your Knowledge of Product Acceptance Criteria

This table shows the product acceptance criteria of the Apples and Pears project.

Schedule Dates	All clothing must be ready for shipment at least two weeks before the stores open.
Functionality	All clothing should fit properly based on the body type for "apples" and "pears."
Appearance	All clothing should match the designs that were approved and the materials that were designated for them. They should be stylish and fresh (wrinkle resistant or wrinkle free).
Performance Levels	The clothing should be well made with tailoring where appropriate. Buttons should be fastened so they will not drop off, and zippers should have no mistakes. There should be no flaws in the fabric.
Practicality	Ninety percent of the clothing should be washable.
Clarity	Clothing tags should be noticeable and understandable.
Capacity	Clothing variety will include bridal, evening wear, daywear, sportswear, outerwear, and lingerie.
Accuracy	Clothing should have correct sizing on the garment and the tag.
Availability	Depending on the market studies, sets of clothing should be available in all sizes.
Maintainability	Extra buttons should be included with clothing, and fabric should be colorfast.
Reliability	The clothes should last for years.
Flexibility	The line of styles should mix and match.

Hands-on 1.15: Testing Your Knowledge of Project Organizational Structures

1. Strong matrix

2. Cimarron has a director of project managers who is on equal footing with other directors.

3. The organization chart for Cimarron is shown here.

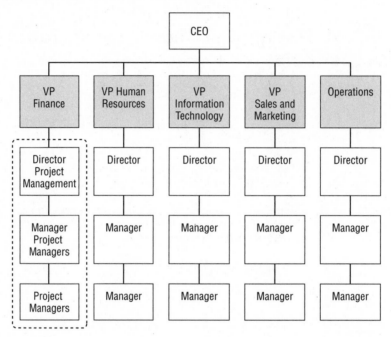

Hands-on 1.16: Testing Your Knowledge of Project Scope Statements

This table shows the completed scope statement of the Apples and Pears project.

High-Level Scope Statement Template	
Describe business goals	• Increase revenue • Promote competitive advantage • Improve customer satisfaction
Describe major objectives of this project	• Build two new stores—one in Bellevue, Washington and the other in Portland, Oregon • Design clothing for apples and pears • Manufacture clothing according to designs • Advertise products in newspapers and television • Develop brand • Stay within approved budget of $8,750,000 • Meet the October 25 due date
Describe background for the project	The clothing line for Cimarron's children's clothing has been very successful. Ms. Ross is aware that one of the major demographics for marketing is the baby boomers who are seniors now. Body shapes have changed over the years and so Ms. Ross wants to develop high quality and stylish clothing that will appeal to this demographic but will not be limited by it. Market studies have been positive and the NPV of the project is positive.
Describe the expected benefits	The expected benefits are increased revenue, increased market share, and customer satisfaction.
List the stakeholders and their role in the project	• Megan Holly is a marketing manager who participated in the original market study. She has a sales background and is already planning her marketing strategy. • James Stevens is on the finance committee with Ms. Reese. He believes that even though the initial numbers looked positive, it is risky to assume that the current economy will support the increasing revenue projections for the project. • Jacob Patrick is the manager of engineering and construction. He believes that the cost of materials is going down because of the slowdown in new home sales and that the project could provide many jobs during its implementation. • Jordyn Kelly is the human resources vice president and is all for the project because it will create new jobs in many new cities. • Skylar Janes is the advertising manager for Cimarron Industries and is eager to pursue the brand project this will create. • Carolyn Lee is the union representative for the manufacturing facility. She represents those who will ultimately design and manufacture the clothing. • Madison Adams is the webmaster of Cimarron's web pages. She wants to know if A&P customers will order clothing through the Internet and if so, will adequate funding be provided for additional servers, and the like. • Allison Jones is the IT manager and is concerned that traffic may double without adequate support systems being added. • Darcy Moore is the operations director for the West Coast children's stores.

	• Louise Rose is the operations director for the East Coast children's stores.
	• Todd Franks is a site superintendant for new stores.
	• Harry Edwards is the procurement director for Cimarron.
Describe the major deliverables	• Brand established for stores that includes logo for the stores, stationery, envelopes, receipts, invoices, business cards, and catalogs
	• Advertising plan to include newspapers and television promos
	• Designs for clothing to include bridal, evening wear, daywear, sportswear, lingerie, and outerwear
	• Clothing for apples and pears manufactured in the United States
	• Hired and trained personnel for counter, sales and management
	• Retail stores open in Belleview, Washington and Portland, Oregon according to construction documents, space planning, lease requirements, and furnishings layout
Describe five high-level requirements	1. Clothing manufactured in the United States
	2. Both stores opened by November 1
	3. Clothing line meets Cimarron's standards of affordability, quality, and style
	4. Order of magnitude budget to be $8,750,000
	5. Advertising plan to be completed by June 30
Describe project boundaries	• There are only two stores—one in Bellevue, Washington and the other in Portland, Oregon.
	• IT will not make any other changes except what the A&P project requires.
	• We will use designers from the United States and Europe if necessary.
	• Clothing will be manufactured in the United States only.
	• We will hire only personnel within the local communities around Bellevue, Washington and Portland, Oregon. Nobody from Cimarron will be transferred.
	• Advertising for the stores will include the Seattle and Portland metro areas only.
	• Advertising will use local publications and television only.
Describe product acceptance criteria	• Schedule dates: All clothing must be ready for shipment at least two weeks before the stores open.
	• Functionality: All clothing should fit properly based on the body type for "apples" and "pears."
	• Appearance: All clothing should match the designs that were approved and the materials that were designated for them. They should be stylish and fresh (no wrinkles).
	• Performance levels: The clothing should be well made with tailoring where apppropriate. Buttons should be fastened so they will not drop off and zippers should have no mistakes. There should be no flaws in the fabric.
	• Practicality: Ninety percent of the clothing should be washable.
	• Clarity: Clothing tags should be noticeable.

	• Capacity: Clothing variety will include bridal, evening wear, daywear, sportswear, outerwear, and lingerie.
	• Accuracy: Clothing should have correct sizing on the garment and the tag.
	• Availability: Depending on the market studies, sets of clothing should be available in all sizes.
	• Maintainability: Extra buttons should be included with clothing, and fabric should be colorfast.
	• Reliability: The clothes should last for years.
	• Flexibility: The line of styles should mix and match.
Describe project organization	The project organization is a strong matrix. It has a director of project management on equal footing with other managers. All project managers and their managers report to the director. All project managers assigned to projects come from here. Training and mentoring are provided.

Hands-on 1.17: Testing Your Knowledge of Milestones

This table shows the milestones associated with the Apples and Pears project.

Milestone	Date
Contracts and lease signed	February 15
Clothing designed	March 15
Advertising plan complete	June 30
Clothing manufactured	August 1
Construction complete	September 15
Personnel hired	October 1
Interior finishes complete	October 1
Stores furnished	October 5
Clothing delivered	October 10
Personnel trained	October 25
Stores open	November 1

Hands-on 1.18: Testing Your Knowledge of an Estimated Budget

This table shows the estimated budget of the Apples and Pears project.

Item	Amount
Advertising	$1,000,000
Space planning	$5,000
Construction	$3,600,000
Noninventoried furnishings	$50,000
Design of clothing	$1,250,000
Hiring and training of personnel	$50,000
Information technology	$700,000
Manufacturing costs	$2,075,000
Delivery and set	$20,000
Total	$8,750,000

Hands-on 1.19: Testing Your Knowledge of High-Level Project Risks

These are the high-level risks associated with the Apples and Pears project:

1. Opportunity: Because of the economic downturn, there may be more qualified employees and construction people available.
2. Risk: Designers may not meet their deadline because of the difference between United States and European vacation time (that is, typically no one works in Europe in August).
3. Risk: The dollar vs. the euro could impact the amount budgeted for European designers.
4. Risk: We may not get all of the products for the stores because of the poor economy.
5. Opportunity: We may be able to buy products at reduced rates now that demand is lower.

Hands-on 1.20: Testing Your Knowledge of Project Assumptions

This table shows the assumptions associated with the Apples and Pears project.

Assumption	T/F?
1. There exists high-level support—the CEO wanted this project and the sponsor is also the champion for the cause.	True
2. The budget is sufficient.	True
3. Local labor force will be available.	True
4. Designers will finish on time.	Not Sure
5. Advertising will be launched on time.	Not Sure
6. Materials will be available when needed.	Not Sure

Hands-on 1.21: Testing Your Knowledge of Project Constraints

This table shows the constraints and response strategies associated with the Apples and Pears project.

Constraint	Response Strategy
1. The project must finish by October 25, so that the store can open by November 1.	Every risk identified that could lengthen the duration will be overcome in the planning phase.
2. The budget available should not exceed $8,750,000.	Ask for management reserves and contingency funds. (More about these in Phase 2.)
3. Designers must finish by March 31, so clothing can be manufactured in time.	Use as many designers as needed. They will be part of team so that the lines of clothing are in keeping with Ms. Ross's vision.

Hands-on 1.22: Testing Your Knowledge of Putting It All Together!

You have finally done it! Here is the completed project charter of the Apples and Pears project.

The Project Charter		
Summary of Milestones	Contracts and Lease Signed	February 15
	Clothing Designed	March 15
	Advertising Plan Complete	June 30
	Clothing Manufactured	August 1
	Construction Complete	September 15
	Personnel Hired	October 1
	Store Finishes Complete	October 5
	Stores Furnished	October 10
	Clothing Delivered	October 25
	Personnel Trained	November 1
	Stores Open	February 15
Summary of Costs	Advertising	$1,000,000.00
	Space planning	$5,000.00
	Construction	$3,600,000.00
	Noninventoried furnishings	$50,000.00
	Design of clothing	$1,250,000.00
	Hiring and training of personnel	$50,000.00
	Information technology	$700,000.00
	Manufacturing costs	$2,075,000.00
	Delivery and set	$20,000.00
	Total	$8,750,000.00
High Level Risks	1. Opportunity: Due to the economic downturn, there may be more qualified employees and construction people available.	
	2. Risk: Designers may not meet their deadline because of the difference between US and European vacation time (i.e., typically no one in Europe works in August).	
	3. Risk: The dollar vs. the euro could impact the amount budgeted for European designers.	
	4. Risk: We may not get all of the products for the stores due to the economy.	
	5. Opportunity: We may be able to buy products at reduced rates now that demand is lower.	
Configuration Management	Configuration management will follow our standard change management process.	

Assumptions	1. There exists high-level support—the CEO wanted this project, and the sponsor is also the champion for the cause.	True
	2. The budget is sufficient.	True
	3. Local labor force will be available.	True
	4. Designers will finish on time.	Not Sure
	5. Advertising will be launched on time.	Not Sure
	6. Materials will be available when needed.	Not Sure

Constraints	Constraints	Response Strategies
	1. The project must finish by October 25, so the store can open by November 1.	Every risk identified that could lengthen the duration will be overcome in the planning phase.
	2. The budget available should not exceed $8,750,000.	Ask for management reserves and contingency funds. (More about these in Phase 2.)
	3. Designers must finish by March 31, so that clothing can be manufactured in time.	Use as many designers as needed. They will be part of team so that the lines of clothing are in keeping with Ms. Ross's vision.

Project approvals	We will follow our progressive business case, and if the scorecard meets or exceeds the minimum score then the project will proceed to planning.

Project acceptance criteria	• All work has been inspected.
	• All deliverables have been accepted.
	• Training of staff has been completed.
	• Manuals and procedures have been provided.
	• As-built drawings have been received and approved.
	• Punch list items are completed and approved.
	• Supplier contracts and agreements have been closed out.
	• Contractors have received final payment.

Phase 2 Solutions

Hands-on 2.1: Testing Your Knowledge of Identifying Team Members

The following table provides a sample defining the team members associated with a given task or set of tasks as well as their responsibilities, accountabilities, the support they may provide, and whether they will provide consulting services or simply provide information. The important thing to remember is that there should be only one accountable person for the task or set of tasks.

Tasks	Project Manager	PMO	Team Members	Line Managers	Dept Manager	Sponsor	Senior Management
Project management	R	S	S	S	I	A	I
Advertising	C	S	S	R	A	I	I
Space planning	I	C	S	R	A	I	I
Construction	C	S	S	R	A	I	I
Noninventoried furnishings	C	S	–	R	A	I	I
Design of clothing	I	–	S	R	A	I	I
Hiring and training of personnel	I	–	–	R	A	I	I
Information technology	I	S	S	R	A	I	I
Manufacturing	C	S	S	R	A	I	I

Hands-on 2.2: Testing Your Knowledge of Roles and Responsibilities in the Planning Phase

The following table represents an up-to-date roles and responsibilities chart for the team members who have been identified thus far. This table is different from the RAM in that you describe the responsibilities and accountabilities of your team members.

Team Member	Role	Category	Responsibility/Accountability
Allison Jones	IT	Project execution	Responsible for Apples and Pears IT issues
Carolyn Lee	Union rep	Project execution	Responsible for ensuring that manufacturing employees follow the union contract
Carrie MacIntyre	Project manager	Project execution	Accountable for project results
Darcy Moore	Operations director	Project execution	Responsible for operations for both Portland and Seattle stores
Eric Nash	Manufacturing director	Project execution	Responsible for meeting delivery dates for all manufactured clothing.
Harry Edwards	Procurement director	Business	Accountable for all procurement needs
Jacob Patrick	Manager engineering and construction	Project execution	Accountable for construction of stores
James Stevens	Project sponsor	Business	Liaison between project management and upper management
Jeness Hopkins	Clothing designer	Project execution	Responsible for designing clothing lines
Jocelyn Greer	Liaison in Europe for clothing design	Project execution	Accountable for all clothing design
Jordyn Kelly	VP HR	Business	Responsible for assisting in resource issues

Team Member	Role	Category	Responsibility/Accountability
Madison Adams	Webmaster	Project execution	Responsible for updating web page to include catalog ordering online
Megan Holly	Marketing manager	Business Project execution	Accountable for marketing strategy and implementation
Michelle Price	Coordinator	Project execution	Responsible for the flow of work between designers and manufacturing
Olivia Ross	CEO	Business	Accountable for funding the project
Skylar Janes	Advertising manager	Project execution	Accountable for advertising
Skylar Reese	CFO	Business	Responsible for financial decisions
Todd Franks	Construction superintendent	Project execution	Responsible for construction of stores in Portland and Seattle

Hands-on 2.3: Testing Your Knowledge of Project Organizational Structures

1.   The challenges associated with working in a horizontal reporting structure are as follows:

   - Some people can't take off their hierarchical hat.
   - If high rank is in the room, it may thwart straight talk.
   - Some people may make their own decision without talking to the PM.

2.   The following are two challenges associated with managing a project within a vertical structure:

   - It is hard to have two bosses; if the performer receives requests from both the project manager and their boss, who do they listen to?
   - The PM may have to follow the chain of command, so it takes longer to make decisions.

3.   You can overcome the challenges of a horizontal structure by doing the following:

   - Setting expectations among the members of the team
   - Using the communications plan
   - Treating everyone as an equal member of the team

4. The following diagram represents a vertical hierarchy project organizational structure.

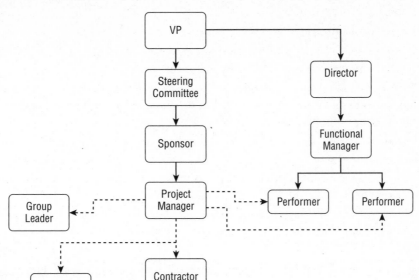

Hands-on 2.4: Testing Your Knowledge of Communications

1. To acquire the information needs of the various stakeholders, you need to carefully analyze them to determine the information that will be provided and the sources of that information. The following lists what can be done to assist in this effort:

- Review the sponsor's, supplier's, and your company's organizational charts to determine official communication channels.

- Interview stakeholders to understand the information needs and the informal communication channels.

- Interview others within your company who may have a history or knowledge of the sponsor or the delivery organization's management.

- Document the information requirements of each stakeholder group in the communications plan.

2. The factors that may influence the selection of communications technology include, but are not limited to, the following:

- Immediacy of the need for information

- Interaction required

- Location of the team

- Availability of technology

- Cost of technology

- Expected project staffing

- Length of the project

3. These are some of the metrics you could put in place that would measure the efficacy of your communications:

   - Tell your team that if at any time they have not received a message they should have, to let you know immediately. The project manager will investigate the cause and take appropriate action. For example:

      - If email messages are not received, make sure you have the correct email address and use the confirm feature.

      - If you are receiving something you should not receive, investigate the distribution of that information.

      - If team members cannot access what you have put in place, make sure they are accessing it correctly.

Hands-on 2.5: Testing Your Knowledge of Creating a List of Work

The following represents a more detailed WBS for the task described as "determine furnishings":

- Furnishings

   - First-floor clothing display area

      - Determine all clothing racks and displays needed.

      - Identify furniture needed.

      - Identify accessories.

      - Identify jewelry displays.

      - Identify accessory displays.

      - Determine mannequins for store front area.

   - First-floor customer service and pay stations

      - Identify types of rubber flooring available.

      - Determine equipment needed for customer service counter.

      - Identify equipment needed for pay stations.

   - Main-floor dressing rooms

      - Determine type of upholstered chairs needed.

      - Determine types of mirrors to be installed.

      - Identify clothing hooks available.

- Restrooms
  - Identify love seat or sofa to be purchased for sitting area.
  - Determine types of end tables to be used in sitting area.
  - Determine types of decorative lamps to be purchased for sitting area.
  - Identify type of decorative 7′ × 9′ Chinese area rug to be used in sitting area.
  - Determine air-dry hand units to be purchased.
  - Determine type of toilet paper dispensers needed.
  - Determine type of soap dispensers to be purchased.
  - Determine accessories for vanity counter.
- Office
  - Identify types of desks with side returns.
  - Determine type of 48″ two-drawer file cabinets needed.
  - Determine type of adjustable ergonomic chairs.
  - Determine hardware and software.
- Break room
  - Identify type of refrigerator to be purchased.
  - Identify microwave to be purchased.
  - Determine set of table and chairs to be used.
  - Identify type of coffeemaker needed.
  - Identify dishes and silverware needed.
  - Determine types of vending machines to be used.
- Bridal room
  - Identify mannequins for bridal area to be purchased.
  - Determine furniture for bridal dressing rooms.
  - Determine type of two-step raised dais.
  - Identify accessories display.
  - Identify type and quantity of bridal gown racks.
  - Identify types of bridesmaid dresses racks.
  - Determine type of veil displays needed.
- Tailoring room
  - Identify types of sewing machines needed.
  - Identify type of sewing station needed.
  - Identify type of ergonomic chair for sewing station.
  - Determine storage needs for tailoring room.

- Inventory storage room
  - Identify storage needs for inventory.
- Maintenance Room
  - Identify storage needs for maintenance items.
  - Determine type of vacuum cleaner needed.
  - Determine other maintenance items needed.

Hands-on 2.6: Testing Your Knowledge of Organizing Tasks into Logical Groupings

1. The following are the logical groupings associated with training of sales personnel, training of marketing personnel, preparation of advertising, and printing brochures and the manual:

Training of Sales Personnel

- Prepare phase 1 of the training program.
- Select sales personnel.
- Send sales personnel to training.
- Conduct phase 1 training.
- Prepare phase 2 training.
- Conduct phase 2 training for sales personnel.
- Familiarize sales with the brochure and customer manual.
- Return sales to territories.

Training of Marketing Personnel

- Determine general marketing approach.
- Select marketing personnel for training.
- Bring marketing personnel to the home office.
- Consolidate specific marketing training.
- Proceed with familiarization course.
- Train marketing personnel.
- Return marketing to territories.

Preparation of Advertising

- Consolidate the advertising plan.
- Prepare an article for a professional journal.

- Publish the article in the professional journal.
- Prepare regional advertising.
- Approve regional advertising.
- Distribute advertising to the proper media.
- Release and prepare to carry regional advertising.

Printing Brochure and Manual

- Draft and approve the brochure.
- Design the layout of the brochure.
- Print the brochure.
- Design the customer instruction manual.
- Approve the customer instruction manual.
- Print the customer instruction manual.
- Deliver brochures and manuals to the training center.

2. These are some of the challenges of *not* using a WBS:

- The scope may not be thoroughly defined.
- Resources may not be fully defined or understood.
- Estimates may not be valid.
- Schedules may not be correct.
- Budgets may not be correct.

Hands-on 2.7: Testing Your Knowledge of Reviewing and Adjusting a WBS

The following construction WBS was reviewed and adjusted. You added tasks and activities that made you feel you can produce appropriate deliverables:

1. Obtain working plans
2. Submit plans for approval
3. Obtain permits
4. Set up temporary power
   - 4.1 Call power company
   - 4.2 Set up temporary power pole
5. Set up job shack
   - 5.1 Bring in temporary trailer
   - 5.2 Bring power to trailer
   - 5.3 Set up temporary phone line

6. Perform dirt work

    6.1   Stake the corners and offsets

    6.2   Establish a monument (set pin) for points of reference

    6.3   Inspect dirt work for grade

    6.4   Dig out foundation

    6.5   Sell or save the dirt

7. Bring utilities to site

    7.1   Establish water lines

    7.2   Establish cable

    7.3   Establish Internet

    7.4   Establish telephone

8. Order materials per plan

    8.1   Order drywall

    8.2   Order acoustical

    8.3   Order doors and jams

    8.4   Order hardware

    8.5   Order millwork

    8.6   Order floor covering

    8.7   Order electrical

    8.8   Order mechanical (HVAC/heating)

    8.9   Order plumbing

    8.10   Order marble/stone/tile

    8.11   Order appliances

    8.12   Order windows

    8.13   Order fire protection

    8.16   Order specialties

9. Foundation

    9.1   Set up forms

    9.2   Install rebar

    9.3   Pour concrete

    9.4   Pour test cylinders

    9.5   Strip and clean forms

9.6   Allow concrete to age

9.7   Analyze test cylinders

9.8   Order inspection

10. Rough in plumbing

11. Rough in electrical

12. Begin framing

12.1   Install floor joists

12.2   Install plywood for floors

12.3   Frame walls

12.4   Frame windows

12.5   Frame doors

13. Set up material delivery in back of building

14. Set up sidewalks, walkways, and blacktop

15. Install rafters

16. Sheet the roof

17. Create traces for wiring

18. Put up roofing

19. Bring electrical to roof

20. Bring plumbing vents to roof

21. Install wiring

21.1   Install electrical wiring

21.2   Install cable TV wiring

21.3   Install Internet wiring

21.4   Install sound system wiring

21.5   Install security wiring

21.6   Inspect wiring

22. Install insulation

23. Install sheetrock

24. Install cabinets

25. Install tile and linoleum

26. Install millwork

27. Install plumbing finishes

28. Install electrical finishes
29. Install heating finishes
30. Clean house
31. Install carpeting

Hands-on 2.8: Testing Your Knowledge of Staffing Risks

See the following table for suggestions on the risks and strategies associated with resources.

Resource	Risk	Strategy
Sole-source human resource	What happens if this resource is no longer able to perform the task?	Create a backup by training someone else to do the work.
Sole-source supplier in your geographic area	What if this supplier has scarce inventory? ▪ What if there are price increases? ▪ What if there are distribution problems? ▪ What if this supplier goes out of business?	▪ Order way in advance. ▪ Lock in price in the contract. ▪ Order materials ahead of time. ▪ Arrange for substitute materials and find backup suppliers.
Internal resources	What if resources are overburdened? ▪ What if they don't have the proper skill set for the task? ▪ What if the resource is not available when needed?	▪ Use resource leveling. ▪ Negotiate in advance with the resource's manager to be sure the skill sets are in place when assigning the resource. ▪ Use Microsoft Project or other project scheduling software to create a resource calendar to remind the resource manager in plenty of time to arrange for the resource to be available when needed.

Hands-on 2.9: Testing Your Knowledge of Network Logic

This diagram represents the answer to the network logic exercise.

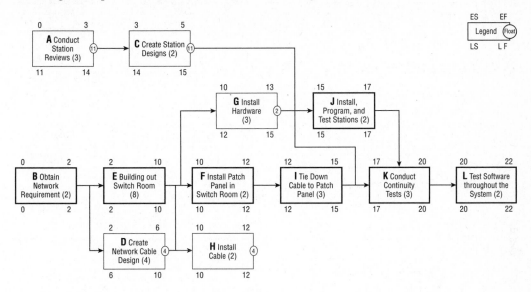

Hands-on 2.10: Testing Your Knowledge of PERT

The following diagram represents the answer to the PERT exercises. The table reveals how the durations and variances to the tasks on the critical path were derived and answers question 4: What is the total variation of the project?

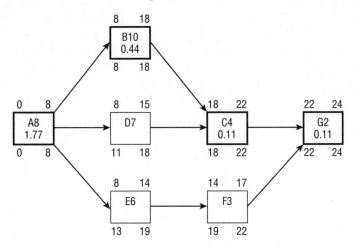

Activity	Predecessor	Successor	Optimistic	Most Likely	Pessimistic	PERT Duration	Variance
A	None	B, D, E	6	7	14	8	1.77
B	A	C	8	10	12	10	0.44
C	B, D	G	3	4	5	4	0.11
D	A	C	6	7	8	7	0.00
E	A	F	5	5.5	9	6	0.00
F	E	G	2	3	4	3	0.00
G	C, F	None	1	2	3	2	0.11
						Total Project Variation	2.43

Answer 4: Variation = 2.43

Answer 5: SD = 1.56

Answer 6: 15.85%

Answer 7: 2.3%

Answer 8: 0.15%

Answer 9: 25.56

Answer 10: 27.12

Answer 11: 28.68

The following diagram represents an illustration of answers 6 through 9.

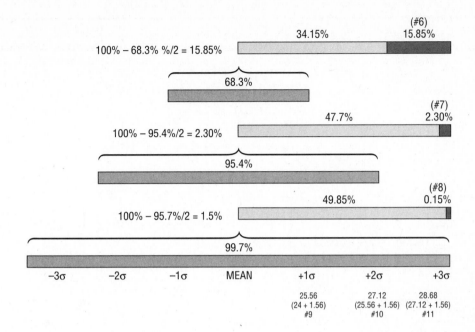

Hands-on 2.11: Testing Your Knowledge of Reducing a Project's Duration

The following diagram is the answer to questions 1 and 2, which were used to reduce a project's duration by "crashing" the project. The table provides the answers to question 3.

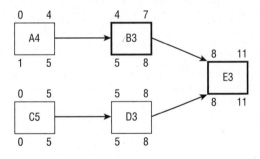

Activity	Predecessor	Successor	Normal Time	Normal Cost	Crash Time	Crash Cost
A	None	B	4	$3,200	2	$5,200
B	A	E	3	$6,000	1	$12,000
C	None	D	5	$5,000	2	$9,500
D	C	E	3	$3,000	1	$5,400
E	B and D	None	3	$1,200	1	$2,200

You start by reducing the least costly task on the critical path. The first task to decrease is the least costly, E. You will reduce it by one week at a cost of $1,000 ($2,200 – $1,200 = $1,000). Path C, D, E is still the critical path, which has been reduced from 11 weeks to 10 weeks.

The next least costly task is C for $2,250. You will reduce this task by one week ($9,500 – $5,000 = $4,500, and then $4500÷2 weeks = $2,250).

The next least costly task on the critical path is D, which is $2,400 ($5,400 – $3,000 = $2,400). By reducing C, you have changed the critical path because path A, B, D is now nine weeks, so you need to reduce it by one week, thus creating two critical paths that have eight weeks each.

The next least costly task is A, at a crash cost of $1,000 ($5,200 – $3,200 = $2,000/2 = $1,000. By result your cost to crash the project to eight weeks is $6,650. You have also introduced total risk to this project because there is no room for error.

Hands-on 2.12: Testing Your Knowledge of Cost Budgeting

1. Activity estimating should be performed by work performers and then compared to historical estimates if they are available.

2. There is a place for both types of estimating. Top-down estimating is often used during the initiation phase to give you an idea of how much the project could cost. The main thing to remember is that these estimates should be qualified as top down and management advised that until you go into bottom-up estimating, those numbers could change. Bottom-up estimating occurs after a detailed WBS has been created, contingency reserves have been established, and management reserves have been approved.

3. Two scenarios:

   - You planned for an expert worker, but that worker is no longer available. Someone with average skills may take a bit longer than planned.

   - A resource manger promised a resource for a task in the future but has forgotten his commitment, and the resource is no longer available.

Hands-on 2.13: Testing Your Knowledge of Quality Planning

1. To make maximum contributions to the project, team members must meet the following qualifications::

   - Know what is expected to meet the specifications
   - Know how to perform the functions to meet the specifications
   - Have adequate tools to perform the function
   - Be able to measure performance during the process
   - Be able to adjust the process to match the desired outcome

2. The differences between product results and project results are detailed here:

   - The *product* result is what you want to end up with at the end of the project. All work products in the project should meet all quality standards associated with it and meet all acceptance criteria negotiated with the client.

   - The *project* result describes whether you met cost, schedule, and performance parameters. Even if you did meet those parameters, the project is not successful unless the customer is happy. An unhappy customer is equal to a failed project.

3. The quality elements that you want to see associated with the construction of the stores include these:

   - Construction work done on time and within budget
   - Construction performed according to state and local building codes
   - Construction performed within safety guidelines
   - Construction follows working plans
   - Millwork done with expert craftsmanship
   - All finishes free of defects
   - All furnishings free of defects

Hands-on 2.14: Testing Your Knowledge of Contract Types

1. The cost plus incentive fee contract is primarily used when contracts involve a long performance period with a substantial amount of hardware development and test requirements. When projects have significant duration (more than five years), the project manager should focus estimates at a defined level for the first phase and at the parametric estimate level beyond that. This means that iterative refinement of the budget and schedule will be the order of the day. The project manager must pay particular attention that change orders are fully analyzed by a technical team. Additionally, projects such as these may be obsolete before they are complete if technology upgrades during the project are not factored in during the course of the project.

2. The project manager assumes high risk, while the seller assumes minimum risk. This type of contract is also susceptible to abuse in that there is a ceiling placed on profit potential, but there is no motivation for the seller to decrease costs.

3. The project manager should keep tight control on labor and material costs. This type of contract is primarily used in research projects in which the effort required to achieve success is uncertain until well after the contract is signed.

4. The seller has no incentive to decrease costs. In fact, increasing the costs will increase profit potential. This type of contract is illegal in the federal government.

5. The project manager should pay particular attention to controlling labor and material costs so that the seller (contractor) will not be able to purposefully increase these costs. Although this type of contract is prohibited for federal government use, it is used in the private sector, particularly in the construction industry. As you can see, 100% of the risk is born by the buyer.

6. The seller bears the greatest degree of risk, while the potential for profit is at a maximum. The seller should be motivated to decrease costs by producing efficiently because regardless of what the costs are, the seller receives the agreed-upon amount. As a consequence, the seller should place emphasis on controlling costs.

Hands-on 2.15: Testing Your Knowledge of Contract Calculations

1. If contractor A's cost was $720,000, what would have been the cost for contractor A's CPPC bid?

    $720,000 (cost)

    + 28,800 (4% of $725,000)

    = $748,800

2. What would the cost of the contract be if Olivia had chosen contractor D's CPIF bid?

    $720,000 (cost)

    + 25,000 (incentive for one month early)

    = $745,000

3. What is the cost of contractor C's CPIF contract if its cost was $700,000 and the cost-sharing ratio was 80% for the client and 20% for the seller?

    target cost = $725,000

    target profit = $20,000

    target price = $745,000

ceiling price = $775,000

actual cost = $700,000

sharing ratio = $5,000 (20% of $25,000 cost underrun)

price of contract = $725,000 (cost $700,000 + $25,000 fee)

4. What is the profit of contractor E's contract if the target cost is $720,000, target profit is $10,000, target price is $730,000, and actual cost was $700,000 and the ceiling price is $750,000?

$10,000 = target profit

$5000 = incentive for bringing schedule in one month early

$2000 = 10% of $20,000

$17,000 = actual profits including incentives

$717,000 = cost of contract

Hands-on 2.16: Testing Your Knowledge of Identifying and Qualifying Risk Events

1. Identify two risk events that could occur on the Apples and Pears Project in each of the following categories:
   - Organizational
     - Key team members may not be available when needed.
     - Reorganization may hinder functional manager commitments.
   - Technical
     - The phone system may not be installed on time.
     - New IT software may not be compatible with current software.
   - Project management
     - The project manager delivers unclear communications and directions.
     - The project manager may have to have surgery.
   - External
     - Inventory may not arrive on time.
     - The labor pool may go on strike.

2. The probability of occurrence, the impact of occurrence, and your risk response can be found in the following table.

TABLE 2.19 Project Risk Register

		Project Risk Register									
RISK #	RISK EVENT DESCRIPTION	PROBABILITY			DESCRIBE IMPACT ON PROJECT	IMPACT			Risk Response	Owner	Status
		Low	Med.	High		Low	Med.	High			
1.	Key team members may not be available when needed.	X			There are three key individuals on the project who are sole source providers.			X	AVOID: Train additional personnel in these three positions.		
2.	Reorganization may hinder functional manager commitments.			X	Schedule will be delayed and costs could increase.			X	AVOID: Discuss problem with sponsor and gain commitment in writing that personnel will engage in the project in spite of reorganization.		
3.	Phone system may not be installed on time.	X			None.	X			ACCEPT: Use cell phones and email.		
4.	New IT software may not be compatible with existing software.			X	Could delay catalog sales.			X	AVOID: Increase test parameters and time for tests—adjust durations for this task.		
5.	Communications overseas may be difficult in August.		X		Issues regarding manufacturing may not be immediately known.			X	AVOID: All overseas personnel will be available for communications whether or not they are on vacation.		
6.	Project manager may need to have surgery.			X	Learning curve for NW PM could stall decision-making at critical intervals in the project.			X	MITIGATE: Assign backup PM who will be kept in the loop.		
7.	Designed clothing inventory may not arrive on time.	X			Could cause delay in store openings.			X	AVOID: Monitor inventories closely and intervene with backup purchases of additional inventory.		
8.	Communications labor pool may go on strike.	X			None.		X		MITIGATE: Hire non-union communications workers.		

Hands-on 2.17: Testing Your Knowledge of Decision Trees and NPV

The following diagram shows how to use expected value and decision trees to formulate an NPV answer. The answer is B, $2,158, and this is a project to pursue.

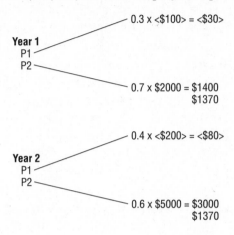

Year 1
P1
P2

0.3 x <$100> = <$30>

0.7 x $2000 = $1400
$1370

Year 2
P1
P2

0.4 x <$200> = <$80>

0.6 x $5000 = $3000
$1370

$$PV = FV/(1 + i)^n$$

Present Value Year 1 = $1370/(1 + 0.10)^1 = $1245

Present Value Year 2 = $2920/(1 + 0.10)^2 = $2413

Present Value = $1245 + $2413   = $3658

Investment   = <$1500>

Net Present Value   = $2158

Phase 3 Solutions

Hands-on 3.1: Testing Your Knowledge of Expertise

1. It takes an exceptional individual to manage a project without project management training. However, it has been done. The assigned project manager must have superior communication skills, excellent conflict-resolution skills, and known organizational and leadership skills. Hiding the fact that you are a novice will quickly be found out. You should acknowledge to your team that you are new to the process and will rely on

them to help you along the way. You should also state that everyone on the team needs to be successful in order for the project to succeed.

When you are assigned work for which you feel you are lacking the skills needed, you should do everything you can to address the issue, such as seeking help from a mentor, attending training classes, speaking to your supervisor about what you perceive are your strengths and weaknesses, and personal research.

If you have a project management office (PMO), many resources should be available to you, such as previous project documentation, books on project management, and the like.

Let your team members know that you need their help and that you would appreciate any feedback as soon as possible so the project doesn't get in trouble.

2. It is time for the team member to have a chat with the project manager. The team member should tell the project manager about the problems as she sees them and say that as a team member, she sees the project beginning to fall apart. She should advise the project manager that the team is willing to help if the project manager gives them a chance, but if things continue the way they are, she will be forced to escalate the problem.

Hands-on 3.2: Testing Your Knowledge of PMIS

1. The elements of an electronic PMIS include the following:
   - Information collection and distribution process
   - Access to intranet or Internet sites
   - Scheduling and presentation software
   - Configuring management databases
   - Project management forms and checklists

2. In the absence of a PMIS, you should create your own. This may be in the form of a literal project control book. This book needs to be current at all times, in a secure location, with access provided to it when needed. Ask yourself, "What if I had to leave the project? What information is needed so that my replacement knows exactly where the project stands?"

3. You should consider who needs access to the PMIS and should create passwords internally for those with a need to know. You should also provide a nonproprietary portal for external contractors working on the project.

Hands-on 3.3: Testing Your Knowledge of Acquiring Resources

1. Challenges associated with obtaining resources include the following:
   - Trying to staff the team with superstars
   - Not looking at personal aspirations of team members (Would they rather manage the project than do the work?)

- Poor interviewing skills
- Not letting resources know their value to the new position
- Accepting a resource without the requisite skills simply because they are available
- Not checking prior commitments of the team member—they may have booked a cruise during a critical portion of your project
- Choosing a technical specialist for a leadership role if you do not know their management and leadership abilities

2. The new member may not know the goals and objectives of the project or the tools that will be used. They may not know where they fit into the project plan. This could make a new team member uncomfortable in their role. They may not speak up because they may assume that they should already know about these things and try to just fit in.

    Mistakes can and will happen. For example, say you have been told to create a report. It sounds easy enough, so you create a report with all of the requested items and put it in the project manager's inbox. You find out later that reports have to follow a certain format and be posted online to a website you didn't even know exists. As a result, the project manager has to explain to critical recipients why the report was not posted on the site.

    As another example, a team member may ask you to do something, and you do it, not knowing that the task has to be done by a particular union person. You find out later that the union has filed a grievance against you.

Hands-on 3.4: Testing Your Knowledge of Developing Your Project Team

1. The following are samples of what can be done to develop a team without using money:

    - Partner a new member of the team with a more-experienced one. This does two things: (1) enables team members to learn more about the project, and (2) enables team members to learn who they can call on for information that relates to their own work.

    - Establish an appreciation system providing ways for people to show appreciation to their team members. This activity reinforces the momentum of the team when someone notices another person's hard work.

    - Meet after work for a game of softball, soccer, or another sport that all can participate in. Seeing your workmates in a casual, nonwork setting changes how you view them. For example, say you see someone you thought was stuffy and unapproachable at a picnic. This stuffy person is in shorts and a T-shirt with his ball cap on backward. He is comforting his small child who just fell down. That picture is different from your first impression of him. You go over and speak to him about children and find him witty and easy-going.

2. The following are additional ground rules:
    - You must all understand the strategic reason for the project in order to test for strategic fit in all planning efforts. For example, your project is aligned with a strategic goal to improve customer satisfaction. Anything else that tries to sneak into your project that doesn't fulfill that goal should not be allowed unless senior management decides differently.
    - If it's not scheduled, it won't get done.
    - Every project leader is to determine the standards of performance and see that all team members adhere.
    - An open-door policy, open communication, no-rank sessions—everyone's input is valuable, and everyone's commitment is to the ultimate goal.
    - Do not use planning sessions to control, but to coordinate.

Hands-on 3.5: Testing Your Knowledge of Managing Your Project Team

1. You let her know how angry you are that she overstepped her boundaries, particularly by signing the invoice. You tell her that she is never to sign her name on an invoice again and that if she doesn't listen to your instructions, you will remove her from the team. You tell her you don't trust her anymore and to leave your office.

2. You invite her in to sit down. You thank her for her quick response but apologize that you must not have communicated your instructions clearly to her. You review what happened and give her guidance on what to do in the future. You also apologize that you did not give her an alternate signatory and that in the future you would provide her with one because it is not appropriate for her to sign for you. You ask for feedback; she reiterates your expectations and thanks you for speaking to her.

In scenario 1 you used coercive power by threatening her with the loss of her participation on the project.

In scenario 2 she leaves feeling that she is still a valuable member of the team and that you, her project manager, provided excellent coaching.

Hands-on 3.6: Testing Your Knowledge of Motivational Theories

1. The concept that managers who hold one of two sets of assumptions about human motivation that will affect the manager's behavior and management style is called theory X and Y. The individual responsible for the theory is Douglas McGregor.

2. The concept of a need being satisfied and no longer motivating until the next-higher need takes its place is called the hierarchy of needs. The individual responsible for the theory is Abraham Maslow.

3. The theory that describes two sets of needs—one as an animal to avoid pain (hygiene needs) and a second as a human being to grow psychologically—is called the hygiene theory. The individual responsible for the theory is Frederick Herzberg.

Hands-on 3.7: Testing Your Knowledge of Types of Power

1. When a senior manager sends specific instructions to his employees and wants immediate action, the type of power being used is *formal* power. Just because an individual has formal power doesn't necessarily mean that the individual deserves that power, however. It happens again and again that a new person gets promoted and is immediately on a "power trip." Most people dislike seeing that type of behavior. But a promotion is a huge deal to some people and can mark a turning point in their career. It might be better to let that person have their "power time" (and see the humor in their actions until they float back to earth and perform as they should).

2. When a project manager has arranged for the project team to attend a three-day retreat to celebrate success, the type of power being used is *reward* power. Reward power also can be misused. Project managers have been offered incentives and gifts by vendors so they will choose that vendor on the next project, for example. It is unethical to partake in that behavior. It is also unethical to promise rewards you may not be able to deliver.

3. When a project manager is asked to be a frequent speaker at industry symposiums, the type of power the project manager has is *expert* power. If you are considered an expert, other people who recognize your expertise (including team members) are more likely to trust your opinion as well as what you say.

4. When a team member has asked to work on another project with the project manager who is leading the current project, the type of power being used is *referent* power. Referent power is the ultimate compliment if it is earned. You should be able to detect whether a person is sincere or simply patronizing.

Hands-on 3.8: Testing Your Knowledge of Managing Conflict

1. You tell Todd, your construction project superintendent, to fire the electrician for gross insubordination. *Forcing* would result in a win/lose for the project.

2. You pretend not to see what is happening and don't say anything to anybody. *Withdrawing* accomplishes nothing.

3. You ask the electrician to come down from the ladder and ask whether he understands that he is not to smoke in the building now that carpet is laid. Assume he says yes and promises not to do it again. This *smoothing* activity produces only a short-term solution.

4. You ask the electrician to come down from the ladder and ask whether he understands that he is not to smoke in the building now that carpet is laid. He says yes. You tell him that he may have as many smoking breaks as he needs but that the work must still be done on time. He agrees not to smoke while working. This *collaboration* effort leads to consensus and commitment as well as providing a long-term solution.

5. You opt for a *confrontation* and ask the electrician to come down from the ladder and to step into your office in 15 minutes. When he arrives, you ask him to sit down at the round table in your office. You join him there and ask, "Do you know why you are here?" He says, "Because I was smoking." You advise him that smoking wasn't the issue; the issue was smoking over new carpet after a specific request not to do so was in place.

You also bring up that by ignoring the rule, he was blatantly insubordinate, not only to his foreman but to you. You ask him what he would do if the tables were turned. He says that he would probably fire the person who did that to him. You reply that, yes, you certainly have grounds to do that, but that he is a valued member of the team and you would like very much to keep him on the project.

You ask him whether there is anything you can do to help him understand this issue more fully. He says that he understands the policy but needs to smoke more often than three times a day (over breaks and lunches). You advise him that he may take as many smoking breaks as he needs during the day but that the work must be done on time. You also tell him that you will discuss this with his foreman so that he is on board. You then ask him whether he understands why there is to be no smoking over carpet. He advises that he does but can't commit that he won't ever do it again.

You say to him, "Then you have left me no choice but to fire you. I will be speaking to your foreman to arrange for you to pick up your pay at the end of the day."

An alternate ending to this scenario would be that if he *does* make a commitment, you will trust that he keeps his promise and send him back to work.

Hands-on 3.9: Testing Your Knowledge of Quality Assurance

1. Several tools can be used to determine a problem:
   - Control charts can be used to capture data in a process over time to determine whether a process is working. The construction steps of a mass-marketed garment depend on the quality of the design and the accompanying garment package. Several processes have to occur before manufacturing even begins. Determine what those processes are, collect and interpret the data, and make improvements accordingly. In this case, however, you may not have the luxury of time to create a control chart.
   - Inspection is another tool that can be used; however, inspection is costly.
   - Statistical sampling can be used but can be risky. For example, say you inspect 10 of 100 garments. They are perfect, so you accept the lot of 100. The risk involved is that you picked out 10 perfect garments, but there may be many more that

are imperfect. Don't forget, in statistical sampling you must know the difference between attribute and variable data. Attribute data indicates product characteristics, which either conform or don't, as in the preceding example. Variable data are rated on a scale to determine the degree of conformance and are infinitely divisible, such as time and money. For example, from start to finish a garment should take one week from design to manufacturing. If manufacturing does not receive the garment in one week, variable data will show how much time passed before they did receive it.

The following could have been used to avoid the problem or reduce its impact:

- Benchmarking: Because Cimarron has never marketed or manufactured wedding dresses before, a team could have been selected that would research how other companies manufacture the gowns.

- Flowcharting: Using a flowchart to map each process would have identified areas of strength or weakness. Those strengths and weaknesses could have been leveraged or avoided.

2. Items that are considered a cost of quality include prevention efforts such as training and appraisals; these appraisal techniques may include testing and inspections as well as quality audits. Costs of nonconformance include internal failures (for example, reworking or scrapping) and external failures (for example, liabilities and the incalculable cost of lost business).

3. The Taguchi method, called design of experiments, works on the premise that quality should be built into the product and measured against the deviation from a specification, rather than by conformance to predetermined tolerance limits. If change is a constant, the Taguchi method may not be the best tool to use because bringing products to market would take longer and competitors would probably achieve market share more quickly. Consider Japanese pickup trucks. It took Japanese manufacturers many years to develop a full-size pickup truck. So even though Japan did not have US market share for full-size pickup trucks for those many years, their trucks today are considered by many to be number one in quality and enjoy a healthy market share today.

4. The purpose of a quality audit is to ensure that planned quality requirements are met, products are safe and fit for use, all applicable laws have been followed, and data systems are in place that track, measure, and report quality attributes so they are adequate and accurate.

5. Cost metrics could include actual vs. planned budgets and the number of approved changes to the budget. Schedule metrics could include whether the end date was met or a list of milestones that were late. Productivity metrics could include work units produced per hour or number of process improvements that saved hours and dollars. Metrics indicating the quality of deliverables could include the number of defects found or the number of hours of rework needed. Metrics indicating the quality of the project could include the number of risks successfully mitigated, or clear and unambiguous acceptance criteria.

Hands-on 3.10: Testing your Knowledge of Communicating with Your Sponsor and Team

1. The sponsor may not trust you to manage the project and may begin to meddle into its minutia. A sponsor may even take over the project or assign another individual. In any case, failure to provide accurate and timely information would be a huge mistake because your credibility as a project manager would diminish. If the project manager begins to hide bad news from the sponsor (even by omission), it places the sponsor in a difficult position of having to explain your behavior when the truth is finally revealed. A sponsor knows that mistakes will occur and expects the project manager to "own up" to them and offer resolutions to the situation without hiding behind bad information or excuses.

2. Be sure to say something to this effect: "I am sorry the information is not to your liking, but my answer is the same. I will tell you the way things really are—not half truths, but the whole truth. I would like to share with you my plan to solve the situation. Would you like to hear that now or should I come back at a later time?"

3. Items that can be informally communicated to the project team include the overall state of the project, progress, performance, and so forth, as well as successes, personnel changes, overview of new technology, and so on.

4. Any type of complaint that is received in writing must have a written response.

Hands-on 3.11: Testing Your Expectations and Commitments

Sponsor expectations of the project manager:

- The project will be delivered on time and within budget.
- Deliverables will meet all quality attributes associated with them.
- True status, good or bad news, will be delivered immediately.
- You will have a recommendation or solution to problems or challenges.
- We will be supportive and respectful of each other.
- You are willing to accept responsibility for the project.
- You will solve conflicts without alienation and accept challenges cheerfully.
- You will apply technical judgment when necessary.
- You will be an honest steward of time and expenses.
- You will assert your creative abilities with flexibility.

Sponsor commitments to the project manager:

- I will involve you in appropriate planning efforts.
- I will value and utilize your input.
- I will honor your role as leader of the project and not micromanage.
- I will keep our lines of communication open.
- I will listen to your challenges and trust you with your solutions to them unless I have information that would not support your solution.
- I will keep you informed of decisions made by senior management that may affect the project.

Hands-on 3.12: Testing Your Knowledge of Listening Habits

You have conducted your listening test and documented your answers in Table 3.15. Table 3.18 interprets your answers.

TABLE 3.18   Test Answers on Listening

Group 1 **Effective listening habits**	The higher the points, the more effective the active listening. 35–40: Excellent active listening 30–35: Good active listening < 30: Active listening needs work
Group 2 **Ineffective listening habits**	The higher the points, the more ineffective the active listening. > 10: Active listening needs work 5–10: Good active listening 0–5: Excellent active listening
Group 3 **Active listening in meetings**	The higher the points, the more ineffective the active listening. > 10: Active listening in meetings needs work 5–10: Good active listening in meetings 0–5: Excellent active listening in meetings

Hands-on 3.13: Testing Your Knowledge of Conduct Procurements

1. The importance of a bidder's conference is to ensure that all potential sellers have an opportunity to ask questions, listen to other sellers' comments and questions, and hear the answers to those questions all at the same time. All potential sellers will then have identical information with which to decide to respond to the buyer or not.

2. The differences and similarities among a weighting system, a screening system, and a compliance matrix are as follows:

   - All are used to assist in selecting sellers.

   - A weighting system tries to minimize the effect of personal prejudice by using the same scale to evaluate potential sellers.

   - A screening system establishes minimum requirements for performance suitable for the buyer.

   - A compliance matrix is used as a tool to be sure that vendors follow certain guidelines; for example, the RFP guidelines the vendor was given prior to their proposal.

3. Research and preparations that need to be made before contract negotiations begin include the following:

   - Decide on the techniques you will use to win your opponent to your point of view.

   - Do your homework on financial and other aspects of the seller.

   - Make sure you know what the contract should cost.

   - Specify where and when the negotiations will occur and other hygiene factors.

   Your confidence level in your ability to win the negotiation is greatly enhanced when you have made through preparations in advance of the negotiation.

Hands-on 3.14: Testing Your Knowledge of Contract Negotiations

1. The project manager should do nothing. Project managers are to provide support to the procurement officer and participate only when asked to do so by the procurement officer.

2. The procurement officer should simply recommend that issues need to be identified before any bargaining or concessions are made. A quick break would be in order so the potential manufacturer can recover and think about the issues. When the meeting resumes, the procurement officer points out issues that Cimarron has and asks whether there are any issues the opposing side would like to see addressed.

3. The next step is bargaining and decision making, during which the two positions are summed up and concessions are made. After that, resolution happens–that is, the two positions are summed up, and final concessions are made and documented. The final step is closing: Both parties have identical agreements, and the negotiations are closed.

Phase 4 Solutions

Hands-On Exercise 4.1: Testing Your Knowledge of Integrated Change Control

1. The documents that must be changed include:
    a. The scope document, which had the requirements of the first set of furniture and now needs the actual furniture information.
    b. Inventory documents
    c. Procurement records to show what was actually purchased
    d. Budget
    e. Risk documents
    f. Change order documents
2. Those that need to be notified of the change include:
    a. The contractor so he won't turn the new furniture away
    b. The interior designers so they can adjust the accessories and color palate to accommodate the change
    c. The sponsor, so there will be no surprises
    d. The store manager, so she will know the plan was changed
3. These answers are based on the scenario.
    a. Original furniture was wrong size and color
    b. $5,000
    c. Yes, these are better quality items.
    d. Yes, they will hold up longer than the original furniture.
    e. None
    f. No
    g. None, as it allows the schedule to stay on target.
    h. This will come out of the management reserve budget.

Hands-On Exercise 4.2: Testing Your Knowledge of Scope Verification

1. Action taken would be to tell the vendor to remove the ducting and prepare the cooling system as per the contract. If the schedule is to remain on track, either of two processes (fast tracking or crashing) can be used to maintain the schedule date if this item impacted the critical path.

2. There would be no payment to the vendor for the time it took to install the ducts or for removing them. There would be no payment for the cost of the ducting, or to reconfigure and test the cooling system.

Hands-On Exercise 4.3: Testing Your Knowledge of Controlling Project Scope

The five steps needed to process a change request are:

1. Submit the change request as per the change management plan.

2. Perform an impact analysis relative to budget schedule, scope, quality, and risk.

3. Make the decision through those authorized to approve changes.

4. Escalate to the change review board or funding board if necessary.

5. Manage the approved change request.

Hands-On Exercise 4.4: Testing Your Knowledge of Controlling the Project Schedule

1. The impacts to the project are:

    a. It changes the ES and EF of task "publish article in professional journal" to 25 and 33.

    b. It changes the ES and EF of task "release and prepare to carry regional advertising" to 33 and 35.

    c. It changes the LS and LF of task "prepare article for professional journal to 17 and 23.

    d. The slack in that path changed from 4 to 1.

2. The impacts to the project are:

   a. It changes the ES and EF of task "publish article in professional journal" to 27 and 35.

   b. It changes the ES and EF of task "release and prepare to carry regional advertising" to 35 and 37.

   c. This path then becomes the only critical path and all the backward pass dates will change.

   d. The slack in the previous critical paths is only 1 which tells you that you now have a very high risk project.

3. The main thing you can do to reduce schedule risk is to communicate to your team exactly what has happened and that they must keep you informed of any deviations to the current project plan. Your performance reports should be done more often, perhaps weekly instead of monthly, or even daily if you are about to reach a major milestone.

4. First the project manager will want to seek tasks on the critical path that may potentially be crashed. Then, if using scheduling software, the critical path can be sorted by length of tasks—the longer the task, the more opportunity to crash. Once you have identified the best tasks to crash, options to crash the schedule include:

   a. Offering overtime to employees whose tasks are on the critical path you have identified

   b. Finding additional resources who can work on tasks on the critical path you have identified to crash

Hands-On Exercise 4.5: Testing Your Knowledge of Earned Value Concepts

1. The earned value is $6,000 (add weeks 1–3, which is 60%). He should have completed $8,000 worth of work (weeks 1–4), but only accomplished $6,000.

2. The project is over budget by $4000 ($10,000 that was spent minus the $6000 worth of work accomplished) and behind schedule by $2000 (80% would have been $8000, so $8000 – $6000 equals $2000.)

3. Table 4.10 provides the answer to the earned value questions.

TABLE 4.12 Earned Value Scenario Answer

Earned Value Elements	What Does the Acronym Stand For?	Formula	Answer	Rationale
PV	Planned value or budgeted cost of work scheduled (BCWS)	None	$8,000	The amount of work scheduled to be completed in four weeks.
AC	The actual cost of work performed (ACWP)	None	$10,000	Provided by the performer. The amount of money spent exceeds what was scheduled to be spent through week 3.
EV	Earned value	None	$6,000	The amount of work that was actually accomplished.
CV	Cost variance	EV – AC	<$4,000>	What this is telling us is that we have thus far spent $4,000 more than we planned to date for the work that was done.
SV	Schedule variance	EV – PV	<$2,000>	What this is really telling us is that we are $2,000 *worth of work* behind schedule. We haven't actually spent this money yet but we have to spend it in the future to make up what we lost.
CPI	Cost performance index	EV/AC	0.60	This shows us how efficiently we are using the project budget. In this example, we can say that for every dollar that we have *spent*, we have *earned* 60 cents, or 60% efficiency.
SPI	Schedule performance index	EV/PV	0.75	This shows us how efficiently we are using the project schedule relative to money. In this example, we can say that for every dollar that we have *spent*, we have *earned* 75 cents, or 75% efficiency.
BAC	Budget at completion	None	$9,000	The sum of all budgets originally allocated to the project. Total of all weeks = $9,000.
ETC	Estimate to complete	EAC – AC	$5,000	The expected additional cost of an activity or group of activities in the project.
EAC	Estimate at completion	AC + ETC	$15,000	The sum of all direct and indirect costs to date plus the estimate of all work remaining.
VAC	Variance at completion	BAC – EAC	$6,000	The difference between what the job was supposed to cost versus what we now expect the project to cost. This amount includes the $4,000 overrun plus the $2,000 worth of work left to do.

Hands-On Exercise 4.6: Testing Your Knowledge of Quality Tools

1. The fishbone diagram is designed to help you understand the root cause of a problem.

2. Histograms are used to determine process capability at a snapshot in time.

3. A Pareto chart is an ordered histogram that shows how many results were generated by type or category of identified causes. It helps to focus on a given problem because it shows the problem that occurs the most, and by focusing on correcting the biggest problem first, this can bring about the most improvement.

4. When data is displayed on a graph that shows observed data in a time sequence in order to see the output or performance of a manufacturing or other business process it is called a run chart.

5. A scatter diagram should be used to see if there is a correlation between dependent and independent variables in a process.

Hands-On Exercise 4.7: Testing Your Knowledge of Performance Reporting

The following answers the questions regarding performance reporting:

1. $2,800,000. The negotiated cost + the target fee = negotiated value; thus $2,500,000 + $300,000 = $2,800,000

2. $2,500,000. All work authorized is equal to negotiated cost.

3. $2,330,000. Contracted funds ($2,500,000) do not need to be released in the budget all at once. In this case, $2,500,000 was the contracted price for authorized work, but the PM built the funding allocation somewhat less ($2,330,000), allowing a buffer, typically called management reserve.

4. $2,380,000. The PM still has a management reserve and so added $50,000 to the original release amount.

5. $170,000. 2,500,000 – $2,330,000 = $170,000.

6. Reduced by $50,000. Revised PV ($2,380,000) – Original PV ($2,330,000) = $50,000

7. Construction A, Construction C, Construction Support. These elements have release amounts less than contracted amounts.

8. $324,000. If the project came in $120,000 under budget, a 20% bonus occurs per the sharing ration concept. Thus $300,000 + 20% ($120,000) = $324,000. (Remember, if the contractor goes over budget then they must pay 20% of the overrun. If the budget is underrun, the contractor receives 20% of the underrun.)

9. $1,190,000. This figure represents 100% overhead of the amount of the revised BCWS, which is also $1,190,000.

10. $73,800 worth of work. This represents the total of the PV.

11. $67,500. By definition, the earned value is equal to the budgeted cost of work performed.

12. Less by $6,300; <8 1/2%>. Schedule variance (SV) = EV ($67,500) - PV ($73,800) = <$6,300>. (SVP) = EV / PV × (100) = <8 1/2%>

13. $78,300. Total of AC.

14. <$10,800>; <16%> Cost Variance (CV) = EV ($67,500) – AC ($78,300) = <$10,800>. Cost variance percentage (CVP) = CV/EV × 100 = <16%>.

15. Construction A, Construction C, Construction Support. A has significant cost and schedule overrun; B has significant schedule variance; and construction support has significant cost and schedule overrun.

16. <$53,100>; <11.4%>. CV ($53,100) = EV ($464,200) – AC ($78,300)
    CVP = CV [EV ($464,200) – AC ($517,300)] ÷ EV ($464,200) × 100 = <11.4%>

17. $23,300; <5.28%>. SV = EV ($464,200) – PV ($440,900) = 23,300.
    SVP = SV [EV ($464,200) – PV ($440,900)] ÷ PV ($440,900) × 100 = <5.28%>

18. Getting worse. The cumulative cost variance is –11.4%. This month is –16%. (See question #14.)

19. Getting worse. The cumulative schedule variance is –5.28%. This month is –8.5%.

20. Cannot be answered without a network diagram (CPM or PERT).

21. $2,652,249. EAC = AC/EV(BAC) thus, $517,300/$464,200 × $2,380,000 = $2,652,000.

22. <$272,249>. VAC = BAC ($2,380,000) – EAC ($2,652,249) = <$272,249>.

23. $50,000. Since the project overran, first compute the difference between the baseline and the ceiling amount:

    Ceiling: $3,000,000: @100% = $150,000

    Budget: $2,500,000: $500,000 × 20% = $100,000

    Then add the two figures = $250,000. Subtract this from the ceiling amount ($3,000,000) = $50,000

Hands-On Exercise 4.8: Testing Your Knowledge of Managing Risk Events

1. The risk events identified include:
   - If we release Cimarron from their obligations to meet the completion date for the switch room, we are still bound to the October 15 date with potential penalties.
   - Project schedule is built too tight to absorb any delays.

- Deadline is unknown for on-site construction of equipment room.
- Implementation could be delayed.
- Lack of environmental protection (fire, dust, etc.) could cause equipment damage.
- Our equipment may not arrive on time.
- Potential damage to equipment due to leakage of steam pipes and/or incorrect power supply.

2. Corrective action for Brendon to consider includes:
   - Negotiate an addendum to the contract to do away with the $5,000 penalty, provide an alternate site for equipment, with Cimarron to absorb the cost and negotiate a phased approach for implementation.
   - Based on the above, negotiate costs associated with additional resources or "fast tracking" to stay on schedule.
   - Negotiate a "drop dead" date for completion of equipment room.
   - Insure against damage and time lost.
   - Carry extra inventory to cover any potential delays.
   - Work closely with Cimarron's contractor.
   - Arrange for a back-up power supply.

3. Brendon can do the following to maintain equilibrium between Cimarron and the recommended mitigation strategy(s):
   - Offer a range of options so the customer can make a choice.
   - Identify the risks and associated costs of the risks.
   - Negotiate with the customer based on their interests—try to determine what the underlying reasons are for the October 15 date. If there is a different way of satisfying their need and still slip the deadline if necessary it would be a win-win for both parties.

4. The following factors produced the circumstances:
   - A need for overall project management by DMPC.
   - DMPC needed to perform risk planning in the beginning of the project.
   - Brendon could have included the Cimarron project team as well as the contractor to improve communications across all facets of the project.

5. The following risk events could have been identified ahead of time:
   - Construction room delay
   - Electrical power issues
   - Steam line may break, given the condition of the existing system

6. Brendon could have done the following to overcome the risk events:

   ▪ Brendon could have integrated the project plans with the construction company and the electric company subcontractor.

   ▪ Brendon could have done a preliminary site survey and physically inspected the conditions or assigned someone to do that task.

   ▪ Brendon could have used a Risk Register noted with risk triggers and assigned owners empowered to take action when triggers were hit.

Hands-On Exercise 4.9: Testing Your Knowledge of Contract Changes

1. These type of changes are called constructive changes.

2. A written order, following change management processes and signed by the contracting officer so that a seller can make a change, is called a change order.

3. Work that has started before a final contract is complete is called an incomplete contractual action.

4. Change that does not affect project work, such as changing mailing addresses or telephone numbers, is called administrative change.

5. A contract modification that is agreed to between the buyer and seller is called a supplemental agreement.

Hands-On Exercise 4.10: Testing Your Knowledge of Legal Contract Issues

1. The difference between a material and immaterial breach of contract is as follows:

   ▪ A material breach involves one of the vital aspects of the agreement, such as a contractor failing to appear on the job site for an extended period of time.

   ▪ An immaterial breach involves a less important aspect of the agreement, such as a contractor failing to clean up the job site at the end the day.

2. Termination for convenience means that a buyer can terminate for convenience at any time. For example, if the project runs out of funds it can be terminated for convenience.

3. Mediation is normally created by contract and uses an objective third party to facilitate an amicable resolution, whereas binding arbitration is normally created by contract and there may be one or three arbitrators. Courts will enforce mediation and arbitration decisions; therefore, they are binding.

4. When a contract is terminated for default, that is, the seller did not perform the work of the contract as stated in the contract, the contractor may not be entitled to payment for work in progress but not yet accepted by the customer. The buyer, depending on the situation, may be entitled to repayment of any payments made to date on the unaccepted work.

5. The three warranties that a seller should provide are:

   a. Materials/equipment will be of good quality and new unless otherwise permitted.

   b. Work will be free of defects not inherent in the quality permitted.

   c. Work will conform to requirements of the contract document.

6. A surety bond is provided by a bonding company. The owner must pay monthly premiums for the bond of choice, which may be a bid bond, performance bond, or payment bond.

Phase 5 Solutions

Hands-on 5.1: Testing Your Knowledge of Project Acceptance

1. Nonacceptance of a deliverable typically requires a review of the original acceptance criteria. Perhaps the client forgot the parameters of acceptance, and the deliverable should be accepted given the acceptance criteria. If the acceptance criteria reveal that the deliverables were not met, then rework has to occur. When the deliverable is accepted, the task is complete—and not before.

2. The contract cannot be closed out until all deliverables are accepted. If the contract was closed out before all of the deliverables were complete and they were accepted, you would have a difficult time asking the vendor to come back and fix the deliverable.

3. The project was not turned over to operations correctly. It is essential that those people who will be maintaining the product or service generated by a project be fully trained and have adequate documentation so they can perform their work.

4. If a product or service is not maintained, most people will be disenchanted and choose not to use it. Whoever created the product will be perceived as not knowing what they are supposed to do.

Hands-on 5.2: Testing Your Knowledge of Performance Reviews

1. Informal feedback is not enough. If you are not the team member's reporting manager, that manager has no way of knowing about their person's performance unless you provide it.

2. No one likes to receive bad news, and it is difficult sometimes to provide that feedback. Some project managers (and managers for that matter) would rather opt for the "satisfactory" category because it is much easier than reporting bad news. However, it is vital that you provide truthful feedback.

   If the project manager had truly "managed" team members as well as the project, unsatisfactory results shouldn't occur. The project manager should have dealt with any performance issues long before project closure. If the team member was never apprised of poor performance up to this point, it is unfair to them to provide negative feedback. If it was important enough to put it in the report, why wasn't it important enough to address it when the problems occurred?

3. There are differences of opinion about whether this is a good idea. We feel that it is not a good idea because some team members will be too hard on themselves and others will overplay their significance in their role as a team member. Honest, truthful, and helpful feedback is always preferred and should be written by the project manager.

Hands-on 5.3: Testing Your Knowledge of Contract Closure

1. She should not close out the contract. Failure to complete all items of the contract is not only a breach of contract, but Cimarron can terminate the contract "with cause" as long as the architect certifies that sufficient cause exists.

2. Typically, money is withheld from the final payment to the contractor until all contracted items are complete. You would have to hire someone else to complete the work, and if the cost exceeds the amount withheld from the contract, Cimarron can bill the contractor for the excess or sue the contractor for that amount if it is not paid.

Hands-on 5.4: Testing Your Knowledge of Lessons Learned

1. No, the project should not be closed out. An action item might include "Collect data over next six months to evaluate realized costs, benefits, operational efficiency, and product performance."

Many times projects are closed out, and ongoing measurements that cannot be completed at the end of the project are forgotten. You may be so anxious for the project to end that you close down the project and move to the next one.

That is not to say that the contract cannot be closed out. As long as all contract items are completed and accepted, the contract can be closed out, but the final report on the project should include the measurable results to see whether the project truly met its goals and objectives.

An action item such as this would typically be given to a person other than the project manager to do, but follow-up on the action item is still the project manager's responsibility.

2. Most project problems occur because of poor management, poor communication, or lack of training. No one comes to work and decides they are going to create problems. (If they do, you have a much bigger problem that should have been addressed as soon as the problem occurred.) It is never appropriate to name an individual as the reason for the problem. Finger-pointing and bad feelings exist, especially if the person is in the room. The problem should be addressed by asking, "What can be done differently to avoid this problem in the future?" For example, suppose your team member failed to do a particular task because they thought the task was unnecessary and reported it as complete. Later, because the task was skipped, a lot of rework had to be done. You ask your team members how to avoid this problem in the future, and they respond as follows:

- You should define those tasks that are significant to the project.

- You should change our ground rules so that if anyone is confused about a task, that person should speak to the project manager about it and never mark a task complete unless it truly is.

- Make sure that team members understand their importance in the overall project effort.

The problem was identified in the lessons learned as: "A task was not completed but was reported as completed. As a result, rework had to be done on tasks 3.1 and 4.6 that were also on the critical path. The schedule was not affected because other tasks were crashed." As you can see, the problem has been addressed without naming an individual.

Hands-on 5.5: Testing Your Knowledge of Creating and Documenting the Project's Final Report

1. If a knowledge database did not exist, a new project manager could not refer to it for necessary background information that would help on a current project. Problems and solutions recorded in a knowledge database can help project managers working on similar projects. For example, say you are a telecommunications project manager with one of the Bell operating companies. Your project was to change out the telephone lines to a newer and more robust system. Your standard process is to check your portion

of the line, and if all goes well, it is turned over to the equipment vendor. You are not responsible for the features—the vendor is. When the customer tries to use their new system, all of the stations have dial tone but many of the features of the phone do not work. According to FCC rules, when the Bell company has completed its work, it is not responsible for the equipment that ties to the system. It doesn't matter who you can blame for the problem; the customer still can't use their system, and you are the project manager. On a previous project, the same thing happened, but the project manager worked with the equipment vendor and arranged for call-through tests to make sure all lines and features worked properly. Having a knowledge database for the previous project would have allowed this solution to be recorded and would have saved the current project time and money.

2. If a knowledge database is not maintained, that is, kept up-to-date, current information would not be available to anyone who uses the knowledge database. If the information has been changed, the project manager will not have access to updated information regarding work-arounds, challenges that were overcome, and so on.

3. Work-arounds performed in the project sometimes work so well that a process change is in order. Any changes to organizational process assets have to be approved by the process owner. Whoever manages the process documentation is responsible for updating the process and making sure that everyone who uses the process is either informed or trained on the new process. Again, this is a follow-up task for the project manager. Otherwise, you may not know that the process was changed.

4. There are different schools of thought on whether team members should be given a copy of the final report. These documents can be several pages long. The team already knows most of the information, and additional information such as vendor and contract information do not fall under "need to know."

Index

Note to the Reader: Throughout this index **boldfaced** page numbers indicate primary discussions of a topic. *Italicized* page numbers indicate illustrations.